Flight
Instructor

ORAL
EXAM
GUIDE

MICHAEL D. HAYES

EIGHTH EDITION

COMPREHENSIVE PREPARATION
FOR THE FAA CHECKRIDE

AVIATION SUPPLIES & ACADEMICS, INC.
NEWCASTLE, WASHINGTON

Flight Instructor Oral Exam Guide
Eighth Edition
by Michael D. Hayes

Aviation Supplies & Academics, Inc.
7005 132nd Place SE
Newcastle, Washington 98059-3153
asa@asa2fly.com | 425-235-1500 | asa2fly.com

See the ASA website at **asa2fly.com/oegcfi** for Reader Resources containing additional information and updates relating to this book.

None of the material in this book supersedes any operational documents or procedures issued by the Federal Aviation Administration, aircraft and avionics manufacturers, flight schools, or the operators of aircraft.

ASA-OEG-CFI8
ISBN 978-1-64425-299-4

Additional formats available:
eBook EPUB   ISBN 978-1-64425-300-7
eBook PDF   ISBN 978-1-64425-301-4

Printed in the United States of America
2027   2026   2025   2024   2023   9 8 7 6 5 4 3 2 1

Library of Congress Cataloging-in-Publication Data:
Names: Hayes, Michael D., author.
Title: Flight instructor oral exam guide : comprehensive preparation for the FAA
    checkride / Michael D. Hayes.
Other titles: Certified flight instructor oral exam guide
Description: Eighth edition. | Newcastle, Washington : Aviation Supplies & Academics,
    Inc., 2023.
Identifiers: LCCN 2023002634 (print) | LCCN 2023002635 (ebook) | ISBN
    9781644252994 (trade paperback) | ISBN 9781644253007 (epub) | ISBN
    9781644253014 (pdf)
Subjects: LCSH: United States. Federal Aviation Administration—Examinations—Study
    guides. | Flight training—Examinations—Study guides. | Airplanes—Piloting—
    Examinations—Study guides. | LCGFT: Study guides.
Classification: LCC TL712 .H39 2023 (print) | LCC TL712 (ebook) | DDC
    629.132/52076—dc23/eng/20230208
LC record available at https://lccn.loc.gov/2023002634
LC ebook record available at https://lccn.loc.gov/2023002635

This guide is dedicated to the many talented students, pilots, and flight instructors I have had the opportunity to work with over the years. Also special thanks to Mark Hayes, David Sickler, the staff at Howell Aircraft Service, and the many others who supplied the patience, encouragement, and understanding necessary to complete the project.

—M.D.H.

Contents

Introduction

The *Flight Instructor Oral Exam Guide* is a comprehensive guide designed for commercial pilots who are involved in training for the initial Flight Instructor Certificate.

This guide was originally designed for use in a Part 141 school but has quickly become popular with those training under 14 CFR Part 61 who are not affiliated with an approved school. It will also prove beneficial to flight instructors who wish to refresh their knowledge or who are preparing to renew their Flight Instructor Certificate.

The *Flight Instructor—Airplane Airman Certification Standards* (FAA-S-ACS-25) specifies the areas in which knowledge and skill must be demonstrated by the applicant before issuance of a Flight Instructor Certificate with the associated category and class ratings. This *Flight Instructor Oral Exam Guide* is designed to evaluate a pilot's knowledge of those areas. Organized around the ACS Areas of Operation and Tasks, this guide provides questions and detailed answers specific to the ACS areas of knowledge, risk management, and skill elements relevant to the tasks. During the exam, an FAA examiner will attempt to determine that the applicant is able to make a practical application of the fundamentals of instructing and is competent to teach the subject matter, procedures, and maneuvers included in the standards to learners with varying backgrounds and levels of experience and ability. Based on very intensive debriefings after flight instructor checkrides, we have provided you with the questions most consistently asked along with the information or the appropriate reference necessary for a knowledgeable response.

This guide may be supplemented with other comprehensive study materials as noted in parentheses after each question; for example: (FAA-H-8083-9). The abbreviations for these materials and their titles are listed below. Ensure that you use the latest revision of these references when reviewing for the test. Also, check the ASA website at asa2fly.com/oegcfi for the most recent updates to this book due to changes in FAA procedures and regulations as well as for Reader Resources containing additional relevant information and updates.

FAA-P-8740-50	*On Landings—Part III*
FAA-P-8740-51	*How to Avoid a Mid Air Collision*
FAA-P-8740-69	*Aeronautical Decision Making*
FAA-S-ACS-6	*Private Pilot—Airplane Airman Certification Standards*
FAA-S-ACS-7	*Commercial Pilot—Airplane Airman Certification Standards*
FAA-S-ACS-8	*Instrument Rating—Airplane Airman Certification Standards*
FAA-S-ACS-25	*Flight Instructor—Airplane Airman Certification Standards*
AIM	*FAA Aeronautical Information Manual*
AIP	*FAA Aeronautical Information Publication*
AIS FAQ	*FAA Aeronautical Information Services: Frequently Asked Questions*
CAMI OK-06-033	*Civil Aerospace Medical Institute, Basic Survival Skills for Aviation*
CAMI OK-21-0375	*Civil Aerospace Medical Institute, Oxygen Equipment Use in General Aviation Operations*
CS	*Chart Supplement U.S. (formerly Aircraft/Facility Directory)*
FAA Safety	*FAA Safety Briefing Magazine/Fly Safe Fact Sheets*
NPRM	*Notice of Proposed Rulemaking 2016-6142-001*
Order 8900.1	*Flight Standards Information Management System*
P/CG	*Pilot/Controller Glossary*
POH/AFM	*Pilot's Operating Handbooks and FAA-Approved Airplane Flight Manuals*
TSA	*Transportation Security Administration*
USRGD	*FAA Aeronautical Chart Users' Guide*

Most of these documents are available on the FAA's website (faa.gov). Additionally, many of the publications are reprinted by ASA (asa2fly.com) and are available from aviation retailers worldwide.

A review of the information and references presented within this guide should provide the necessary preparation for the FAA initial Flight Instructor Practical Test.

Fundamentals of
Instructing

1

A. Effects of Human Behavior and Communication on the Learning Process

1. What is the definition of *human behavior*? (FAA-H-8083-9)

Human behavior is the product of factors that cause people to act in predictable ways. It can also be defined as the result of a person's attempt to satisfy certain needs. A working knowledge of human behavior can help an instructor better understand learners.

2. Why is understanding human behavior important for effective flight instruction? (FAA-H-8083-9)

By observing human behavior, instructors can gain the knowledge needed to better understand themselves as instructors as well as the learning needs of learners. Understanding human behavior leads to successful instruction.

3. What are examples of how human behavior can affect motivation and learning? (FAA-H-8083-9)

a. Aviation learners are usually out of their normal surroundings during training, and their need for association and belonging is more pronounced. Instructors should make every effort to help new learners feel at ease and to reinforce their decision to pursue a career or hobby in aviation.

b. A learner may have a repressed fear of flying that inhibits his or her ability to learn how to fly.

c. A death in the family, a divorce, or even a failing grade on an important test may trigger harmful defensive reactions.

d. Physiological and emotional factors, such as anxiety, may have a potent effect on a person's actions and the ability to learn from perceptions and may result in hesitation or impulsive actions. When introducing stalls, learner anxiety can be minimized by first reviewing the aerodynamic principles and explaining how stalls affect flight characteristics. Also, carefully describing the physical sensations to be expected, as well as the recovery procedures can help reduce anxiety.

4. Explain why the relationship between the instructor and learner is so important. (FAA-H-8083-9)

The instructor/learner relationship has a significant impact on how effective an instructor's teaching will be and how much a learner will learn.

5. How does personality type affect instructors and learners? (FAA-H-8083-9)

Based on personality type, everyone has an individual style of learning. Recognizing that learning style and working with it, rather than against it, benefits both the instructor and the learner.

6. Why is it important to recognize personal instruction style? (FAA-H-8083-9)

The match or mismatch between the way an instructor teaches and the way an individual learns contributes to instructional satisfaction or dissatisfaction. Learners whose styles are compatible with the teaching styles of their instructors tend to retain information longer, apply it more effectively, learn more, and have a more positive attitude toward the course in general.

7. Define *motivation*. (FAA-H-8083-9)

A motivation is a need or desire that causes a person to act. Motivation can be positive or negative, tangible or intangible, subtle or obvious.

8. Where does a learner's motivation to learn come from? (FAA-H-8083-9)

A motivation to learn can come from many sources. All of these sources of motivation have one thing in common: they all offer some type of reward in exchange for performing the hard work. Examples include:

a. A fundamental interest in and fascination with aircraft or with the experience of flight.

b. A way to boost the learner's self-image or ego.

c. Pursuit of aviation training because it offers a promising career.

d. A belief that aviation offers fun and excitement or simply a more convenient form of transportation.

9. **Explain why it's important for an instructor to understand what motivates a learner.** (FAA-H-8083-9)

   Motivation is the most dominant force that governs the learner's progress and ability to understand and can be used to the advantage of the instructor.

10. **What can an instructor do to maintain a learner's motivation and progress?** (FAA-H-8083-9)

    Make each lesson a pleasant experience.

11. **How effective is the use of negative motivation in promoting efficient learning when compared with the use of positive motivation?** (FAA-H-8083-9)

    Negative motivation may engender fear; while negative motivation may be useful in certain situations, it is not as effective in promoting efficient learning as positive motivation.

    Positive motivation is provided by the promise or achievement of rewards. These rewards may be personal or social, and they may involve financial gain, satisfaction of the self-concept, personal gain, or public recognition.

12. **You've noticed that your learner has begun arriving for ground and flight lessons unprepared (e.g., reading assignments are not completed). As their instructor, what should you do?** (FAA-H-8083-9)

    Instructors must be prepared to deal with a number of circumstances in which motivation levels drop. It is natural for motivation to wane somewhat after the initial excitement of the student's first days of training or between major training events, such as solo, evaluations, or practical tests. Students may come to lessons unprepared or give the general sense that aviation training is no longer a priority. During these times, it is often helpful to remind students of their own stated goals for seeking aviation training.

13. What methods can an instructor use to ensure that a learner continues to work hard and do their best? (FAA-H-8083-9)

a. Ask new learners about their aviation training goals.

b. Reward incremental successes in learning.

c. Present new challenges.

d. Occasionally remind learners about their own stated goals for aviation training.

e. Assure learners that learning plateaus are normal and that improvement will resume with continued effort.

14. Control of human behavior involves understanding human needs. What are these basic needs, and how are they important to the instructor-learner relationship? (FAA-H-8083-9)

a. *Physiological*—The need for air, food, and water; unless these biological needs are met, a person cannot concentrate fully on learning.

b. *Security*—If a learner does not feel safe, they cannot concentrate on learning.

c. *Belonging*—Learners are usually out of their normal surroundings during training, and their need for association and belonging is more pronounced.

d. *Esteem*—Humans have a need for a stable, firmly based, high level of self-respect (internal) and respect from others (external). High self-esteem results in self-confidence, independence, achievement, competence, and knowledge.

e. *Cognitive*—Humans have a deep need to understand what is going on around them. When a person understands what is going on, he or she can either control the situation or make an informed choice about what steps might be taken next.

f. *Aesthetic*—These needs connect directly with human emotions. When someone likes another person or an object, the reasons are not examined—he or she simply likes it. This need can factor into the learner-instructor relationship.

g. *Self-actualization*—A person's need to be and do that which the person was "born to do." Helping a learner achieve his or her individual potential in aviation offers the greatest challenge as well as greatest reward to the instructor.

15. What are defense mechanisms? (FAA-H-8083-9)

Defense mechanisms are subconscious, ego-protecting reactions to unpleasant situations. They soften feelings of failure, alleviate feelings of guilt, help an individual cope with reality, and protect one's self-image.

16. Explain the eight common defense mechanisms a person will use that may prevent learning. (FAA-H-8083-9)

Repression—When a person places uncomfortable thoughts into inaccessible areas of the unconscious mind. Things a person is unable to cope with now are pushed away, to be dealt with at another time, or hopefully never. *Example:* A student pilot may have a repressed fear of flying that inhibits his or her ability to learn how to fly.

Denial—A refusal to accept external reality because it is too threatening. Denial is the refusal to acknowledge what has happened, is happening, or will happen. *Example:* The instructor finds the gas cap on the wing unsecured after a student completed the preflight inspection. The student, unwilling to accept reality that their inattention could have caused an inflight problem, denies that they missed it during preflight inspection.

Compensation—Students often attempt to disguise the presence of a weak or undesirable quality by emphasizing a more positive one. Compensation is the process of psychologically counterbalancing perceived weaknesses by emphasizing strength in other areas. *Example:* A philosophy of "I'm not a fighter, I'm a lover."

Projection—When students relegate the blame for personal shortcomings and mistakes to others or attribute their personal motives, desires, and characteristics to others. *Example*: If a student pilot who fails a flight exam says, "I failed because I had a poor examiner," the student is projecting blame onto a perceived "unfair" examiner instead of accepting his or her own lack of personal skill or knowledge.

Rationalization—Justifying actions that otherwise would be unacceptable; the substitution of excuses for reasons. *Example:* A student performs poorly on a test and then justifies the poor grade by claiming there was not enough time to learn the required information.

Reaction Formation—Faking a belief opposite to the true belief because the true belief causes anxiety. *Example:* A student may develop a "who-cares-how-other-people-feel" attitude to cover up feelings of loneliness and a hunger for acceptance.

Fantasy—When a student engages in daydreams about how things should be rather than doing anything about how things are. *Example:* A transitioning pilot is having trouble mastering a more complex aircraft, which jeopardizes his or her dream of becoming an airline pilot. It becomes easier to daydream about the career than to achieve the certification.

Displacement—An unconscious shift of emotion, affect, or desire from the original object to a more acceptable, less threatening substitute. Displacement avoids the risk associated with feeling unpleasant emotions and puts them somewhere other than where they belong.

17. Explain how an instructor can deal with a learner that continually uses excuses to justify substandard performance. (FAA-H-8083-9)

A perceptive instructor can assist the learner by using common sense and discussing the problem with the learner. The main objective should be to restore motivation and self-confidence.

18. What are several examples of emotional reactions that may inhibit learning during flight training? (FAA-H-8083-9)

a. Anxiety and stress
b. Impatience
c. Worry or lack of interest
d. Physical discomfort, illness, fatigue, and dehydration
e. Apathy due to inadequate instruction

19. What is the definition of *anxiety*, and why is a learner's anxiety of concern to an instructor? (FAA-H-8083-9)

Anxiety is a feeling of worry, nervousness, or unease, often about something that is going to happen—typically something with an uncertain outcome. It results from the fear of anything, real or imagined, that threatens the person who experiences it, and it may have a potent effect on actions and the ability to learn from perceptions.

20. Describe how a learner might react to a stressful situation. (FAA-H-8083-9)

Normal reaction—The learner responds rapidly and exactly within the limits of their experience and training; the individual thinks rationally, acts rapidly, and is extremely sensitive to all aspects of their surroundings.

Abnormal reaction—The individual's response to anxiety or stress may be completely absent or at least inadequate; the response may be random or illogical or the person may do more than is called for by the situation.

21. Describe several student reactions you might observe that are indicative of abnormal reactions to stress. (FAA-H-8083-9)

Extreme over-cooperation, painstaking self-control, inappropriate laughter or singing, and very rapid changes in emotions. Another example is marked changes in mood across different lessons, such as excellent morale followed by deep depression.

22. How can an instructor help learners to counter their anxieties? (FAA-H-8083-9)

Anxiety can be countered by reinforcing the learner's enjoyment of flying and by teaching them to cope with their fears. An instructor can treat fears as a normal reaction, rather than ignoring them.

23. Explain the difference between acute fatigue and chronic fatigue. (AIM 8-1-1)

Acute (short-term) fatigue—The tiredness felt after long periods of physical and mental strain. Fatigue is the primary consideration in determining the length and frequency of flight instruction periods. It is important for a flight instructor to be able to detect fatigue, both in assessing a learner's substandard performance early in a lesson and also in recognizing the deterioration of performance.

Chronic fatigue—This occurs when there is not enough time for full recovery between episodes of acute fatigue. Performance will continue to fall off, and judgment becomes impaired so that unwarranted risks may be taken. Recovery from chronic fatigue requires a prolonged period of rest.

24. What are some of the signs that indicate a learner may be experiencing acute fatigue? (FAA-H-8083-9)

Acute fatigue is characterized by inattention, distractibility, errors in timing, neglect of secondary tasks, loss of accuracy and control, lack of awareness of error accumulation, and irritability.

25. Describe the physical discomforts learners may experience during flight training that may affect their rate of learning. (FAA-H-8083-9)

Extremes of temperature, poor ventilation, inadequate lighting, or noise and confusion have a detrimental effect on learning. Minor illnesses such as a cold, as well as conditions such as airsickness, fatigue, dehydration and heatstroke, are also of concern.

26. Describe the steps an instructor may take if they believe that a learner may have a disqualifying psychological defect. (FAA-H-8083-9)

a. Arrange to have another instructor, who is not acquainted with the learner, conduct an evaluation flight.

b. After the flight, the instructors should confer to determine whether they agree that further investigation or action is justified.

c. If, after consultation with an unbiased instructor, the instructor believes that the learner may have a serious psychological deficiency, any endorsement of the learner to be competent for solo flight operations, or recommendation for a practical test leading to certification as a pilot, should be withheld.

27. What primary responsibility does an instructor have after determining that a learner may have serious psychological problems? (FAA-H-8083-9)

A flight instructor who believes a learner may be suffering from a serious psychological abnormality has a responsibility to refrain from instructing that learner. In addition, a flight instructor has the personal responsibility of assuring that such a person does not continue flight training or become certificated as a pilot.

28. Explain several methods an instructor can use to address the needs of adult learners. (FAA-H-8083-9)

a. Provide a training syllabus that is organized with clearly defined course objectives to show learners how the training helps them attain specific goals.

b. Help learners integrate new ideas with what they already know to ensure they keep and use the new information.

c. Recognize the learner's need to control the pace and start/stop time.

d. Take advantage of the adult preference to self-direct and self-design learning projects by giving the learner frequent scenario-based training opportunities.

e. Use books, programmed instruction, and computers, which are popular with adult learners.

f. Refrain from spoon-feeding information to the learner.

g. Create a cooperative learning climate.

29. What are the three basic elements of communication? (FAA-H-8083-9)

Source—speaker, writer, or instructor.

Symbols—words or signs.

Receiver—listener, reader, or learner.

30. Explain the three characteristics that instructors must understand about their learners before effective communication can take place. (FAA-H-8083-9)

a. *Abilities*—An instructor needs to determine the abilities of the learner in order to properly communicate.

b. *Attitudes*—The attitudes that learners exhibit may indicate resistance, willingness, or passive neutrality.

c. *Experiences*—Learner experience, background, and educational level determine the approach an instructor takes.

31. What are the four barriers to effective communication? (FAA-H-8083-9)

*C*onfusion between the symbol and the symbolized object—This results when a word is confused with what it is meant to represent. Words and symbols do not always represent the same thing to every person.

*O*veruse of abstractions—Abstractions are words that are general rather than specific. They stand for ideas that cannot be directly experienced and things that do not call forth mental images in the minds of learners. The word "aircraft" is an abstract word that might mean an airplane, a helicopter, an airship, etc.

*I*nterference—The prevention of a process or activity from being carried out properly; composed of factors outside the control of the instructor, which include physiological (e.g., hearing loss, injury, or physical illness), environmental (e.g., noise), and psychological (e.g., fear of a situation or mistrust between the instructor and learner).

*L*ack of common experience between the instructor and the learner; this is the greatest single barrier to effective communication; communication can be effective only when the experiences (physical, mental, and emotional) of the people concerned are similar.

32. How can flight instructors develop their instructional communication skills? (FAA-H-8083-9)

Role playing—Instructional communication experience comes from actually doing it and is learned by role playing during the instructor's initial training. For example, an instructor applicant can fly with a CFI who assumes the role of a learner pilot.

Instructional communication—Instructors must always determine whether the learner has actually received and retained the knowledge. Communication has not occurred unless the desired results of the communication have taken place. Also, instructors should not be afraid to use examples of past experiences to illustrate particular points.

Listening—Instructors must know something about their learners in order to communicate effectively. One way to accomplish this is to be a good listener. In addition, instructors can improve information transfer by teaching their learners how to listen.

(continued)

Questioning—Good questioning can determine how well the learner understands what is being taught. It also shows the learner that the instructor is paying attention and is interested in the learner's response.

Instructional enhancement—The more an instructor knows about a subject, the better the instructor is at conveying that information. Additional knowledge and training improves the instructor's confidence and gives the instructional presentation more depth.

33. Name several techniques instructors can use to become better at listening to their learners. (FAA-H-8083-9)

a. Do not interrupt.
b. Do not judge.
c. Think before answering.
d. Be close enough to hear.
e. Watch non-verbal behavior.
f. Beware of biases.
g. Look for underlying feelings.
h. Concentrate.
i. Avoid rehearsing answers while listening.
j. Do not insist on having the last word.

B. Learning Process

1. What is the definition of *learning*? (FAA-H-8083-9)

Learning can be defined as a change in the behavior of the learner as a result of experience. If a change in your learner's behavior has not occurred, then the learner probably has not learned what you have taught.

2. Define the term *learning theory*. (FAA-H-8083-9)

Learning theory is the body of principles that explain how people acquire skills, knowledge, and attitudes.

3. Modern learning theories grew out of two concepts of how people learn: behaviorism and cognitive theory. Explain these two concepts. (FAA-H-8083-9)

Behaviorism is the theory of learning that stresses the importance of having a particular form of behavior reinforced by someone other than the learner to shape or control what is learned. Classic behaviorist theory stressed a system of rewards and punishments, or the carrot-and-stick approach to learning.

Cognitive theory focuses on what is going on inside the learner's mind and is concerned with cognition (the process of thinking and learning). Learning is not just a change in behavior; it is a change in the way a learner thinks, understands, or feels.

4. **Cognitive theory has led to theories such as information processing and constructivism. Briefly explain these theories.** (FAA-H-8083-9)

   Information processing theory uses a computer system as a model for human learning. The human brain processes incoming information, stores and retrieves it, and generates responses to the information. This involves a number of cognitive processes, which include gathering and representing information (encoding), retaining of information, and retrieving the information when needed.

   Constructivism holds that learners do not acquire knowledge and skills passively but rather actively build or construct them based on their experiences. Constructivism emphasizes the constructing or building that goes on during the learning process, and it therefore creates a learner-centered environment in which they assume responsibility for their own learning.

5. **Why are perceptions so important to learning?** (FAA-H-8083-9)

   Perceptions result when a person gives meaning to external stimuli or sensations. Initially, all learning comes from perceptions, which are directed to the brain by one or more of the five senses: sight, hearing, touch, smell, and taste. Meaning derived from perception is influenced by an individual's experience and many other factors.

6. **Explain the factors that affect an individual's perception.** (FAA-H-8083-9)

   Both internal and external factors affect an individual's ability to perceive:

   a. *Physical organism*—Provides individuals with the perceptual apparatus for sensing the world around them: the ability to see, hear, feel, and respond.

(continued)

b. *Goals and values*—Every experience and sensation that is funneled into a person's central nervous system is colored by the individual's own beliefs and value structures.

c. *Self-concept*—A learner's self-image, described in such terms as "confident" or "insecure," has a great influence on the total perceptual process.

d. *Time and opportunity*—Learning some things depends on other perceptions that have preceded that learning, and on the availability of time to sense and relate those new things to the earlier perceptions.

e. *Element of threat*—Confronted with a threat, learners tend to limit their attention to the threatening object or condition. Fear adversely affects perception by narrowing the perceptual field.

7. Define *insight*. (FAA-H-8083-9)

Insight involves the grouping of perceptions into meaningful wholes. It is the mental relating and grouping of associated perceptions. As perceptions increase in number, the learner develops insight by assembling them into larger blocks of learning. Creating insight is one of the instructor's major responsibilities.

8. How can an instructor ensure that a learner develops insight during flight training? (FAA-H-8083-9)

a. Help the learner understand how each piece relates to all other pieces of the total pattern of the task to be learned.

b. Provide a secure and non-threatening environment in which to learn.

c. Help the learner acquire and maintain a favorable self-concept.

9. Define the word *knowledge* and explain how a learner acquires knowledge (3 phases). (FAA-H-8083-9)

Knowledge refers to information that humans are consciously aware of and can articulate. Acquiring knowledge involves three phases:

a. *Memorization*—learner acquires and memorizes facts.

b. *Understanding*—learner begins to organize knowledge to formulate understanding.

c. *Application*—learner learns to use the knowledge they have compiled to solve problems and make decisions.

10. How can an instructor help learners in acquiring knowledge? (FAA-H-8083-9)

The instructor should:

a. Ask learners to recite or practice newly acquired knowledge.

b. Ask questions that probe learners' understanding and prompt them to think about what they have learned.

c. Present opportunities for learners to apply what they know to solving problems or making decisions.

d. Present learners with problems and decisions that test the limits of their knowledge.

e. Demonstrate the benefits of understanding and being able to apply knowledge.

f. Introduce new topics as they support the objectives of the lesson, whenever possible.

11. What are the six principles (laws) of learning? (FAA-H-8083-9)

They are rules and principles that apply generally to the learning process. The first three are the basic laws; the last three are the result of experimental studies:

*R*eadiness—Individuals learn best when they are ready to learn, and they do not learn well if they see no reason for it or lack motivation. If learners have a strong purpose, a clear objective, and a true reason for learning something, they make more progress.

*E*xercise—Memory and connections between concepts are strengthened with practice and weakened when practice is discontinued, which reflects the adage "use it or lose it." The learner needs to practice what has been learned in order to understand and remember it.

*E*ffect—Learning is strengthened when accompanied by a pleasant or satisfying feeling, but it is weakened when associated with an unpleasant feeling.

*P*rimacy—The state of being first often creates a strong, almost unshakable impression and underlies the reason that an instructor must teach correctly the first time and the learner's initial learning must be right.

(continued)

Intensity—A vivid, dramatic, or exciting learning experience teaches more than a routine or boring experience.

Recency—The things most recently learned are best remembered.

12. What are the three domains of learning? (FAA-H-8083-9)

Cognitive (thinking)—A grouping of levels of learning associated with mental activity. The six major levels, in order of increasing complexity, are knowledge, comprehension, application, analysis, synthesis, and evaluation.

Affective (feelings)—A grouping of levels of learning associated with a person's attitudes, personal beliefs, and values. The levels (in order of increasing complexity) include receiving, responding, valuing, organization, and characterization.

Psychomotor (doing)—A grouping of levels of learning associated with physical skill levels, which include (in order of increasing complexity) perception, set, guided response, mechanism, complex overt response, adaptation, and origination.

13. What are the four basic levels of learning? (FAA-H-8083-9)

Rote—the ability to repeat something back that was learned but not necessarily understood.

Understanding—to comprehend or grasp the nature or meaning of something.

Application—the act of putting something to use that has been learned and understood.

Correlation—associating what has been learned, understood, and applied with previous or subsequent learning; this level is the overall objective of aviation instruction.

14. Briefly describe the six major levels of the cognitive (thinking) domain. (FAA-H-8083-9)

a. *Knowledge*—the least complex level; remembering information.

b. *Comprehension*—understanding and explaining the meaning of information.

c. *Application*—using abstractions in concrete situations.

d. *Analysis*—breaking down a whole into component parts.

   e. *Synthesis*—putting parts together to form a new and integrated whole.

   f. *Evaluation*—making judgments about the merits of ideas, materials, and phenomena; the most complex level.

15. Briefly describe the five levels of the affective (feeling) domain. (FAA-H-8083-9)

   a. *Receiving*—willingness to pay attention; least complex level.

   b. *Responding*—reacts voluntarily or complies.

   c. *Valuing*—acceptance.

   d. *Organization*—rearrangement of value system.

   e. *Characterization*—incorporates value into life; most complex level.

16. Briefly describe the seven educational objective levels of the psychomotor (doing) domain. (FAA-H-8083-9)

   a. *Perception*—awareness of sensory stimulus.

   b. *Set*—relates cues/knows.

   c. *Guided response*—performs as demonstrated.

   d. *Mechanism*—performs simple acts well.

   e. *Complex overt response*—skillful performance of complex acts.

   f. *Adaptation*—modifies for special problems.

   g. *Origination*—new movement patterns, creativity.

17. What are the four practical instructional levels of the psychomotor domain? (FAA-H-8083-9)

Observation—The learner observes a more experienced person perform the skill.

Imitation—The learner attempts to copy the skill under the watchful eye of the instructor.

Practice—The learner tries a specific activity over and over with or without the instructor.

Habit—The learner can perform the skill in twice the time that it takes the instructor or an expert to perform it.

18. What are the basic characteristics of learning?
(FAA-H-8083-9)

Learning is:

*P*urposeful—Each learner is a unique individual whose past experience affects readiness to learn and understanding of the requirements involved. Learners have fairly definite ideas about what they want to do and achieve.

*E*xperience—Learning is an individual process from personal experiences. Previous experience conditions a person to respond to some things and ignore others. Knowledge cannot be poured into the learner's head.

*M*ultifaceted—Learning may include verbal elements, conceptual elements, perceptual elements, emotional elements, and problem-solving elements all taking place at once.

*A*ctive process—Learners do not soak up knowledge like a sponge absorbs water. For learners to learn, they must react and respond—perhaps outwardly, or perhaps only inwardly, emotionally, or intellectually.

19. Explain the VAK learning styles model of learning.
(FAA-H-8083-9)

The visual, auditory, and kinesthetic (VAK) model is one of the most popular learning styles and is based on the three main sensory receptors: vision, hearing, and touch. Learners generally use all three styles to receive information, but one of these three ways of receiving information is dominant. VAK learning style traits and teaching tips:

Learning Style	Traits	Teaching Tips
Visual	Seeing, reading	Use graphs, charts, and videos.
Auditory	Hearing, speaking	Have learner verbalize questions.
Kinesthetic	Touching, doing	Use demonstration of skills.

20. How might understanding learning styles help in the design of lesson plans? (FAA-H-8083-9)

It can help instructors make adjustments in how material is presented. Learners whose learning styles are compatible with the teaching styles of an instructor tend to retain information longer, apply it more effectively, learn more, and have a more positive attitude toward the course in general.

21. What are the three stages of acquiring skill knowledge? (FAA-H-8083-9)

Cognitive—Cognitive learning has a basis in factual knowledge; since the learner has no prior knowledge of flying, the instructor first introduces him or her to a basic skill. The learner then memorizes the steps required to perform the skill.

Associative—As the storage of skill knowledge through practice continues, the learner learns to associate individual steps in performance with likely outcomes. They no longer perform a series of memorized steps but are able to assess their progress along the way and make adjustments in performance.

Automatic Response Stage—As procedures become automatic, less attention is required to carry them out, so it is possible to do other things simultaneously, or at least do other things more comfortably.

22. Why is it important for an instructor to always make certain that a learner is aware of their progress? (FAA-H-8083-9)

It is as important for learners to know when they are right as to know when they are wrong. Learners should be told as soon after the performance as possible and should not be allowed to practice mistakes. It's more difficult to unlearn a mistake, and then learn the skill correctly, than to learn it correctly in the first place.

23. How does a learner develop and become proficient at a skill? (FAA-H-8083-9)

Progress depends on repeated practice, and it tends to follow what is known as the "power law of practice." This law states that the speed of performance of a task improves as a power of the number of times that the task is performed. Simply stated, practice improves performance.

24. What is a learning plateau? Explain how an instructor can help a learner who has reached a learning plateau. (FAA-H-8083-9)

A learning plateau is a learning phenomenon where progress appears to cease or slow down for a significant period of time before once again increasing. Instructors can help learners experiencing a learning plateau by moving to a different place in the curriculum and giving the current task a break, or by better explaining the lesson, the reason for the lesson, and how it applies to the learner. Instructors should be aware that they can bring on a learning plateau by over practice.

25. What are the three types of practice? (FAA-H-8083-9)

Deliberate—Practice aimed at a particular goal. The learner practices specific areas for improvement and receives specific feedback after practice; the feedback points out discrepancies and the learner focuses on eliminating those discrepancies.

Blocked—Practicing the same drill until the movement becomes automatic. Doing the same task over and over leads to better short-term performance but poorer long-term learning; it tends to fool not only the learner but the instructor into thinking the skills have been well learned.

Random—Mixing up the skills to be acquired throughout the practice session, which results in better retention. By performing a series of separate skills in a random order, the learner begins to recognize the similarities and differences of each skill, which makes it more meaningful.

26. How much practice is needed by a learner in order to attain proficiency? (FAA-H-8083-9)

A beginning learner reaches a point where additional practice is not only unproductive but may even be harmful. When this point is reached, errors increase and motivation declines. As a learner gains experience, longer periods of practice are profitable.

27. Explain the difference between an evaluation and a critique. (FAA-H-8083-9)

Evaluation—Evaluation of a learner's ability refers to judging a learner's ability to perform a maneuver or procedure. It is usually teacher-oriented and provides a check on teaching effectiveness. It can be used to predict eventual learner learning proficiency and can help the teacher locate special problem areas.

Critique—An instructor ensures a skill is practiced correctly by monitoring the practice and providing feedback about the skill development. The learner profits by having someone watch the performance and provide constructive criticism to help eliminate errors.

28. What is the purpose of using distractions during flight training? (FAA-H-8083-9)

The purpose is to determine that the learner possesses the skills required to cope with distractions while maintaining the degree of aircraft control required for safe flight. Pilots at all skill levels should be aware of the increased risk of entering into an inadvertent stall or spin while performing tasks that are secondary to controlling the aircraft.

29. How should an instructor incorporate the use of distractions into flight instruction? (FAA-H-8083-9)

Instructor responsibilities include teaching the learner to divide his or her attention between the distracting task and maintaining control of the aircraft. Following are examples of distractions that can be used for this training:

a. Drop a pencil. Ask the learner to pick it up.
b. Ask the learner to determine a heading to an airport using a chart.
c. Ask the learner to reset the clock.
d. Ask the learner to get something from the back seat.
e. Ask the learner to compute the aircraft's true airspeed.
f. Ask the learner to identify terrain or objects on the ground.
g. Ask the learner to identify a field suitable for a forced landing.

30. How would an instructor identify a learner having fixation or inattention problems? (FAA-H-8083-9)

Try to follow where learners look. Watch a learner's eyes/head position to determine where they are looking. If they appear to look at one instrument for an extended period of time, they might have a problem with fixation. Learners whose gaze is never directed toward engine instruments might have a problem with inattention.

31. **Explain the two kinds of errors.** (FAA-H-8083-9)

    Slip—A slip occurs when a person plans to do one thing but then inadvertently does something else. Slips are errors of action. Simply neglecting to do something is one common form of a slip. Someone being asked to perform a routine procedure in a slightly different way can result in a slip. Time pressure is another common source of slips. The more hurried one's work becomes the more slips he or she is likely to make.

    Mistake—A mistake occurs when a person plans to do the wrong thing and is successful. Mistakes are errors of thought. They are sometimes the result of gaps or misconceptions in a learner's understanding. For example, overly simplistic understanding of weather frequently leads inexperienced learners into situations that are unexpected.

32. **Although errors cannot be eliminated entirely, what are several ways to reduce them?** (FAA-H-8083-9)
    a. Learning and practicing
    b. Taking time
    c. Checking for errors
    d. Using reminders
    e. Developing routines
    f. Raising awareness

33. **How can learners be prepared for some of the more common errors that they could make?** (FAA-H-8083-9)

    It is a worthwhile exercise to practice recovering from commonly made errors, or those that pose more serious consequences. For example, all learners should learn and practice lost procedures to ensure that they can recover from the situation in which they have become lost. It is useful to devote the same sort of preparation to other common learner errors.

34. **How can errors be a valuable learning resource?** (FAA-H-8083-9)

    When a learner makes an error, it is useful to ask the learner to consider why the error happened and what could be done differently to prevent the error from happening again in the future.

In some cases, errors are slips that simply reveal the need for more practice. In other cases, errors point to aspects of learner methods or habits that might be improved.

35. How can an instructor help learners to learn from errors they've made and be prepared for errors in the future? (FAA-H-8083-9)

a. Explain that pilots at all levels of skill and experience make occasional errors.

b. Explain that the magnitude and frequency of errors tend to decrease as skill and experience increases.

c. Explain the difference between slips and mistakes and provide examples of each.

d. Explain ways in which the learner can help minimize errors.

e. Allow the learner to practice recovering from common errors.

f. Point out errors when they occur and ask the learner to explain why they occurred.

36. Define *memory*. (FAA-H-8083-9)

Memory is the ability of people to encode (initial perception and registration of information), store (retention of encoded information over time), and retrieve (processes involved in using stored information) information.

37. What are the three types of memory? (FAA-H-8083-9)

Sensory memory—receives and processes input from the environment according to the individual's pre-conceived concept of what is important. Information is then sent to short-term memory.

Short-term memory—the part of the memory where information is stored briefly (30 seconds), after which it may rapidly fade or be consolidated into long-term memory.

Long-term memory—relatively permanent storage of unlimited information; it is possible for memories in long-term memory to remain there for a lifetime.

38. The ability to retrieve knowledge from memory depends on what two things? (FAA-H-8083-9)

Frequency—how often the knowledge has been used in the past.

Recency—how recently the knowledge has been used.

39. What are several threats to remembering what has been learned during training? (FAA-H-8083-9)

a. *Lack of frequent usage in the past*—Learners must engage in regular practice of what they have learned in order to retain that knowledge.

b. *Lack of understanding*—Learners may lack understanding that might serve to assist them in recalling what they've learned. The repetition of knowledge with efforts to understand that knowledge leads to the best results.

40. Why do learners forget information? (FAA-H-8083-9)

Several theories exist on why people forget, including:

Fading—a person forgets information that is not used for an extended period of time.

Interference—people forget because a certain experience has overshadowed it or the learning of similar things has intervened.

Repression or suppression—a memory is pushed out of reach because the individual does not want to remember feelings associated with it.

Retrieval failure—the inability to retrieve information.

41. What principles facilitate retention of learning or remembering? (FAA-H-8083-9)

a. *Praise*—stimulates remembering; absence of praise or recognition discourages remembering.

b. *Association*—recall is promoted by association.

c. *Attitudes*—favorable attitudes aid retention; people learn and remember only what they wish to know.

d. *Senses*—learning with all senses is most effective.

e. *Repetition*—meaningful repetition aids recall, but mere repetition does not guarantee retention.

f. *Mnemonics*—pattern of letters, ideas, visual images, or associations assist in remembering information.

42. How can an instructor help learners remember what they have learned? (FAA-H-8083-9)

The instructor should:

a. Discuss the difference between short-term memory and long-term memory.

b. Explain the effect of frequent and recent usage of knowledge on remembering and forgetting.

c. Explain the effect of depth of understanding on remembering and forgetting.

d. Encourage the learner's use of mnemonic devices while studying.

e. Explain the benefits of studying at regularly spaced intervals, and the disadvantages of cramming.

43. What is meant by the term *transfer of learning*? (FAA-H-8083-9)

Transfer of learning is defined as the ability to apply knowledge or procedures learned in one context to new contexts. Learning occurs more quickly and a deeper understanding of the task develops if the learner brings some knowledge or skills from previous learning.

44. When learning two skills, when does a positive transfer of learning occur and when does a negative transfer of learning occur? (FAA-H-8083-9)

Positive transfer—occurs if the learning of skill A helps to learn skill B.

Negative transfer—occurs if the learning of skill A hinders the learning of skill B.

Examples: The practice of slow flight helps the learner learn short-field landings (positive transfer). Practice in making a landing approach in an airplane may hinder learning to make an approach in a helicopter (negative transfer).

45. Why does use of the building block technique of instruction ensure proper habits and correct techniques are learned during training? (FAA-H-8083-9)

New learning and habit patterns are based on a solid foundation of experience and/or old learning. Everything from intricate cognitive processes to simple motor skills depends on what the learner already knows and how that knowledge can be applied in the present. As knowledge and skill increase, there is an expanding base upon which to build for future learning.

C. Course Development, Lesson Plans, and Classroom Training Techniques

1. What is teaching? (FAA-H-8083-9)

Teaching is to instruct or train. Teachers often complete some type of formal training, have specialized knowledge, have been certified or validated in some way, and adhere to a set of standards of performance.

2. Define the term *good instructor*. (FAA-H-8083-9)

In *The Essence of Good Teaching*, psychologist Stanford C. Ericksen wrote, "good teachers select and organize worthwhile course material, lead learners to encode and integrate this material in memorable form, ensure competence in the procedures and methods of a discipline, sustain intellectual curiosity, and promote how to learn independently."

3. Explain the four basic steps involved in the teaching process. (FAA-H-8083-9)

Preparation—determining the scope of the lesson, the objectives, and the goals to be attained, and ensuring that the necessary supplies are available.

Presentation—consists of delivering information or demonstrating the skills that make up the lesson. Delivery could be through the lecture method, guided discussion method, demonstration-performance method, etc.

Application—the learner performs the procedure or demonstrates the knowledge required in the lesson.

Review and evaluation—consists of a review of all material and an evaluation of the learner's performance.

4. Explain the four essential skills that are necessary to be an effective instructor. (FAA-H-8083-9)

People skills—Effective instructors relate well to people, and effective communication underlies people skills.

Subject matter expertise—A subject matter expert (SME) is a person who possesses a high level of expertise, knowledge, or skill in a particular area.

Assessment skills—Assessment of learning is another important skill of an effective instructor. Assessment of learning is a complex process, and it is important to be clear about the purposes of the assessment.

Management skills—These generally include the ability to plan, organize, lead, and supervise. For the effective instructor, this translates into being able to plan, organize, and carry out a lesson.

5. Explain what it means to have good people skills. (FAA-H-8083-9)

Good people skills include the ability to:

a. Interact with learners respectfully.
b. Detect when learners are not learning.
c. Provide motivation.
d. Adapt to learner needs when necessary.
e. Challenge learners intellectually while supporting their efforts.
f. Display enthusiasm for the subject matter.
g. Express yourself clearly.

6. Define the following terms: *course of training*, *curriculum*, *training course outline*, and *syllabus*. (FAA-H-8083-9)

Course of training—a complete series of studies leading to attainment of a specific goal such as a certificate of completion, graduation, or an academic degree.

Curriculum—a set of courses in an area of specialization offered by an educational institution. A curriculum for a pilot school usually includes courses for various pilot certificates and ratings.

Training course outline—the content of a particular course within a curriculum; it normally includes statements of objectives,

(continued)

descriptions of teaching aids, definitions of assessment criteria, and indications of desired outcomes.

Syllabus—a summary or outline of a course of study that generally contains a description of each lesson, including objectives and completion standards.

7. What are the initial steps in planning a course of training? (FAA-H-8083-9)

a. Determine the overall objectives and standards.
b. Identify the foundation blocks of learning.
c. Design and develop the blocks of learning.

8. What are the two types of training objectives used in aviation training? (FAA-H-8083-9)

Performance-based objectives define what needs to be done and how it will be done. They consist of three elements: a description of the skill or behavior, conditions, and criteria.

Decision-based objectives teach critical thinking skills such as risk management and aeronautical decision-making (ADM). They facilitate a higher level of learning and application through the use of dynamic and meaningful scenarios.

9. Explain the importance of the ACS in aviation training curricula. (FAA-H-8083-9)

ACS documents hold an important position in aviation training curricula because they supply the instructor with specific performance objectives based on the standards for the issuance of a particular aviation certificate or rating. The ACS Areas of Operation and Tasks are frequently reviewed by the FAA to maintain their relevance to the current aviation environment.

10. Once a learner has progressed through higher levels of performance and understanding, an instructor should shift the training focus to what type of training objectives? (FAA-H-8083-9)

The training focus should shift to decision-based training objectives, which rely on a more dynamic training environment, are ideally suited to scenario-based training, and teach aviation learners critical thinking skills, such as risk management and aeronautical decision-making.

11. Explain how use of performance-based and decision-based training objectives can help an instructor design a lesson plan. (FAA-H-8083-9)

An instructor can use the standards of assessment, objectives, conditions, and criteria to fashion many of the details of the lesson plan:

a. Objective components may be used to determine the elements of the lesson and the schedule of events.

b. The equipment necessary and the instructor and learner actions anticipated during the lesson have been specified.

c. By listing the criteria for the training objectives, the instructor has already established the completion standards normally included as part of the lesson plan.

12. The traditional organization for a lesson consists of what steps? (FAA-H-8083-9)

Introduction—consists of three elements:

- Attention—the instructor gains the learner's attention and focuses it on the subject.

- Motivation—the instructor offers the learner specific reasons why the lesson content is important.

- Overview—the instructor gives a clear concise presentation of what is to be covered during the lesson.

Development—the main part of the lesson in which the instructor logically organizes the material to show the relationships of the main points in one of the following ways: from past to present, simple to complex, known to unknown, or most-frequently used to least-frequently used.

Conclusion—retraces the important elements of the lesson and relates them to the objective. This review reinforces learner learning and improves the retention of what has been learned. No new ideas should be introduced.

13. **Explain the different ways an instructor can develop the subject matter of a lesson.** (FAA-H-8083-9)

    Past to present—Subject matter is arranged chronologically from present to the past or from the past to present. Time relationships are most suitable when history is an important consideration (e.g., in describing development of radio navigation systems).

    Simple to complex—This pattern helps the instructor lead the learner from simple facts or ideas to an understanding of the phenomena or concepts involved. For example, when studying jet propulsion, the lesson might start by considering forces involved when releasing air from a toy balloon and finish with a discussion of a complex gas turbine.

    Known to unknown—By using something the learner already knows as the point of departure, the instructor can lead into new ideas and concepts. For example, when developing a lesson on heading indicators, the instructor could begin with a discussion of the magnetic compass before proceeding to a description of gyroscopic indicators.

    Most frequently used to least used—This organizational pattern starts with common usage before progressing to the rarer ones. For example, even though some aircraft are equipped with a computerized navigational system, instructors should begin by teaching learners the basics of navigation since all pilots use the basic skills.

14. **What are several common teaching methods an instructor may use to present instructional material?** (FAA-H-8083-9)

    a. *Lecture method*—delivered by an instructor to a group of learners.

    b. *Discussion method*—short lecture followed by instructor–learner and learner–learner discussion.

    c. *Guided discussion method*—instructor participates only as necessary to keep the group focused on the subject.

    d. *Problem-based learning*—instructor confronts learners with problems encountered in real life that force them to reach real-world solutions.

e. *E-learning*—computer-based method of delivery.

f. *Cooperative or group learning*—learners organized into small groups that work together to maximize their own and each other's learning.

g. *Demonstration-performance method*—instructor first shows the learner the correct way to perform an activity and then has the learner attempt the same activity.

h. *Drill and practice method*—based on the principle that connections are strengthened with practice.

15. Describe the lecture method of teaching. (FAA-H-8083-9)

In the lecture method, the instructor delivers knowledge via lectures to learners who are more or less silent participants. Lectures are best used when an instructor wishes to convey a general understanding of a subject. Lectures may introduce new subjects, summarize ideas, show relationships between theory and practice, and reemphasize main points. Types of lectures include the teaching lecture, illustrated talk, briefing, and formal lecture. Lectures may be conducted in a formal or informal manner.

16. Explain the four ways a lecture is usually delivered. (FAA-H-8083-9)

a. Reading from a typed or written manuscript.

b. Reciting memorized material without the aid of a manuscript.

c. Speaking extemporaneously from an outline.

d. Speaking impromptu without preparation.

17. Describe the advantages and disadvantages of the lecture method of teaching. (FAA-H-8083-9)

Advantages:

a. A lecture is a convenient way to instruct a large group.

b. The instructor can present many ideas in a relatively short time.

c. It is suitable for introducing a new subject and for explaining necessary background information.

d. It can be used to present information that would be difficult for the learners to get in other ways.

(continued)

Disadvantages:

a. It does not allow the instructor a precise measure of learner understanding.

b. It can sometimes be difficult to hold the attention of all learners throughout a lecture.

c. The pure lecture format inhibits learner participation.

d. It does not foster attainment of certain types of learning outcomes, such as motor skills.

18. Explain the discussion method of teaching.
(FAA-H-8083-9)

This method relies on discussion and the exchange of ideas. Everyone has the opportunity to comment, listen, think, and participate. By being actively engaged in discussing the lecture, learners improve their recall and ability to use the information. It is important for the instructor to keep the discussion focused on the subject matter. The instructor may need to initiate leading questions, comment on any disagreements, ensure that all learners participate, and summarize what has been learned.

19. Explain the guided discussion method of teaching.
(FAA-H-8083-9)

This method relies on learner possession of a level of knowledge about the topic to be discussed, either through reading prior to class or a short lecture to set up the topic to be discussed. It employs instructor-guided discussion with the instructor maintaining control of the discussion. The goal of guided discussions is to draw out what the learners know.

20. Explain the demonstration-performance method of teaching. (FAA-H-8083-9)

This method is based on the principle that people learn by doing. The instructor first shows the learner the correct way to perform an activity and then has the learner attempt the same activity. Learners observe the skill and then try to reproduce it. This method is best used for the mastery of mental or physical skills that require practice.

21. What are the five essential phases of the demonstration-performance method of teaching? (FAA-H-8083-9)

Explanation—must be clear, be pertinent to the objectives of the lesson presented, and convey to learners the precise actions they are to perform.

Demonstration—the instructor must show learners the actions necessary to perform a skill.

Learner performance—requires learners to act and do. Through doing, learners learn to follow correct procedures and to reach established standards.

Instructor supervision—instructor supervises and coaches as necessary.

Evaluation—the instructor judges learner performance and determines effectiveness of instruction.

22. Explain the steps involved in the telling-and-doing technique of flight instructing. (FAA-H-8083-9)

This technique is a variation of the demonstration-performance method and is very effective in teaching procedures and maneuvers. The steps are as follows:

a. Instructor tells—Instructor does
b. Learner tells—Instructor does
c. Learner tells—Learner does
d. Instructor evaluates—Learner does

23. Describe the drill and practice method of teaching. (FAA-H-8083-9)

The drill and practice method is based on the learning principle of exercise, which holds that connections are strengthened with practice. It promotes learning through repetition because those things most often repeated are best remembered.

24. What is meant by the term *e-learning*? (FAA-H-8083-9)

Electronic learning, or e-learning, is an umbrella term for any type of education that involves an electronic component. It can be a stand-alone software application that takes a learner from lecture to exam, or it can be an interactive, web-based course. E-learning offers many advantages: It is time-flexible, cost-competitive, learner-centered, easily updated, and accessible anytime and anywhere.

25. **Explain the difference between instructional aids and training media.** (FAA-H-8083-9)

    Instructional aids—devices that assist an instructor in the teaching-learning process. They are not self-supporting; they support, supplement, or reinforce what is being taught.

    Training media—any physical means that communicates an instructional message to learners. Examples include printed text, interactive computer programs, flight training devices, etc.

26. **Describe the characteristics of good instructional teaching aids.** (FAA-H-8083-9)

    Instructional aids should cover the key points and concepts, be straightforward and factual, and be relatively simple. Carefully selected charts, graphs, pictures, or other well-organized visual aids are examples of items that help the learner understand, as well as retain, essential information.

27. **When planning a lesson, describe the process that can be used to determine if and where instructional aids are necessary.** (FAA-H-8083-9)

    a. Clearly establish the lesson objective; be certain of what is to be communicated.

    b. Gather the necessary data by researching for support material.

    c. Organize the material into an outline or a lesson plan. The plan should include all key points that need to be covered.

    d. Select the ideas to be supported with instructional aids. The aids should be concentrated on the key points.

28. **When is use of instructional aids appropriate?** (FAA-H-8083-9)

    a. For long segments of a technical description.

    b. When a point is complex and difficult to put into words.

    c. When instructors find themselves forming visual images.

    d. When learners are puzzled by an explanation or description.

29. Why are instructional aids useful in helping learners learn? (FAA-H-8083-9)

Instructional aids help:

a. Gain and hold the attention of learners.

b. Increase learners' knowledge retention.

c. Provide an accurate visual image and make learning easier for the learner.

d. Clarify the relationships between material objects and concepts.

e. Instructors teach more in a shorter time frame.

30. Describe the different types of instructional aids you might use. (FAA-H-8083-9)

Marker boards, supplemental print materials, projected material, video, interactive systems, computer-assisted learning, models, mock-ups, and cut-away diagrams.

31. Define the term *integrated flight instruction*. (FAA-H-8083-9)

Integrated flight instruction is flight instruction during which learners are taught to perform flight maneuvers both by outside visual references and by reference to flight instruments. For this type of instruction to be fully effective, the use of instrument references should begin the first time each new maneuver is introduced.

32. Describe the problem-based approach to teaching. (FAA-H-8083-9)

Problem-based learning (PBL) presents lessons in a way that confronts learners with problems that are encountered in real life, which forces them to reach real-world solutions. It starts with a carefully constructed problem for which there is no single solution. The benefit of PBL lies in helping learners gain a deeper understanding of the information and in improving their ability to recall the information.

33. What are the three types of problem-based instruction? (FAA-H-8083-9)

Scenario based—training that uses a highly structured script of real-world experiences to address aviation training objectives in an operational environment.

Collaborative problem-solving—collaboration (two or more people working together) to solve problems.

Case study—a written or oral account of a real-world situation that contains a message that educates the learner.

34. What is scenario-based training and what makes a good scenario? (FAA-H-8083-9)

Scenario-based training (SBT) is a training method that uses a highly structured script of real-world experiences to address aviation training objectives in an operational environment. A good scenario has a clear set of objectives, is tailored to the needs of the learner, and capitalizes on the nuances of the local environment.

35. For SBT instruction to be effective, what information should the instructor and learner establish before training begins? (FAA-H-8083-9)

a. Scenario destination(s)
b. Desired learner learning outcome(s)
c. Desired level of learner performance
d. Possible inflight scenario changes

36. What are the characteristics of a good scenario? (FAA-H-8083-9)

A good scenario:
a. Is not a test.
b. Will not have a single correct answer.
c. Does not offer an obvious answer.
d. Engages all three learning domains.
e. Is interactive.
f. Should not promote errors.
g. Should promote situational awareness and opportunities for decision-making.

37. Explain how an instructor would use the collaborative problem-solving method of instruction during a ground school class. (FAA-H-8083-9)

The instructor provides a problem to a group who then proceeds to solve it. The instructor provides assistance when needed but understands that learning to solve the problem without assistance is part of the learning process. Using open-ended "what if" problems encourages the learners to develop higher-order thinking skills (HOTS).

38. Explain the building blocks of learning theory. (FAA-H-8083-9)

Training for any complicated and involved task, such as piloting or maintaining an aircraft, requires the development and assembly of many segments or blocks of learning in their proper relationships. A learner can master the segments or blocks individually and can progressively combine these with other related segments until their sum meets the overall training objectives. When an instructor organizes instructional material into blocks, it enables a learner to gain insights, and completion of each of the blocks provides the learner with a boost in self-confidence.

39. During the process of identifying the blocks of learning for a proposed training activity, the instructor should also examine each block to ensure that it is an integral part of the structure. Explain. (FAA-H-8083-9)

a. Each block constitutes the necessary parts of the total objective.

b. Some blocks can be submerged in the structure, but each is an integral and necessary part.

c. The various blocks are not isolated but an essential part of the whole.

d. Each block should be fairly consistent in scope.

e. The blocks should represent units of learning that can be measured and evaluated, not a sequence of periods of instruction.

40. Explain the purpose and content of a training syllabus. (FAA-H-8083-9)

A training syllabus is a step-by-step, building block progression of learning with provisions for regular review and assessments at prescribed stages of learning. The syllabus defines the unit of training, states by objective what the learner is expected to accomplish during the unit of training, shows an organized plan for instruction, and dictates the assessment process for either the unit or stages of learning.

41. What is a lesson plan? (FAA-H-8083-9)

A lesson plan is an organized outline for a single instructional period. It is a necessary guide for the instructor because it tells what to do, in what order to do it, and what procedure to use in teaching the material of a lesson.

42. Explain the purpose of a lesson plan. (FAA-H-8083-9)

Lesson plans are designed to ensure that each learner receives the best possible instruction under the existing conditions. Lesson plans help instructors keep a constant check on their own activity as well as that of their learners. The development of lesson plans by instructors signifies, in effect, that they have taught the lessons to themselves prior to attempting to teach the lessons to learners.

43. What are the characteristics of a well-planned lesson? (FAA-H-8083-9)

Unity—Each lesson should be a unified segment of instruction. A lesson is concerned with certain limited objectives, which are stated in terms of desired learning outcomes. All teaching procedures and materials should be selected to attain these objectives.

Content—Each lesson should contain new material. However, the new facts, principles, procedures, or skills should be related to the lesson previously presented. A short review of earlier lessons is usually necessary, particularly in flight training.

Scope—Each lesson should be reasonable in scope. A person can master only a few principles or skills at a time—the number depends on the complexity. Too much material in a lesson results in confusion; too little material results in inefficiency.

Practicality—Each lesson should be planned in terms of the conditions under which the training is to be conducted. Lesson plans conducted in an airplane or ground trainer will differ from those conducted in a classroom.

Flexibility—Although the lesson plan provides an outline and sequence for the training to be conducted, a degree of flexibility should be incorporated.

Relation to course of training—Each lesson should be planned and taught so that its relation to the course objectives is clear to each learner.

Instructional steps—Every lesson, when adequately developed, falls logically into the four steps of the teaching process: preparation, presentation, application, and review and evaluation.

44. Describe common elements found in most aviation lesson plans. (FAA-H-8083-9)

The lesson objectives, content, schedule, equipment, instructor's actions, learner's actions, and completion standards.

45. Explain the steps necessary in preparing a lesson plan. (FAA-H-8083-9)

a. Determine the objective of the lesson.

b. Research the subject as defined by the objective.

c. Determine the method of instruction and lesson plan format.

d. Decide how to organize the lesson and select suitable supporting material.

e. Assemble training aids.

f. Write the lesson plan outline.

D. Student Evaluation, Assessment, and Testing

1. **What term describes the process of gathering measurable information to meet evaluation needs?** (FAA-H-8083-9)

   Assessment.

2. **What is the purpose of an assessment? Why is an effective assessment an important component in the teaching and learning process?** (FAA-H-8083-9)

   a. It provides the instructor and learner with information on how well the learner is progressing.

   b. It provides feedback to the learner, including direction and guidance on how to improve performance.

   c. It contributes to the development of aeronautical decision-making (ADM) and judgment skills by helping develop the learner's ability to accurately evaluate their own knowledge and performance.

   d. It helps the instructor see where more emphasis is needed by highlighting the areas in which a learner's performance is incorrect or inadequate.

3. **What are the general characteristics of an effective assessment?** (FAA-H-8083-9)

   An effective assessment is:

   Objective—The assessment should be focused on learner performance; it should not reflect the personal opinions, likes, dislikes, or biases of the instructor.

   Flexible—The assessment should evaluate the entire performance in the context in which it was accomplished; it should be designed and executed so that the instructor can allow for variables. The challenge for the instructor is deciding what to say, what to omit, what to stress, and what to minimize at the proper moment.

   Acceptable—The learner must accept the instructor in order to accept his or her assessment willingly. The learner must have confidence in the instructor's qualifications, teaching ability, sincerity, competence, and authority.

Comprehensive—It must cover strengths as well as weaknesses; it should not be unnecessarily long, nor must it treat every aspect of the performance in detail. The instructor's task is to determine how to balance the two.

Constructive—Praise can be very effective in reinforcing and capitalizing on things that are done well; negative comments that do not point toward improvement or a higher level of performance should be omitted.

Organized—Almost any pattern of organization is acceptable as long as it is logical and makes sense to the learner.

Thoughtful—An effective assessment reflects the instructor's thoughtfulness toward the learner's need for self-esteem, recognition, and approval.

Specific—At the conclusion of an assessment, learners should have no doubt about what they did well and what they did poorly—and most importantly, specifically how they can improve.

4. What are the two broad categories of assessment? (FAA-H-8083-9)

Traditional assessment—generally refers to written testing, such as multiple choice, matching, true/false, or fill-in-the-blank; normally used to judge or evaluate the learner's progress at the rote and understanding levels of learning.

Authentic assessment—asks the learner to perform real-world tasks and demonstrate a meaningful application of skills and competencies. Authentic assessment requires the learner to use critical thinking skills and exhibit in-depth knowledge by generating a solution instead of merely choosing a response.

5. Describe the characteristics of an effective test. (FAA-H-8083-9)

Reliability—the test results are consistent with repeated measurements.

Validity—the test measures what it is supposed to measure.

Usability—the test is easy to read, has clear and concise wording, and is easily graded.

(continued)

Objectivity—refers to the singleness of scoring of a test; the test must minimize the bias of the instructor giving the test.

Comprehensiveness—the degree to which a test measures the overall objective.

Discrimination—the degree to which a test distinguishes the difference between learners.

6. **Explain the four-step series of open-ended questions an instructor can use to guide the learner through a complete self-assessment.** (FAA-H-8083-9)

Replay—the instructor asks the learner to verbally replay the flight or procedure.

Reconstruct—encourages learning by identifying the key things that the learner would have, could have, or should have done differently during the flight or procedure.

Reflect—insights come from investing perceptions and experiences with meaning, requiring reflection on the events.

Redirect—help the learner relate lessons learned in this session to other experiences and consider how they might help in future sessions.

7. **What are the four outcomes (grades) of the rubric for assessing flight training maneuvers or procedures?** (FAA-H-8083-9)

- *Describe*—The learner can describe the physical characteristics and cognitive elements of the scenario activities but needs assistance to execute the maneuver or procedure successfully.

- *Explain*—The learner can describe the scenario activity and understand the underlying concepts, principles, and procedures that comprise the activity, but needs assistance to execute the maneuver or procedure successfully.

- *Practice*—The learner can plan and execute the scenario. Coaching, instruction, and/or assistance will correct deviations and errors identified by the instructor.

- *Perform*—The learner can perform the activity without instructor assistance and can identify and correct errors and deviations in an expeditious manner. At no time is the successful completion of the activity in doubt. ("Perform" is used to signify that the learner is satisfactorily demonstrating proficiency in traditional piloting and systems operation skills.)

- *Not observed*—any event not accomplished or required.

8. What are the three outcomes (grades) of the rubric for assessing risk management skills? (FAA-H-8083-9)

- *Explain*—The learner can verbally identify, describe, and understand the risks inherent in the flight scenario but needs to be prompted to identify risks and make decisions.

- *Practice*—The learner is able to identify, understand, and apply single-pilot resource management (SRM) principles to the actual flight situation. Coaching, instruction, and/or assistance corrects minor deviations and errors identified by the instructor. The learner is an active decision maker.

- *Manage-Decide*—The learner can correctly gather the most important data available both inside and outside the flight deck, identify possible courses of action, evaluate the risk inherent in each course of action, and make the appropriate decision. Instructor intervention is not required for the safe completion of the flight.

9. Explain the four-step process an instructor can follow when choosing an effective assessment method. (FAA-H-8083-9)

a. *Determine level-of-learning objectives*—objectives should measure one of the learning levels of the cognitive, affective, or psychomotor domains.

b. *List indicators of desired behaviors* that give the best indication of achievement of the objective.

c. *Establish criterion objectives*—define criterion (performance-based) objectives and conditions under which the behavior is to be performed.

d. *Develop criterion-referenced test items*—develop written test questions and performance tests (maneuvers/procedures).

10. Explain the different methods for conducting a critique of a learner's performance. (FAA-H-8083-9)

a. *Instructor/learner critique*—The instructor leads a group discussion in which members of the class are invited to offer criticism of a performance. This method should be carefully controlled by the instructor. It must have a clear purpose, be organized, and not be allowed to degenerate into a random free-for-all.

b. *Learner-led critique*—The instructor asks a learner to lead the assessment. Because of learner inexperience in the lesson area, learner-led assessments may not be efficient, but they can generate learner interest and learning.

c. *Small group critique*—The class is divided into small groups, each of which is assigned a specific area to analyze. Each group presents its findings to the class and the combined reports from the groups result in a comprehensive assessment.

d. *Individual learner critique by another learner*—The instructor may require another learner to present the entire assessment. Discussion of the performance and the assessment can often allow the group to accept more ownership of the ideas expressed.

e. *Self-critique*—A learner critiques their personal performance. A self-critique must be controlled and supervised by the instructor.

f. *Written critique*—This method has three advantages. First, the instructor can devote more time and thought to it than to an oral assessment. Second, learners can keep written assessments and refer to them whenever they wish. Third, the learner has a permanent record of all suggestions, recommendations, and opinions.

11. During a learner's training, when is an assessment more appropriate than a critique? (FAA-H-8083-9)

In the initial stages of skill acquisition, practical suggestions are more valuable to the learner than a grade. Early assessment is usually teacher-oriented and provides a check on teaching effectiveness. It can be used to predict eventual learner learning proficiency and can help the teacher locate special problem areas.

12. What is one of the most common forms of assessment used by instructors? (FAA-H-8083-9)

Direct or indirect oral questioning. Questions may be loosely classified as *fact questions* or *HOTS questions*. Answers to fact questions are based on memory or recall and usually concern *who, what, when*, and *where*. HOTS questions involve *why* or *how* and require the learner to combine knowledge of facts with an ability to analyze situations, solve problems, and arrive at conclusions.

13. What are several desirable results an instructor should achieve when quizzing a learner? (FAA-H-8083-9)

The quizzing should:

a. Reveal the effectiveness of the instructor's training methods.

b. Check learner retention of what has been learned.

c. Review material already presented to the learner.

d. Be usable in retaining learner interest and stimulating thinking.

e. Emphasize the important points of training.

f. Identify points that need more emphasis.

g. Check comprehension of what has been learned.

h. Promote active learner participation, which is important to effective learning.

14. What are the characteristics of effective questions that instructors must consider? (FAA-H-8083-9)

Effective questions:

a. Apply to the subject of instruction.

b. Are brief and concise but also clear and definite.

c. Are adapted to the ability, experience, and stage of training of the learners.

d. Center on only one idea (limited to who, what, when, where, how, or why—not a combination).

e. Present a challenge to the learners.

15. **Effective oral assessment should never include what types of questions?** (FAA-H-8083-9)

    Yes/No—such as "Do you understand?" or "Do you have any questions?"

    Puzzle—questions with many subparts.

    Oversize—questions that are too general, covering a wide subject area.

    Toss-up—questions for which there is more than one correct answer.

    Bewilderment—questions with unclear content.

    Irrelevant—questions that are unrelated to what is being discussed.

    Trick—questions that cause learners to think they are in a battle of wits with the instructor.

16. **Describe the strategies an instructor can use when responding to learner questions.** (FAA-H-8083-9)

    a. Be sure to clearly understand the question before attempting to answer.

    b. Display interest in the learner's question and frame an answer that is as direct and accurate as possible.

    c. After responding, determine whether or not the learner is satisfied with the answer.

17. **Your learner asks you a question for which you don't know the answer. How will you respond?** (FAA-H-8083-9)

    Occasionally, a learner asks a question that the instructor cannot answer. In such cases, the instructor should freely admit not knowing the answer, but should promise to get the answer or, if practicable, offer to help the learner look it up in available references.

18. **Assessment of demonstrated ability during flight instruction is based upon what factors?** (FAA-H-8083-9)

    Assessment of demonstrated ability is based upon established standards of performance, suitably modified to apply to the learner's experience and stage of development as a pilot. The assessment must consider the learner's mastery of the elements involved in the maneuver rather than merely the overall performance.

19. **What methods does a flight instructor generally use to conduct an assessment of piloting ability?** (FAA-H-8083-9)

    There are many types of assessment, but the flight instructor generally uses the review, collaborative assessment (LCG), written tests, and performance-based tests to ascertain knowledge or practical skill levels.

E. Elements of Effective Teaching in a Professional Environment

1. **What are the main responsibilities of all flight instructors with regards to the learning process?** (FAA-H-8083-9)

    a. *Helping learners learn*—make learning interesting and enjoyable.

    b. *Providing adequate instruction*—analyze learner's personality, thinking, and ability.

    c. *Demanding appropriate standards of performance*—in all subject matter areas, procedures, and maneuvers of the appropriate ACS/PTS.

    d. *Emphasizing the positive*—the way instructors conduct themselves and the attitudes they display make an impression on the learner.

    e. *Ensuring aviation safety*—emphasize safety by example.

2. What additional responsibilities do all flight instructors have? (FAA-H-8083-9)

   a. Evaluation of learner's piloting ability

   b. Pilot supervision

   c. Practical test recommendations

   d. Flight instructor endorsements

   e. Additional training and endorsements

   f. Pilot proficiency

   g. Responsibility to see and avoid

   h. Learner's pre-solo flight thought process

3. How can an instructor minimize learner frustrations during training? (FAA-H-8083-9)

   a. *Motivate learners*—They will gain more if they want to learn than if they are forced to learn.

   b. *Keep learners informed*—Tell learners what is expected of them and what they can expect in return.

   c. *Approach learners as individuals*—Each individual has a unique personality.

   d. *Give credit when due*—Praise and credit from the instructor provides incentive to do better.

   e. *Criticize constructively*—It is important to identify mistakes and failures and explain how to correct them.

   f. *Be consistent*—The instructor's philosophy and actions must be consistent.

   g. *Admit errors*—No one, including learners, expects an instructor to be perfect.

4. Why is it important to use standards of performance when training learners? (FAA-H-8083-9)

The use of standards, and measurement against standards, is key to helping learners learn. Meeting standards holds its own satisfaction for learners. People want to feel capable, and they are proud of the successful achievement of difficult goals.

5. **When should application of the minimum acceptable standards for passing a checkride be introduced during flight training?** (FAA-H-8083-9)

   The minimum standards to pass the checkride should be kept in the proper perspective, with emphasis on the learner meeting test standards increasing later in the training—the ACS (PTS) is a testing document, not a teaching document.

6. **To teach effectively, why must an instructor make sure that a learner's physiological needs are met first?** (FAA-H-8083-9)

   During flight training, learners may react to unfamiliar noises or vibrations, experience unfamiliar sensations due to G-force, or have an uncomfortable feeling in their stomach. To teach effectively, instructors cannot ignore the existence of these negative factors, nor should they ridicule learners who are adversely affected. These negative sensations can usually be overcome by understanding the nature of their causes. Remember, a sick learner does not learn well.

7. **How can an instructor ensure that an adequate level of instruction is provided to a learner?** (FAA-H-8083-9)

   No two learners are alike, and a particular method of instruction cannot be equally effective for all learners. An instructor should tailor teaching techniques to the learner by first analyzing the learner's personality, thinking, and ability. The instructor should also be prepared to change instruction methods as the learner advances through successive stages of training.

8. **How can an instructor ensure that a learner has developed the ability and required skills necessary to conduct their first solo flight safely?** (FAA-H-8083-9)

   Generally, a learner is ready for the first solo flight when the instructor observes the learner from preflight to engine start to engine shutdown, and the learner performs consistently, without the need for instructor assistance. The learner pilot should demonstrate consistency in the required solo tasks: takeoffs and landings, ability to prioritize maintaining control of the aircraft, proficiency in flight, traffic pattern operation, proper navigation skills, and proper radio procedure and communication skills.

9. **What important responsibility do all flight instructors have with respect to pilot supervision?** (FAA-H-8083-9)

   Flight instructors have the responsibility to provide guidance and restraint with respect to the solo operations of their learners. The flight instructor is the only person in a position to make the determination a learner is ready for solo operations. Before endorsing a learner for solo flight, the instructor should require the learner to demonstrate consistent ability to perform all of the fundamental maneuvers.

10. **Describe your overall responsibility as an instructor regarding endorsements and recommendations for knowledge tests and practical tests.** (FAA-H-8083-9)

    Making an endorsement or signing a recommendation imposes a serious responsibility on the flight instructor. If an instructor fails to ensure a learner pilot or additional rating pilot meets the requirements of regulations prior to making endorsements or recommendations, that instructor is exhibiting a serious deficiency in performance. The FAA holds him or her accountable. It is also a breach of faith with the learner or applicant.

11. **Professionalism can be achieved by demonstrating certain characteristics when teaching a learner. What are some of those characteristics?** (FAA-H-8083-9)

    a. *Sincerity*—Instructors should be straightforward and honest.

    b. *Acceptance of the learner*—Instructors should accept learners as they are, including faults and problems.

    c. *Personal appearance and habits*—These have an important effect on the professional image of the instructor.

    d. *Demeanor*—The attitude and behavior of the instructor contributes much to professional image.

    e. *Proper language*—The use of profane/obscene language leads to distrust and lack of confidence in the instructor.

12. **When evaluating a learner's ability to perform a maneuver or procedure, an instructor should follow what general guidelines?** (FAA-H-8083-9)

    Evaluation of learner's ability is based upon:

    a. Established standards of performance suitably modified to the learner's experience and stage of development.

    b. Consideration of the learner's mastery of the elements involved in the maneuver or procedure, rather than merely the overall performance.

    c. Keeping the learner informed of their progress by identifying deficiencies and suggesting corrective measures.

    d. Not immediately correcting learner errors when a mistake is made (safety permitting). It is difficult for learners to learn if they seldom have the opportunity to correct an error.

13. **How can instructors improve upon their effectiveness and qualifications as teachers?** (FAA-H-8083-9)

    a. Continuing Education—Instructors should continually update their knowledge and skills. Possible resources to use for this are:

       • *Government*—FAA safety seminars, workshops, Pilot Proficiency Program, Gold Seal CFI certificates, etc.

       • *Educational/training institutions*—local community colleges, technical schools, or universities.

       • *Commercial organizations*—provide videos, computer-based training, printed material, etc.

       • *Industry organizations*—provide educational articles in their publications, training programs, etc.

    b. Sources of material—Instructors should maintain access to current flight publications, which include FAA regulations, the *Aeronautical Information Manual*, Airman Certification Standards, Practical Test Standards, and FAA handbooks.

       • *Printed Material*—GPO and NTIS, numerous publishers, and book suppliers.

       • *Electronic Sources*—internet access via computer, tablets, and smartphones to aviation websites and apps.

14. What is the Instructor's Code of Ethics? (FAA-H-8083-9)

An aviation instructor has the responsibility of developing a good aviation citizen—a pilot or maintenance technician who will be an asset to the rest of the aviation community. The instructor needs to remember that they are teaching a pilot or technician who should:

a. Make safety the number one priority.

b. Develop and exercise good judgment in making decisions.

c. Recognize and manage risk effectively.

d. Be accountable for his or her actions.

e. Act with responsibility and courtesy.

f. Adhere to prudent operating practices and personal operating parameters.

g. Adhere to applicable laws and regulations.

In addition, an aviation instructor needs to remember he or she is teaching a pilot who should:

a. Seek proficiency in control of the aircraft.

b. Use flight deck technology in a safe and appropriate way.

c. Be confident in a wide variety of flight situations.

d. Be respectful of the privilege of flight.

F. Elements of Effective Teaching That Include Risk Management and Accident Prevention

1. Explain, as you would to a learner, the basic three-step process used in risk management. (FAA-H-8083-9)

Step 1: Identify the Hazard—A hazard is defined as any real or potential condition that can cause degradation, injury, illness, death, or damage to or loss of equipment or property. Experience, common sense, and specific analytical tools (PAVE) help identify the hazards and associated risks. Once the pilot determines that a hazard poses a potential risk to the flight, it may be further analyzed.

Step 2: Assess the Risk—Each identified risk may be assessed in terms of its likelihood (probability) and its severity (consequences) that could result from the hazards based upon the exposure of humans or equipment to the hazards. An assessment of overall risk is then possible, typically by using a risk assessment matrix, such as an online flight risk assessment tool (FRAT). This process defines the probability and severity of an accident.

Step 3: Mitigate the Risk—Investigate specific strategies and tools that reduce, mitigate, or eliminate the risk. High risks may be mitigated by taking action to lower the likelihood and/or severity to lower levels. For serious risks, such actions may also be taken. Medium and low risks do not normally require mitigation. Effective control measures reduce or eliminate the most critical risks. The analysis may consider the overall costs and benefits of remedial actions, providing alternative choices when possible.

2. What risk management tool can your learners use to identify risk? (FAA-H-8083-9)

The PAVE checklist is an effective and accepted means for identifying risk. Its four categories (**P**ilot, **A**ircraft, en**V**ironment, **E**xternal pressures) capture broad areas of risk and provide the learner with convenient "buckets" for risk identification. Instructors should coach learners to ensure they use the PAVE checklist methodically and consider all the sub-elements in each bucket.

3. Explain how a learner would use a PAVE checklist to identify hazards. (FAA-H-8083-9)

By incorporating the PAVE checklist into all stages of flight planning, the pilot divides the risks of flight into four categories: Pilot-in-command (PIC), Aircraft, enVironment, and External pressures (PAVE), which form part of a pilot's decision-making process. With the PAVE checklist, pilots have a simple way to remember each category to examine for risk prior to each flight. Once a pilot identifies the risks of a flight, he or she needs to decide whether the risk or combination of risks can be managed safely and successfully. If not, the flight should be canceled. If the pilot decides to continue with the flight, he or she should develop strategies to mitigate the risks.

4. What are the sub-elements within each PAVE category that the learner should consider? (FAA-H-8083-9)

Pilot—experience/recency (takeoffs/landings, hours in make/model), physical/mental condition (IMSAFE).

Aircraft—fuel reserves, VFR day/night, aircraft performance (weight and balance, density altitude, etc.), aircraft equipment (avionics familiarity, charts, survival gear).

EnVironment—airport conditions (runway condition/length), weather (winds, ceilings, visibilities).

External pressures—allowance for delays, diversion, cancellation, and alternate plans; personal equipment available for alternate plans (phone numbers, credit cards, medications).

5. What is a flight risk assessment tool (FRAT)? (FAA-H-8083-9)

Because every flight has some level of risk, it is critical that pilots can differentiate, in advance, between a low-risk flight and a high-risk flight, establish a review process, and develop risk mitigation strategies. A flight risk assessment tool (FRAT) enables proactive hazard identification, is easy to use, and can visually depict risk. Many of these FRATs have numerical scoring systems. A fixed list of hazards and associated risks are presented and assigned scores based on the severity of the hazard. If the total score is below a certain number, the pilot can begin the flight. If the score is above a certain number, then some sort of mitigating action is required.

6. When should an instructor introduce risk management principles into flight training? (FAA-H-8083-9)

The importance of risk management suggests that it should be taught at the very start of flight training and should be integrated into any actual flight training, rather than taught as a separate subject. Risk management activity and discussion should be included in all preflight and postflight briefings.

7. **What teaching method can an instructor use to introduce risk management concepts into flight training?** (FAA-H-8083-9)

Instructors should teach risk management using a building block approach. This method will be effective with both new pilots as well as existing pilots who have not previously been exposed to formal risk management training.

8. **Explain the risk management (RM) teaching objectives when providing instruction through the Private Pilot level.** (FAA-H-8083-9)

Pre-solo—RM should be part of every preflight and postflight brief. The instructor should introduce the learner to a non-numerical FRAT and demonstrate its use during the first few flights. By first solo, the learner should be able to conduct a basic RM analysis.

Post-solo prior to XC training—During initial solo and dual flights after solo, the learner should be able to perform RM of the planned flight, with occasional coaching from the instructor. The instructor should review the learner's risk analysis for all solo flights and provide feedback. At completion of solo flights, the learner should debrief the instructor on the RM aspects of the flight.

Cross-country training—Learners should master RM techniques commensurate with the complexity of flights and terrain along the route to destination(s). The learner should provide full risk analysis for every dual and solo XC flight. Risk analysis should include use of a FRAT or other method of analysis. The instructor should review and approve the risk analysis along with the learner's preflight preparation and calculations.

9. **Explain how an instructor could include risk management training into training events for pilots who are already certificated.** (FAA-H-8083-9)

Instrument training—Risk management training is vital during instruction for the Instrument Rating because of the potential hazards related to IMC. Instructors should emphasize broad risk management techniques and strategies that will allow a pilot to analyze and evaluate complex weather and other elements that generate risk.

(continued)

Transition training—Pilots transitioning to more advanced aircraft will encounter additional types of risk associated with such aircraft. In addition to risk management, other SRM skills such as automation management, task and workload management, and maintaining situational awareness should be emphasized.

Recurrent training, flight reviews, and instrument proficiency checks—Instructors should consider using scenarios to evaluate pilot risk management proficiency. The scenarios should be constructed in a way that mirrors the pilot's typical operating profile.

10. What can an instructor do to manage risk when providing flight instruction? (FAA-H-8083-9)

The risk management techniques are the same as those taught to learners; however, there are a few hazards that are unique to flight instruction. The resulting risk can be identified, assessed, and mitigated. Following are a few ways to mitigate risk:

a. Ask the learner to fly specific maneuvers after giving appropriate training.

b. Choose practice locations that provide safe options.

c. Perform maneuvers with sufficient altitude.

d. Stay alert for the unexpected either from the learner or external elements.

e. Be prepared to take over the control of the aircraft.

11. How can an instructor identify hazards and the associated risk when giving flight instruction? (FAA-H-8083-9)

There are many potential risks when conducting flight instruction and instructors should always conduct a risk analysis prior to flight. The best process for analyzing flight instruction risks is to identify them as you would on any other flight, using the PAVE checklist.

12. What are several examples of common risks in the PAVE "Pilot" category that instructors should be aware of when providing flight instruction? (FAA-H-8083-9)

Qualifications—Learners are generally less proficient, and instructors may also have qualification, currency, and proficiency issues. Instructors should be familiar with the aircraft, avionics, and procedures. Any unfamiliarity creates a hazard and the associated risk.

Aeromedical—These risks require that the instructor be aware of the aeromedical status of both the instructor and the learner. Medical problems with the instructor or learner results in additional risk.

Learner/instructor proficiency—Pilot risk includes both the learner pilot and the instructor pilot. The learner will make mistakes and the instructor needs to be prepared for the learner to make mistakes.

13. What are several examples of common risks in the PAVE "Aircraft" category that instructors should be aware of when providing flight instruction? (FAA-H-8083-9)

Maintenance—Aircraft used in flight instruction may not always be under the direct control and maintenance supervision of the instructor, which means that the instructor may not be aware of inoperative systems and equipment or overdue inspections.

Performance—For two-place trainer aircraft, payload is often limited, requiring a reduction in the amount of fuel carried. Performance may also be marginal in high density altitude situations.

14. What are examples of common risks in the PAVE "EnVironment" category that instructors should be aware of when providing flight instruction? (FAA-H-8083-9)

Airspace—The airspace used for flight training may be crowded, creating a potential collision hazard. Restricted visibility due to haze, pollution, or other factors can increase the risk of a potential collision hazard. Complex airspace may be subject to restrictions.

Maneuvers—Certain maneuvers can create hazards and potential risks. Practicing full stalls can result in inadvertent spins. Simulated engine failures, if performed incorrectly, can create real emergencies and cause accidents. Practice approaches without ATC surveillance can concentrate aircraft along the same path.

15. What are examples of common risks in the PAVE "External" category that instructors should be aware of when providing flight instruction? (FAA-H-8083-9)

Instructors and learners often experience scheduling problems, and this can be aggravated by aircraft problems, weather issues, and other unpredictable events. Instructors and learners are also subject to other external pressures involving work, family, finances, and other issues. All of these can create distractions, anxiety, and other responses that can degrade learner performance.

16. Briefly explain how an instructor can manage risk while in flight and providing flight instruction. (FAA-H-8083-9)

In flight, instructors can manage risk by constantly being aware of potential risk elements and managing them in real time. To do this, the instructor needs to maintain situational awareness of pertinent information, not only of the state of the aircraft, the surrounding traffic, the weather, the airspace, and the surrounding area but also of what the learner is doing and planning to do.

17. What are several special considerations an instructor should have when providing instruction in takeoffs? (FAA-H-8083-9)

a. Information an instructor may be trying to convey during the takeoff may not be heard or processed by the learner. The majority of teaching (airspeeds, pitch attitudes, etc.) should occur prior to the takeoff.

b. Conveying important information prior to takeoff will avoid overstimulating the learner's senses, help maintain a sterile flight deck, and support situational awareness and collision avoidance.

c. Use realistic scenarios for the different takeoffs, but do not create hazards that result in the learner attempting unsafe climb rates or excessive pitch attitudes.

d. Be alert for insufficient spacing from preceding aircraft during takeoffs. Insufficient spacing can result in various hazards such as encountering wake turbulence, insufficient in-trail spacing, and insufficient separation from an aircraft that is on final approach to land.

18. Describe several special considerations an instructor should have when providing instruction in landings? (FAA-H-8083-9)

a. The instructor may want to convey a lot of information while simultaneously verifying that the aircraft is being flown safely. This can cause a decrease in attention to collision avoidance or loss of situational awareness.

b. Excessive teaching and coaching on final approach may cause missed radio transmissions from air traffic control or aircraft in the pattern.

c. Certain landings present unique risks. The instructor should teach appropriate pre-landing reconnaissance for unfamiliar landing areas or uncontrolled fields.

d. During landings in strong winds, the instructor should have sufficient skill to deal with the wind conditions.

e. Short-field approaches and landings require operating an aircraft at slower approach speeds, which reduces safety margins and increases risk.

19. When teaching flight maneuvers, what instructional risk management concepts should an instructor always keep in mind? (FAA-H-8083-9)

a. Identify relevant hazards systematically and keep track of hazards during maneuvering; the learner manipulating controls may be a significant hazard.

b. Avoid creating a hazard by attempting to teach something at an inappropriate time or at an inappropriate altitude.

c. Discuss hazards and risk mitigation in detail during preflight and postflight.

d. Prompt the learner to identify hazards in flight and on their own and to verbalize thought processes and risk mitigations.

Technical Subject
Areas

2

A. Human Factors

1. What is hypoxia? (AIM 8-1-2)

Hypoxia is a state of oxygen deficiency in the body sufficient to impair functions of the brain and other organs.

2. Give a brief explanation of the four forms of hypoxia. (FAA-H-8083-25)

Hypoxic—The result of insufficient oxygen available to the body as a whole. The reduction in partial pressure of oxygen at high altitude is an example for pilots.

Hypemic—Occurs when the blood is unable to transport a sufficient amount of oxygen to the cells. It is the result of oxygen deficiency in the blood, rather than a lack of inhaled oxygen. CO_2 poisoning is an example.

Stagnant—This results when the oxygen-rich blood in the lungs is not moving. It can result from shock, the heart failing to pump blood effectively, a constricted artery, and excessive acceleration of gravity (Gs).

Histotoxic—The inability of the cells to effectively use oxygen; it can be caused by alcohol and other drugs.

3. Where does hypoxia usually occur, and what symptoms should one expect? (AIM 8-1-2)

Although a deterioration in night vision occurs at a cabin pressure altitude as low as 5,000 feet, other significant effects of altitude hypoxia usually do not occur in the normal healthy pilot below 12,000 feet. From 12,000 feet to 15,000 feet of altitude, judgment, memory, alertness, coordination, and ability to make calculations are impaired, and headache, drowsiness, dizziness and either a sense of well-being or belligerence occur.

4. What factors can make a pilot more susceptible to hypoxia? (AIM 8-1-2)

a. Carbon monoxide inhaled in smoking or from exhaust fumes.

b. Anemia (lowered hemoglobin).

c. Certain medications.

d. Small amounts of alcohol.

e. Low doses of certain drugs (antihistamines, tranquilizers, sedatives, analgesics, etc.).

f. Extreme heat or cold, fever, and anxiety increase the body's demand for oxygen, and hence its susceptibility to hypoxia.

5. How can hypoxia be avoided? (AIM 8-1-2, FAA-H-8083-25)

Hypoxia is prevented by heeding factors that reduce tolerance to altitude, by enriching the inspired air with oxygen from an appropriate oxygen system, and by maintaining a comfortable, safe cabin pressure altitude. For optimum protection, pilots are encouraged to use supplemental oxygen above 10,000 feet during the day and above 5,000 feet at night. If supplemental oxygen is not available, a fingertip pulse oximeter can be very useful in monitoring blood oxygen levels.

6. What is hyperventilation? (AIM 8-1-3)

Hyperventilation is an abnormal increase in the volume of air breathed in and out of the lungs, and it can occur subconsciously when a stressful situation is encountered in flight. This results in a significant decrease in the carbon dioxide content of the blood. Carbon dioxide is needed to automatically regulate the breathing process.

7. What symptoms can a pilot expect from hyperventilation? (AIM 8-1-3)

As hyperventilation "blows off" excessive carbon dioxide from the body, a pilot can experience symptoms of lightheadedness, suffocation, drowsiness, tingling in the extremities, and coolness, and react to them with even greater hyperventilation. Incapacitation can eventually result from uncoordination, disorientation, and painful muscle spasms. Finally, unconsciousness can occur.

8. How can a hyperventilating condition be reversed? (AIM 8-1-3)

The symptoms of hyperventilation subside within a few minutes after the rate and depth of breathing are consciously brought back to normal. The buildup of carbon dioxide in the body can be hastened by controlled breathing in and out of a paper bag held over the nose and mouth.

9. What is ear block? (AIM 8-1-2)

As the aircraft cabin pressure decreases during ascent, the expanding air in the middle ear pushes open the Eustachian tube and escapes down to the nasal passages, thereby equalizing in pressure with the cabin pressure. But this does not occur automatically during descent; the pilot must periodically open the Eustachian tube to equalize pressure. An upper respiratory infection or a nasal allergic condition can produce enough congestion around the Eustachian tube to make equalization difficult. Consequently, the difference in pressure between the middle ear and aircraft cabin can build to a level that holds the Eustachian tube closed, making equalization difficult if not impossible. An ear block produces severe pain and loss of hearing that can last from several hours to several days.

10. How is ear block normally prevented from occurring? (AIM 8-1-2)

Ear block can normally be prevented by swallowing, yawning, tensing muscles in the throat or, if these do not work, by the combination of closing the mouth, pinching the nose closed, and attempting to blow through the nostrils (Valsalva maneuver). It is also prevented by not flying with an upper respiratory infection or nasal allergic condition.

11. What is spatial disorientation? (FAA-H-8083-15)

Orientation is the awareness of the position of the aircraft and of oneself in relation to a specific reference point. Spatial disorientation specifically refers to the lack of orientation with regard to position in space and to other objects.

12. What causes spatial disorientation? (FAA-H-8083-15)

Orientation is maintained through the body's sensory organs in three areas:

a. *Visual*—the eyes maintain visual orientation.

b. *Vestibular*—the motion-sensing system in the inner ear maintains vestibular orientation.

c. *Postural*—the nerves in the skin, joints, and muscles of the body maintain postural orientation.

When human beings are in their natural environment, these three systems work well. However, when the human body is subjected to the forces of flight, these senses can provide misleading information resulting in disorientation.

13. What is the cause of motion sickness, and what are its symptoms? (FAA-H-8083-25)

Motion sickness is caused by continued stimulation of the inner ear, which controls the pilot's sense of balance. The symptoms are progressive. First, the desire for food is lost. Then, saliva collects in the mouth and the person begins to perspire freely. Eventually, the person becomes nauseated and disoriented and may have a headache and a tendency to vomit. If the air sickness becomes severe enough, the pilot may become completely incapacitated.

14. What action should be taken if a pilot or passenger suffers from motion sickness? (FAA-H-8083-25)

If suffering from airsickness while piloting an aircraft, open up the air vents, loosen clothing, use supplemental oxygen, and keep the eyes on a point outside the airplane. Avoid unnecessary head movements. Then cancel the flight and land as soon as possible.

15. What is carbon monoxide poisoning? (AIM 8-1-4)

Carbon monoxide is a colorless, odorless, and tasteless gas contained in exhaust fumes. When inhaled, even in minute quantities over a period of time, it can significantly reduce the ability of the blood to carry oxygen. Consequently, effects of hypoxia occur.

16. How does carbon monoxide poisoning occur, and what symptoms should a pilot be alert for? (AIM 8-1-4)

Most heaters in light aircraft work by air flowing over the manifold. Use of these heaters while exhaust fumes are escaping through manifold cracks and seals is responsible for several nonfatal and fatal aircraft accidents from carbon monoxide poisoning each year. A pilot who detects the odor of exhaust or experiences symptoms of headache, drowsiness, or dizziness while using the heater should suspect carbon monoxide poisoning.

17. What action should be taken if a pilot suspects carbon monoxide poisoning? (AIM 8-1-4)

A pilot who suspects this condition exists should immediately shut off the heater and open all air vents. If symptoms are severe or they continue after landing, the pilot should seek medical treatment.

18. Define the term *stress* and explain what the two main categories of stress are. (FAA-H-8083-25)

Stress is the body's response to physical and psychological demands placed upon it. The two main categories are:

Acute stress (short term)—involves an immediate threat that is perceived as danger. This is the type of stress that triggers a fight-or-flight response in an individual, whether the threat is real or imagined.

Chronic stress (long term)—a level of stress that presents an intolerable burden, exceeds the ability of an individual to cope, and causes individual performance to fall sharply.

19. What is dehydration and why is it a problem for pilots? (FAA-H-8083-25)

Dehydration is the term given to a critical loss of water from the body. Causes of dehydration for pilots can range from hot flight decks and flight lines to diuretic drinks like coffee, tea, and caffeinated soft drinks. Flying for long periods in hot summer temperatures or at high altitudes increases the susceptibility to dehydration because these conditions tend to increase the rate of water loss from the body.

20. Describe some common signs of dehydration. (FAA-H-8083-25)

Headache, fatigue, cramps, sleepiness, and dizziness. The first noticeable effect of dehydration is fatigue, which in turn makes top physical and mental performance difficult if not impossible.

21. What is the definition of *hypothermia*? (CAMI OK-06-033)

The average body temperature for the human body is 98.6°F. Any deviation from this normal temperature, even as little as one to two degrees, will reduce efficiency. Hypothermia, or *exposure*, is defined as body core temperature less than 95°F. As the body core temperature drops, so does mental and physical efficiency.

22. Explain how heat can be lost from the body.
(CAMI OK-06-033)

a. *Conduction*—The primary cause of heat loss, conduction is a transfer of heat that occurs when the body comes in contact with something colder than itself.

b. *Radiation*—The body will continually radiate heat from exposed areas. Fifty percent of body heat is lost from the head.

c. *Convection*—An air current blows heat away from the body faster than it is produced.

d. *Evaporation*—Sweat (or other moisture) can moisten clothing and accelerate conduction.

e. *Respiration*—In a cold environment, cold air enters the body and leaves as warm air. The body loses heat by warming the colder air.

23. What are the symptoms of hypothermia?
(CAMI OK-06-033)

Body temperature	Signs and symptoms
99–96°F	Intense shivering and impaired ability to perform complex tasks.
95–91°F	Violent shivering, difficulty in speaking, sluggish thinking, amnesia.
90–86°F	Shivering is replaced by muscular rigidity. Exposed skin is blue or puffy. Movements are jerky.

24. What is the first line of defense against hypothermia?
(CAMI OK-06-033)

The first line of defense against hypothermia is shelter. The most readily available shelter at a pilot's disposal is the aircraft fuselage. Clothing is considered shelter, in the sense that it is your first immediate measure to retain body heat. An important fact to keep in mind is that when clothing becomes wet, it will lose its insulative quality. Wet clothing in wind will draw off body heat 200 times faster than wind alone.

25. Explain how rain on the windscreen (water refraction), haze, and fog can create optical illusions.
(FAA-H-8083-25)

Water Refraction—Rain on the windscreen can create an illusion of being at a higher altitude due to the horizon appearing lower than it is. This can result in the pilot flying a lower approach.

Haze—Atmospheric haze can create an illusion of being at a greater distance and height from the runway. As a result, the pilot will have a tendency to be low on the approach.

Fog—Flying into fog can create an illusion of pitching up. Pilots who do not recognize this illusion will often steepen the approach quite abruptly.

26. Explain the effects of nitrogen excesses from scuba diving upon a pilot or passenger in flight. (AIM 8-1-2)

A pilot or passenger who intends to fly after scuba diving should allow the body sufficient time to rid itself of excess nitrogen absorbed during diving. If this is not done, decompression sickness due to evolved gas can occur during exposure to low altitude and create a serious inflight emergency. The recommended waiting times before flight are as follows:

a. Flight altitudes up to 8,000 feet:
  • Wait at least 12 hours after a dive that did not require a controlled ascent.
  • Wait at least 24 hours after a dive in which a controlled ascent was required.

b. Flight altitudes above 8,000 feet:
  • Wait at least 24 hours after any scuba dive.

Note: The recommended altitudes are actual flight altitudes above mean sea level and not pressurized cabin altitudes. This takes into consideration the risk of decompression of the aircraft during flight.

27. What regulations apply, and what common sense should prevail, concerning the use of alcohol? (14 CFR 91.17, AIM 8-1-1)

The regulations prohibit pilots from performing crewmember duties within 8 hours after drinking any alcoholic beverage or while under the influence of alcohol. However, due to the slow destruction of alcohol, a pilot may still be under its influence 8 hours after drinking a moderate amount of alcohol. Therefore, an excellent rule is to allow at least 12 to 24 hours from "bottle to throttle," depending on the amount of alcoholic beverage consumed.

28. No person may act as a crewmember of a civil aircraft with a blood alcohol level of what value? (14 CFR 91.17)

No person may act or attempt to act as a crewmember of a civil aircraft while having an alcohol concentration of 0.04 or greater in a blood or breath specimen.

29. For a pilot who has been taking an over-the-counter (OTC) cold medication, how do the various environmental factors the pilot is exposed to in flight affect the drug's physiological impact on the pilot? (FAA-H-8083-25)

Drugs that cause no apparent side effects on the ground can create serious problems at relatively low altitudes. Even at typical general aviation altitudes, the changes in concentrations of atmospheric gases in the blood can enhance the effects of seemingly innocuous drugs and result in impaired judgment, decision-making, and performance.

30. Explain how the IMSAFE checklist can help a pilot mitigate risk. (FAA-H-8083-9)

Prior to flight, pilots should assess their fitness, just as they evaluate the aircraft's airworthiness:

Illness—Do I have any symptoms?

Medication—Have I been taking prescription or over-the-counter drugs?

Stress—Am I under psychological pressure from the job?

Alcohol—Have I been drinking within 8 hours? Within 24 hours?

Fatigue—Am I tired and not adequately rested?

Eating—Am I adequately nourished?

31. Define the term *aeronautical decision making* **(ADM).** (FAA-H-8083-9)

Aeronautical decision making (ADM) is a systematic approach to the mental process used by aircraft pilots to consistently determine the best course of action in response to a given set of circumstances. The two most commonly used models for practicing ADM are the DECIDE model and the 3P model.

32. The DECIDE model of decision-making involves which elements? (FAA-H-8083-9)

Detect a change needing attention.

Estimate the need to counter or react to a change.

Choose the most desirable outcome for the flight.

Identify actions to successfully control the change.

Do something to adapt to the change.

Evaluate the effect of the action countering the change.

33. Describe the 3P model used in ADM. (FAA-H-8083-2)

The Perceive, Process, Perform (3P) model for ADM offers a simple, practical, and systematic approach that can be used during all phases of flight. To use it, the pilot will:

Perceive the given set of circumstances for a flight. Think through circumstances related to the: **P**ilot, **A**ircraft, en**V**ironment, and **E**xternal pressures (**PAVE**). The fundamental question to ask is, "What could hurt me, my passengers, or my aircraft?"

Process by evaluating their impact on flight safety. Think through the **C**onsequences of each hazard, **A**lternatives available, **R**eality of the situation, and **E**xternal pressures (**CARE**) that might influence their analysis.

Perform by implementing the best course of action. **T**ransfer (can the risk decision be transferred to someone else; can you consult someone?); **E**liminate (is there a way to eliminate the hazard?); **A**ccept (do the benefits of accepting risk outweigh the costs?); **M**itigate (what can you do to reduce the risk?) (**TEAM**).

34. How is the 3P model different from the DECIDE model of ADM? (FAA-H-8083-2)

The Perceive, Process, Perform (3P) model is a continuous loop of the pilot's handling of hazards. The DECIDE model and naturalistic decision-making focus on particular problems requiring resolution. Therefore, pilots exercise the 3P process continuously, while the DECIDE model and naturalistic decision-making result from the 3P process.

35. How should a pilot use the 3P model to recognize and mitigate risks throughout a flight? (FAA-H-8083-9)

Once a pilot has completed the 3P decision process and selected a course of action, the process begins again because the circumstances brought about by the course of action requires analysis. The decision-making process is a continuous loop of perceiving, processing and performing.

36. Identify the hazards that all pilots should consider when evaluating human factors. (FAA-S-ACS-25)

a. Aeromedical and physiological issues.

b. Hazardous attitudes.

c. Distractions, task prioritization, loss of situational awareness, or disorientation.

d. Confirmation and expectation bias.

B. Visual Scanning and Collision Avoidance

1. Name several factors that can degrade a pilot's vision. (AIM 8-1-6, 8-1-8)

a. *Visibility conditions*—Smoke, haze, dust, rain, and flying towards the sun can greatly reduce the ability to detect targets.

b. *Windshield conditions*—Dirty or bug-smeared windshields can greatly reduce the ability to see other aircraft.

c. *Bright illumination*—Reflections off clouds, water, snow, and desert terrain can produce glare resulting in eye strain and the inability to see effectively.

(continued)

  d. *Dim illumination*—Small print and colors on aeronautical charts and aircraft instruments become unreadable.

  e. *Dark adaptation*—Eyes must have at least 20 to 30 minutes to adjust to reduced light conditions.

2. Briefly describe the various vestibular illusions a pilot can experience in flight. (FAA-H-8083-15, AIM 8-1-5)

The leans—An abrupt correction of a banked attitude, which has been entered too slowly to stimulate the motion-sensing system in the inner ear, can create the illusion of banking in the opposite direction. Examples include Coriolis illusion, graveyard spin, graveyard spiral, somatogravic illusion, inversion illusion, elevator illusion, false horizon and autokinesis.

Coriolis illusion—This illusion occurs when a pilot has been in a turn long enough for the fluid in the ear canal to move at the same speed as the canal. A movement of the head in a different plane, such as looking at something in a different part of the flight deck, may set the fluid moving and create the illusion of turning or accelerating on an entirely different axis.

Graveyard spiral—As in other illusions, a pilot in a prolonged, coordinated, constant-rate turn will have the illusion of not turning. During the recovery to level flight, the pilot experiences the sensation of turning in the opposite direction.

Somatogravic illusion—A rapid acceleration, such as experienced during takeoff, stimulates the otolith organs in the same way as tilting the head backwards. This action creates the somatogravic illusion of being in a nose-up attitude, especially in situations without good visual references.

Inversion illusion—An abrupt change from climb to straight-and-level flight can stimulate the otolith organs enough to create the illusion of tumbling backwards (inversion illusion). The disoriented pilot may push the aircraft abruptly into a nose-low attitude, possibly intensifying this illusion.

Elevator illusion—An abrupt upward vertical acceleration, as can occur in an updraft, can stimulate the otolith organs to create the illusion of being in a climb. The disoriented pilot may push the aircraft into a nose-low attitude. An abrupt downward vertical acceleration, usually in a downdraft, has the opposite effect with the disoriented pilot pulling the aircraft into a nose-up attitude.

3. **Describe the various visual illusions that a pilot may experience in flight.** (FAA-H-8083-15, AIM 8-1-5)

False horizon—A sloping cloud formation, an obscured horizon, an aurora borealis, a dark scene spread with ground lights and stars, and certain geometric patterns of ground lights can provide inaccurate visual information, or false horizon, for aligning the aircraft correctly with the actual horizon. The disoriented pilot may place the aircraft in a dangerous attitude.

Autokinesis—In the dark, a stationary light will appear to move about when stared at for many seconds. The disoriented pilot could lose control of the aircraft in attempting to align it with the false movements of this light, called autokinesis.

Runway width illusion—A narrower-than-usual runway can create the illusion that the aircraft is at a higher altitude than it actually is. A pilot who does not recognize this illusion may fly a lower approach, with the risk of striking objects along the approach path or landing short. A wider-than-usual runway can have the opposite effect, with the risk of leveling out high and landing hard or overshooting the runway.

Runway and terrain slope illusion—An upsloping runway, upsloping terrain, or both can create the illusion that the aircraft is at a higher altitude than it actually is; if unrecognized, this may cause the pilot to fly a lower approach. A downsloping runway, downsloping approach terrain, or both can have the opposite effect.

Featureless terrain illusion—An absence of ground features, such as when landing over water, darkened areas, and terrain made featureless by snow, can create the illusion that the aircraft is at a higher altitude than it actually is. If the illusion is not recognized, the pilot may fly a lower approach.

4. **Explain the *see and avoid* concept.** (14 CFR 91.113)

When weather conditions permit, regardless of whether the flight is conducted under instrument flight rules or visual flight rules, vigilance shall be maintained by each person operating an aircraft so as to see and avoid other aircraft.

5. **What is a good visual scanning technique?** (AIM 8-1-6)

   Effective scanning is accomplished with a series of short, regularly spaced eye movements that bring successive areas of the sky into the central visual field. Each movement should not exceed 10 degrees, and each area should be observed for at least 1 second to enable detection. Although horizontal back-and-forth eye movements seem preferred, each pilot should develop a scanning pattern that is most comfortable and then adhere to it to ensure optimum scanning.

6. **Explain the importance of peripheral vision.** (FAA-H-8083-3)

   Peripheral vision can be most useful in spotting collision threats from other aircraft. Each time a scan is stopped and the eyes are refocused, the peripheral vision takes on more importance because it is through this element that movement is detected. Apparent movement is almost always the first perception of a collision threat and probably the most important, because it is the discovery of a threat that triggers the events leading to proper evasive action.

7. **Explain how an aircraft's blind spots can require specific clearing procedures.** (FAA-H-8083-3)

   When in the traffic, pilots must continue to scan for other aircraft and check blind spots caused by fixed aircraft structures, such as doorposts and wings. High-wing airplanes have restricted visibility above, while low-wing airplanes have limited visibility below. The worst-case scenario is a low-wing airplane flying above a high-wing airplane. Banking from time to time can uncover blind spots. The pilot should also occasionally look to the rear of the airplane to check for other aircraft.

8. **Studies of mid-air collisions reveal certain warning patterns or visual cues. Explain.** (FAA-P-8740-51)

   a. Mid-air collisions generally occur during daylight hours.

   b. Most mid-air collisions occur under good visibility.

   c. A mid-air collision is most likely to occur between two aircraft going in the same direction.

   d. The majority of pilots involved in mid-air collisions are not on a flight plan.

e. Nearly all accidents occur at or near uncontrolled airports and at altitudes below 1,000 feet.

f. Pilots of all experience levels are involved in mid-air collisions.

9. Explain the recommended collision avoidance procedures and considerations in the following situations: (a) before takeoff; (b) climbs and descents; (c) straight-and-level flight; (d) traffic patterns; (e) traffic at VOR sites; (f) training operations. (FAA-H-8083-25)

a. *Before takeoff*—Before taxiing onto a runway or landing area in preparation for takeoff, scan the approach area for possible landing traffic, executing appropriate maneuvers to provide a clear view of the approach areas.

b. *Climbs and descents*—During climbs and descents in flight conditions that permit visual detection of other traffic, make gentle banks left and right at a frequency that allows continuous visual scanning of the airspace.

c. *Straight and level*—During sustained periods of straight-and-level flight, execute appropriate clearing procedures at periodic intervals.

d. *Traffic patterns*—Entries into traffic patterns while descending should be avoided.

e. *Traffic at VOR sites*—Due to converging traffic, maintain sustained vigilance in the vicinity of VORs and intersections.

f. *Training operations*—Maintain vigilance and make clearing turns before a practice maneuver. During instruction, the pilot should be asked to verbalize the clearing procedures (call out clear "left, right, above, below"). High-wing and low-wing aircraft have their respective blind spots: For high-wing aircraft, momentarily raise the wing in the direction of the intended turn and look for traffic prior to commencing the turn; for low-wing aircraft, momentarily lower the wing.

10. Explain the practice of timesharing your attention inside and outside the cockpit. (AIM 8-1-6)

Studies show that the time a pilot spends on visual tasks inside the cabin should represent no more than one-quarter to one-third of the time spent scanning outside, or no more than 4 to 5 seconds on the instrument panel for every 16 seconds outside.

11. **Identify the hazards that all pilots should consider with regards to visual scanning and collision avoidance.** (FAA-S-ACS-25)

    a. Distractions to visual scanning.

    b. Relaxed intermediate focal distance.

    c. High volume operational environments.

    d. Collision reaction time.

    e. Use of a safety pilot—appropriately rated, required endorsements, currency, qualifications, ability to act as PIC if necessary.

C. Runway Incursion Avoidance

1. What is a runway incursion? (FAA-H-8083-25)

A runway incursion is "any occurrence in the airport runway environment involving an aircraft, vehicle, person, or object on the ground that creates a collision hazard or results in a loss of required separation with an aircraft taking off, intending to take off, landing, or intending to land."

2. Describe the challenges a learner may encounter during taxi operations. (FAA-H-8083-25)

A pilot taxiing an airplane to or from a runway or otherwise moving about an airport may encounter one or a combination of challenging scenarios. Construction, airport unfamiliarity, time of day, distractions, fatigue, and miscommunications with ATC can add greatly to the challenge of taxiing an airplane safely at an airport.

3. Explain why it's important to record taxi instructions and review taxi routes on an airport diagram prior to taxi. (AC 91-73)

At many airports, taxi clearance can be very complex. The instruction can involve numerous turns as well as intermediate hold short lines of other runways. Written taxi instructions can be used as a reference for reading back the instructions to ATC and as a means of confirming the taxi route and any restrictions during the airport surface taxi operation. This will mitigate any misunderstanding or forgetting of any part of the taxi clearance, which can lead to a runway incursion.

4. **Preflight planning for taxi operations should be an integral part of the learner's flight planning process. What information should this include?** (FAA-H-8083-25, AC 91-73)

   a. Review and understand airport signage, markings, and lighting.

   b. Review the airport diagram and planned taxi route, and identify any hot spots.

   c. Review the latest airfield NOTAMs and ATIS (if available) for taxiway/runway closures, construction activity, etc.

   d. Conduct a pre-taxi/pre-landing briefing that includes the expected/assigned taxi route and any hold short lines and restrictions based on ATIS information or previous experience at the airport.

   e. Plan for critical times and locations on the taxi route (complex intersections, crossing runways, etc.).

   f. Plan to complete as many aircraft checklist items as possible prior to taxi.

   g. Brief passengers on the importance of minimizing discussions, questions, and conversation during taxi (maintain a sterile cockpit).

5. **What are some recommended practices that can assist a pilot in maintaining situational awareness during taxi operations?** (AC 91-73)

   a. A current airport diagram should be available for immediate reference during taxi.

   b. Monitor ATC instructions/clearances issued to other aircraft for the big picture.

   c. Focus attention outside the cockpit while taxiing.

   d. Use all available resources (airport diagrams, airport signs, markings, lighting, and ATC) to keep the aircraft on its assigned taxi route.

   e. Cross-reference heading indicator to ensure turns are being made in the correct direction and that the aircraft is on the assigned taxi route.

   f. Prior to crossing any hold short line, visually check for conflicting traffic; verbalize "clear left, clear right."

(continued)

    g. Be alert for other aircraft with similar call signs on the frequency.

    h. Understand and follow all ATC instructions and if in doubt—ask!

6. What practical classroom exercise can an instructor use to assist a learner in learning to taxi safely at an airport with multiple runways and taxiways?

    a. Have the learner obtain an airport diagram.

    b. Give the learner a taxi instruction from aircraft parking to a runway or from a runway to parking.

    c. Ask the learner to indicate on the airport diagram how they would comply with the instruction.

7. During calm or nearly calm wind conditions, at an airport without an operating control tower, a pilot should be aware of what potentially hazardous situations? (AC 91-73)

Aircraft may be landing and/or taking off on more than one runway at the airport. Also, aircraft may be using an instrument approach procedure to runways other than the runway in use for VFR operations. The instrument approach runway may intersect the VFR runway. It is also possible that an instrument arrival may be made to the opposite end of the runway from which a takeoff is being made.

8. When taxiing an aircraft at a non-towered airport, what are several precautionary measures a pilot should take prior to entering or crossing a runway? (AC 91-73)

Listen on the appropriate frequency (CTAF) for inbound aircraft information and always scan the full length of the runway, including the final approach and departure paths, before entering or crossing the runway. Self-announce your position and intentions and remember that not all aircraft are radio-equipped.

9. **Identify the hazards all pilots should consider in avoiding runway incursions.** (FAA-S-ACS-25)

   a. Distractions, task prioritization, loss of situational awareness, or disorientation.

   b. Confirmation or expectation bias as related to taxi instructions.

   c. Entering or crossing runways.

   d. Night taxi operations.

   e. Low visibility taxi operations.

   f. Runway incursion after landing.

   g. Operating on taxiways between parallel runways.

D. Principles of Flight

1. **Define the following terms: airfoil; angle of attack; angle of incidence; camber; chord line; laminar flow; load factor; stagnation point; wing planform.** (FAA-H-8083-25)

   Airfoil—any surface designed to obtain reaction, such as lift, from the air through which it moves.

   Angle of attack—the angle between the chord line of the wing and the direction of the relative wind.

   Angle of incidence—the angle formed by the chord line of the wing and the longitudinal axis of the airplane.

   Camber—the curvature of the airfoil from the leading edge to the trailing edge.

   Chord line—an imaginary straight line drawn from the leading edge to the trailing edge of a cross section of an airfoil.

   Laminar flow—airflow in which the air passes over the surface in smooth layers with a minimum of turbulence.

   Load factor—the ratio of a specified load to the total weight of the aircraft.

   Stagnation point—the point on the leading edge of a wing at which the airflow separates, with some flowing over the top of the wing and the rest below the wing.

   Wing planform—the shape or form of a wing as viewed from above. It may be long and tapered, short and rectangular, or various other shapes.

2. **Define the term** *stability* **and name the two basic types.**
(FAA-H-8083-25)

Stability is the inherent characteristic designed into an airplane to correct for conditions that may disturb its equilibrium, and to return or to continue on the original flightpath. The two types of stability are static stability, which is the *initial* tendency that the airplane displays after its equilibrium is disturbed, and dynamic stability, which is the *overall* tendency the airplane displays after its equilibrium is disturbed.

3. **What do the terms** *maneuverability* **and** *controllability* **of an aircraft refer to?** (FAA-H-8083-3)

Maneuverability—The quality of an aircraft that permits it to be maneuvered easily and to withstand the stresses imposed by the maneuvers. It is governed by the aircraft's weight, inertia, size and location of flight controls, structural strength, and powerplant.

Controllability—The capability of an aircraft to respond to the pilot's control, especially with regard to flightpath and attitude. It is the quality of the aircraft's response to the pilot's control application when maneuvering the aircraft, regardless of its stability characteristics.

4. **Explain the effect of wing downwash on longitudinal stability.** (FAA-H-8083-25)

In level flight, there will be a downwash of air from the wings that strikes the top of the horizontal stabilizer and produces a downward pressure, which at a certain speed will be just enough to balance the airplane's nose-heaviness. The faster the airplane is flying, the greater the downwash and the greater the downward force on the horizontal stabilizer. If the airplane's speed decreases, the speed of the airflow over the wing is decreased, which reduces downwash resulting in a lesser downward force on the horizontal stabilizer. In turn, nose-heaviness is accentuated, causing the airplane's nose to pitch down more. With the airplane in a nose-low attitude, this lessens the wings' angle of attack and drag and allows the airspeed to increase. As the airplane continues in the nose-low attitude and its speed increases, the downward force on the horizontal stabilizer is once again increased. Consequently the tail is again pushed downward and the nose rises into a climbing attitude.

5. What causes an airplane to turn? (FAA-H-8083-25)

An object at rest or moving in a straight line will remain at rest or continue to move in a straight line until acted upon by some other force. An airplane requires a sideward force to make it turn; in a normal turn, this is done by banking the airplane so that lift is exerted inward as well as upward. This force of lift is separated into two components: one that acts vertically and opposite to weight (gravity) is called the *vertical component of lift*; the other that acts horizontally, toward the center of the turn, is called the *horizontal component of lift* or centripetal force. The latter is the force that pulls the airplane from a straight flightpath to make it turn. Centrifugal force is the "equal and opposite reaction" of the airplane to the change in direction and acts equal and opposite to the horizontal component of lift. This explains why, in a correctly executed turn, it is not rudder-supplied force that turns the airplane.

6. What are the four factors that contribute to torque effect? (FAA-H-8083-25)

a. *Torque reaction of the engine and propeller*—For every action there is an equal and opposite reaction. The rotation of the propeller (from the cockpit) to the right tends to roll or bank the airplane to the left.

b. *Gyroscopic effect of the propeller*—Gyroscopic precession applies here, the resultant action or deflection of a spinning object when a force is applied to the outer rim of its rotational mass. If the axis of a propeller is tilted, the resulting force will be exerted 90 degrees ahead in the direction of rotation and in the same direction as the applied force. It is most noticeable on takeoffs in taildraggers.

Remember: Nose yaws to the right when nose is moving upwards (tail down). Nose yaws to the left when nose is moving downwards (tail up).

c. *Corkscrewing effect of the propeller slipstream*—High-speed rotation of an airplane propeller results in a corkscrewing rotation to the slipstream as it moves rearward. Most noticeable at high propeller speeds and low forward speeds (as in a takeoff), the slipstream strikes the vertical tail surface on the left side, pushing the tail to the right and yawing the airplane to the left.

(continued)

d. *Asymmetrical loading of the propeller (P-Factor)*—When an airplane is flying with a high angle of attack, the bite of the downward-moving propeller blade is greater than the bite of the upward moving blade. This is due to the downward-moving blade meeting the oncoming relative wind at a greater angle of attack than the upward-moving blade. Consequently, there is greater thrust on the downward moving blade on the right side, and this forces the airplane to yaw to the left.

7. What are the four dynamic forces that act on an airplane during all maneuvers? (FAA-H-8083-25)

The airplane in straight-and-level, unaccelerated flight is acted on by four forces:

Lift—opposes the downward force of weight, is produced by the dynamic effect of the air acting on the airfoil, and acts perpendicular to the flightpath through the center of lift.

Weight—pulls the aircraft downward because of the force of gravity. It opposes lift, and acts vertically downward through the aircraft's center of gravity (CG).

Thrust—the forward force produced by the powerplant/propeller or rotor. It opposes or overcomes the force of drag. As a general rule, it acts parallel to the longitudinal axis. However, this is not always the case, as explained later.

Drag—a rearward, retarding force caused by disruption of airflow by the wing, rotor, fuselage, and other protruding objects. Drag opposes thrust and acts rearward parallel to the relative wind.

8. Explain how an airfoil produces lift. (FAA-H-8083-25)

An airfoil (wing or rotor blade) produces the lift force by making use of the energy of the free airstream. Whenever an airfoil is producing lift, the pressure on its lower surface is greater than that on its upper surface (Bernoulli's Principle). As a result, the air tends to flow from the high-pressure area below the tip upward to the low pressure area on the upper surface. In the vicinity of the tips, there is a tendency for these pressures to equalize, resulting in a lateral flow outward from the underside to the upper surface. This lateral flow imparts a rotational velocity to the air at the tips, creating vortices that trail behind the airfoil.

9. **Explain *Bernoulli's Principle* and *Newton's Third Law* as they relate to the production of lift.** (FAA-H-8083-25)

   Bernoulli's principle—states in part that the internal pressure of a fluid (liquid or gas) decreases at points where the speed of the fluid increases. In other words, high-speed flow (above the wing) is associated with low pressure, and low-speed flow (below the wing) with high pressure.

   Newton's Third Law—since for every action there is an opposite and equal reaction, an additional upward force is generated as the lower surface of the wing deflects air downward.

10. **Explain the forces acting on an airplane when operating in straight-and-level, unaccelerated flight.** (FAA-H-8083-25)

    In steady flight, the sum of lift, weight, thrust and drag is always zero. There can be no unbalanced forces in steady, straight flight based upon Newton's Third Law, which states that for every action or force there is an equal, but opposite, reaction or force. This is true whether flying level or when climbing or descending. It does not mean the four forces are equal but means the opposing forces are equal to, and thereby cancel, the effects of each other. In straight-and-level unaccelerated flight, lift equals weight and thrust equals drag; said another way, the sum of all upward forces equals the sum of all downward forces, and the sum of all forward forces equals the sum of all backward forces.

    Note: The statement that thrust equals drag and lift equals weight can be misleading. In straight, level, unaccelerated flight, it is true that the opposing lift/weight forces are equal, but they are also greater than the opposing forces of thrust/drag that are equal only to each other. Therefore, in steady flight:

    • The sum of all upward forces (not just lift) equals the sum of all downward forces (not just weight).
    • The sum of all forward forces (not just thrust) equals the sum of all backward forces (not just drag).

11. **Explain the effects of speed on load factor.**
(FAA-H-8083-25)

The amount of excess load that can be imposed on the wing depends on how fast the airplane is flying. At slower speeds, the maximum allowable lifting force of the wing is only slightly greater than the amount necessary to support the weight of the airplane. Consequently, the load factor should not become excessive even if the controls are moved abruptly or the airplane encounters severe gusts. The reason for this is the airplane will stall before the load can become excessive. However, at high speeds, the lifting capacity of the wing is so great that a sudden movement of the elevator controls or a strong gust may increase the load factor beyond safe limits.

12. **Explain the relationship between the center of lift and the center of gravity.** (FAA-H-8083-25)

Most aircraft are designed so that the wing's center of lift (CL) is to the rear of the center of gravity (CG). This makes the aircraft nose heavy and requires that there be a slight downward force on the horizontal stabilizer in order to balance the aircraft and keep the nose from continually pitching downward. Compensation for this nose heaviness is provided by setting the horizontal stabilizer at a slight negative angle of attack (AOA). The downward force this produces holds the tail down, counterbalancing the "heavy" nose.

13. **Explain how wingtip vortices are created and when they are the most hazardous.** (FAA-H-8083-3)

Wingtip vortices are created when an airplane generates lift. When an airplane generates lift, air spills over the wingtips from the high pressure areas below the wings to the low pressure areas above them. This flow causes rapidly rotating whirlpools of air called wingtip vortices, also referred to as wake turbulence. The intensity of the turbulence depends on the airplane's weight, speed, and configuration. Vortices from heavy aircraft may be extremely hazardous to small aircraft.

E. Airplane Flight Controls and Operation of Systems

1. What are the primary and secondary flight controls in an aircraft? (FAA-H-8083-25)

Primary flight controls—the ailerons, elevator (or stabilator), and rudder.

Secondary flight controls—wing flaps, leading edge devices, spoilers, and trim systems.

2. Explain the purpose of the elevators. (FAA-H-8083-25)

The elevators are attached to the horizontal portion of the empennage—the horizontal stabilizer. The elevators provide control of the pitch attitude about the airplane's lateral axis. The elevator is connected to the control column in the flight deck by a series of mechanical linkages.

3. What are ailerons? (FAA-H-8083-25)

The movable portions of each wing are the ailerons. They are located on the trailing edge of each wing near the outer tips. When deflected up or down, they in effect change the wing's camber (curvature) and its angle of attack, and therefore change the wing's lift/drag characteristics.

4. Explain the purpose of the rudder. (FAA-H-8083-25)

The rudder is attached to the fixed vertical portion of the empennage—the vertical fin or vertical stabilizer. It is used to control direction (left or right) of yaw about the airplane's vertical axis.

5. What are movable trim devices and what is their function? (FAA-H-8083-25)

A trim tab is a small auxiliary control surface hinged at the trailing edge of a primary control surface (elevator, aileron, rudder). They are commonly used to relieve the pilot of maintaining continuous pressure on the primary controls when correcting for an unbalanced flight condition resulting from changes in aerodynamic forces or weight. A trim tab acts on the primary flight control surface, which in turn acts upon the entire airplane. A trim tab is a part of the control surface but may be moved up or down independently of the surface itself.

6. Describe the direction of movement of the elevator trim tab and elevator when the pilot is applying "up" or "down" elevator trim. (FAA-H-8083-25)

An upward deflection of the trim tab will force the elevator downward with the same result as moving the elevator downward with the elevator control, and conversely a downward deflection of the trim tab will force the elevator upward. The direction the trim tab is deflected will always cause the entire elevator to be deflected in the opposite direction.

7. What are flaps and what is their function? (FAA-H-8083-25)

The wing flaps are movable panels on the inboard trailing edges of the wings. They are hinged so that they may be extended downward into the flow of air beneath the wings to increase both lift and drag. Their purpose is to permit a slower airspeed and a steeper angle of descent during a landing approach. In some cases, they may also be used to shorten the takeoff distance.

8. Name four basic types of flaps. (FAA-H-8083-25)

Plain flap—The simplest design of the four types, this flap when extended increases the airfoil camber, resulting in a significant increase in the coefficient of lift as well as drag at a given angle of attack. This moves the center of pressure aft on the airfoil, resulting in a nose-down pitching moment.

Split flap—Deflected from the lower surface of the airfoil, this flap produces a slight increase in lift compared to the plain flap. However, more drag is created because of the turbulent air pattern produced behind the airfoil.

Slotted flap—The most popular flap on airplanes today, it increases the lift coefficient significantly more than plain or split flaps. When the flap is lowered, it forms a duct between the flap well in the wing and the leading edge of the flap. In this way, high-energy air from the lower surface is ducted to the flap's upper surface. The high-energy air from the slot accelerates the upper surface boundary layer and delays airflow separation, providing a higher coefficient of lift.

Fowler flap—This is a type of slotted flap that not only changes the camber of the wing but also increases the wing area. It slides backward on tracks in the first portion of extension, significantly increasing lift with little additional drag. As extension continues, the flap deflects downward, increasing drag with little additional increase in lift.

9. **What is the most common type of engine found in small general aviation aircraft? Explain the two primary designs of this engine.** (FAA-H-8083-25)

   The reciprocating engine is the most common type in small general aviation aircraft. The two primary reciprocating engine designs are the spark ignition and the compression ignition. The main difference between spark ignition and compression ignition is the process of igniting the fuel. Spark ignition engines use a spark plug to ignite a premixed fuel-air mixture. A compression ignition engine first compresses the air in the cylinder, raising its temperature to a degree necessary for automatic ignition when fuel is injected into the cylinder.

10. **Explain the term *normally aspirated*.** (FAA-H-8083-25)

    The term *normally aspirated* means that the engine has no supercharger or turbocharger to maintain sea level atmospheric pressure at the engine's induction air intake when operating at higher altitudes. This results in the engine's maximum available power output decreasing with an increase in altitude.

11. **Explain the primary and secondary functions of an aircraft's powerplant.** (FAA-H-8083-25)

    The powerplant usually includes both the engine and the propeller. The primary function of the engine is to provide the power to turn the propeller. It also generates electrical power, provides a vacuum source for some flight instruments, and in most single-engine airplanes, provides a source of heat for the pilot and passengers.

12. **Explain how a four-stroke engine converts chemical energy into mechanical energy.** (FAA-H-8083-25)

    The conversion occurs over a four-stroke operating cycle. The intake, compression, power, and exhaust processes occur in four separate strokes of the piston in the following order.

    a. The *intake* stroke begins as the piston starts its downward travel. When this happens, the intake valve opens and the fuel-air mixture is drawn into the cylinder.

    b. The *compression* stroke begins when the intake valve closes, and the piston starts moving back to the top of the cylinder. This phase of the cycle is used to obtain a much greater power output from the fuel-air mixture once it is ignited.

    c. The *power* stroke begins when the fuel-air mixture is ignited. This causes a tremendous pressure increase in the cylinder and forces the piston downward away from the cylinder head, creating the power that turns the crankshaft that is connected to the propeller.

    d. The *exhaust* stroke is used to purge the cylinder of burned gases. It begins when the exhaust valve opens, and the piston starts to move toward the cylinder head once again.

13. **Explain the purpose of an engine crankshaft.** (FAA-H-8083-32)

    The crankshaft is the backbone of the reciprocating engine. The crankshaft, as the name implies, is a shaft composed of one or more cranks located at specified points along its length. Its main purpose is to transform the reciprocating motion of the piston and connecting rod into rotary motion for rotation of the propeller.

14. **Explain the term *fixed-pitch propeller*.** (FAA-H-8083-25)

    A propeller with fixed blade angles is a fixed-pitch propeller. There are two types of fixed-pitch propellers:

    a. *Climb propellers* have a lower pitch and therefore less drag, which results in higher RPM and more horsepower capability. This increases performance during takeoffs and climbs but decreases performance during cruising flight.

b. *Cruise propellers* have a higher pitch and therefore more drag, which results in lower RPM and less horsepower capability. This decreases performance during takeoffs and climbs but increases efficiency during cruising flight.

15. Why are the propeller blades twisted? (FAA-H-8083-25)

The reason for the twist is to produce uniform lift from the hub to the tip. As the blade rotates, there is a difference in the actual speed of the various portions of the blade. The tip of the blade travels faster than the part near the hub, because the tip travels a greater distance than the hub in the same length of time. Changing the angle of incidence (pitch) from the hub to the tip to correspond with the speed produces uniform lift throughout the length of the blade. A propeller blade designed with the same angle of incidence throughout its entire length would be inefficient because as airspeed increases in flight, the portion near the hub would have a negative angle of attack while the blade tip would be stalled.

16. Explain how a variable-pitch (constant-speed) propeller operates. (FAA-H-8083-25)

An airplane equipped with a constant-speed propeller is capable of continuously adjusting the propeller blade angle to maintain a constant engine speed. For example, if engine RPM increases as a result of a decreased load on the engine (descent), the system automatically increases the propeller blade angle (increasing air load) until the RPM has returned to the preset speed. The propeller governor can be regulated by the pilot with a control in the cockpit so that any desired blade angle setting (within its limits) and engine operating RPM can be obtained, thereby increasing the airplane's efficiency in various flight conditions.

17. Explain the term *direct-drive propeller*. (FAA-H-8083-32)

The term *direct drive* means that the propeller is bolted to and turns at the same speed as the crankshaft. No reduction gearing is used.

18. Why do some propellers require reduction gearing?
(FAA-H-8083-32)

The increased brake horsepower delivered by a high-horsepower engine results partly from increased crankshaft RPM. It is therefore necessary to provide reduction gears to limit the propeller rotation speed to a value at which efficient operation is obtained. Whenever the speed of the blade tips approaches the speed of sound, the efficiency of the propeller decreases rapidly.

19. Describe tricycle-type landing gear. (POH/AFM)

This landing gear consists of a tricycle-type system using two main wheels and a steerable nose wheel. Tubular spring steel main gear struts provide main gear shock absorption, while nose gear shock absorption is provided by a combination air/oil shock strut.

20. Explain how the air/oil shock strut provides shock absorption for the nose gear. (FAA-H-8083-31)

A shock strut is constructed of two telescoping cylinders or tubes that are closed on the external ends. The upper cylinder is fixed to the aircraft and does not move. The lower cylinder is called the piston and is free to slide in and out of the upper cylinder. The lower chamber is always filled with hydraulic fluid and the upper chamber is filled with compressed air or nitrogen. An orifice located between the two cylinders provides a passage for the fluid from the bottom chamber to enter the top cylinder chamber when the strut is compressed.

21. Explain the purpose of the torque links on the landing nose gear. (FAA-H-8083-31)

Torque links keep the nose landing gear pointed in a straight-ahead direction; one torque link connects to the shock strut cylinder, while the other connects to the piston. The links are hinged at the center so that the piston can move up or down in the strut.

22. What is the purpose of a shimmy damper?
(FAA-H-8083-31)

A shimmy damper is a small hydraulic shock absorber installed between the nose wheel fork and the nose wheel cylinder attached to the aircraft structure. Its purpose is to control oscillations of the nose gear during taxi, takeoff, and landing.

23. How are the rudder pedals connected to the steerable nose wheel? (POH/AFM)

A spring-loaded steering bungee connects the nose gear to the rudder pedals.

24. Briefly describe an aircraft fuel system. (FAA-H-8083-25)

The fuel system is designed to provide an uninterrupted flow of clean fuel from the fuel tanks to the engine. The fuel must be available to the engine under all conditions of engine power, altitude, and attitude and during all approved flight maneuvers. Two common classifications apply to fuel systems in small aircraft: gravity-feed and fuel-pump systems.

25. Describe a gravity-feed fuel system. (FAA-H-8083-25)

The gravity-feed system utilizes the force of gravity to transfer the fuel from the tanks to the engine. On high-wing airplanes, the fuel tanks are installed in the wings. This places the fuel tanks above the carburetor, and the fuel is gravity fed through the system and into the carburetor. If the design of the aircraft is such that gravity cannot be used to transfer fuel, fuel pumps are installed. Low-wing airplanes utilize this system.

26. Explain the purpose of the fuel tank vents. (FAA-H-8083-25)

As the fuel level in an aircraft fuel tank decreases, without vents a vacuum would be created within the tank, which would eventually result in a decreasing fuel flow and finally engine stoppage. Fuel system venting provides a way of replacing fuel with outside air, preventing formation of a vacuum. Tanks may be vented through the filler cap or through a tube extending through the surface of the wing.

27. The engine oil system performs several important functions. What are they? (FAA-H-8083-25)

a. Lubrication of the engine's moving parts.
b. Cooling of the engine by reducing friction.
c. Removing heat from the cylinders.
d. Providing a seal between the cylinder walls and pistons.
e. Carrying away contaminants.

28. Describe how a basic hydraulic system works.
(FAA-H-8083-25)

Hydraulic fluid is pumped through the system to an actuator or a single-acting/double-acting servo based on the needs of the system. Fluid can be applied in one direction with a single-acting servo and in both directions with a double-acting servo. A selector valve allows the fluid direction to be controlled. This is necessary for operations like the extension and retraction of landing gear where the fluid must work in two different directions. A relief valve provides an outlet for the system in the event of excessive fluid pressure in the system.

29. What type of hydraulic fluid does your aircraft use and what is its color? (FAA-H-8083-25; FAA-H-8083-31)

Refer to your POH/AFM. A mineral-based hydraulic fluid (MIL-H-5606) is the most widely used type for small aircraft. It has an odor similar to penetrating oil and is dyed red. A newer, fire-resistant fluid (MIL-H-83282) is also used in small aircraft and is dyed red.

30. Explain the purpose for each of the following basic aircraft electrical system components: (a) alternator; (b) battery; (c) master/battery switch; (d) alternator/ generator switch; (e) bus bar, fuses, and circuit breakers; (f) voltage regular; (g) ammeter/loadmeter.
(FAA-H-8083-25)

Most aircraft are equipped with either a 14- or a 28-volt direct current (DC) electrical system that consists of the following components:

a. *Alternator*—engine-driven alternators or generators supply electric current to the electrical system. It also maintains a sufficient electrical charge in the battery.

b. *Battery*—provides a source of electrical power for starting the engine and a limited supply of electrical power for use in the event the alternator or generator fails.

c. *Master/battery switch*—turns electrical system on or off. Turning the master switch to the ON position provides electrical energy to all the electrical equipment circuits except the ignition system.

   d. *Alternator/generator switch*—permits the pilot to exclude the alternator from the electrical system in the event of alternator failure. With the alternator half of the switch in the OFF position, the entire electrical load is placed on the battery.

   e. *Bus bar, fuses, and circuit breakers*—used as a terminal in the aircraft electrical system to connect the main electrical system to the equipment using electricity as a source of power. This simplifies the wiring system and provides a common point from which voltage can be distributed throughout the system.

   f. *Voltage regulator*—controls the rate of charge to the battery by stabilizing the generator/alternator electrical output. The generator/alternator voltage output should be higher than the battery voltage. For example, a 12-volt battery would be fed by a generator/alternator system of approximately 14 volts. The difference in voltage keeps the battery charged.

   g. *Ammeter/loadmeter*—used to monitor the performance of the aircraft electrical system. The ammeter shows if the alternator/ generator is producing an adequate supply of electrical power. It also indicates whether or not the battery is receiving an electrical charge. A loadmeter indicates the load (in amps) being placed on the aircraft's alternator/generator by the electrical system.

31. Explain the operation of a magneto. (FAA-H-8083-25)

A magneto uses a permanent magnet (coupled to the engine) to generate an electrical current completely independent of the aircraft's electrical system. The magneto generates sufficiently high voltage to jump a spark across the spark plug gap in each cylinder. The system begins to fire when the starter is engaged and the crankshaft begins to turn. It continues to operate whenever the crankshaft is rotating.

32. How many magnetos are installed in an aircraft with a magneto ignition system? (FAA-H-8083-32)

Most standard certificated aircraft incorporate a dual ignition system with two individual magnetos, separate sets of wires, and spark plugs to increase reliability of the ignition system. Each magneto operates independently to fire one of the two spark plugs in each cylinder.

33. Explain what would happen if the master switch were switched off in flight.

In an airplane with a magneto ignition-equipped engine, the electrical system can be turned off and the engine will continue to run. Each engine-driven magneto (usually two) is independent and provides electricity to its own set of spark plugs. As long as the engine continues to run, the magnetos will continue to provide electricity to the spark plugs, which will continue to ignite the fuel-air mixture, which will cause the engine to continue to run.

34. Briefly describe an aircraft pitot/static system.
(FAA-H-8083-25)

The pitot-static system is a combined system that utilizes the static air pressure and the dynamic pressure due to the motion of the aircraft through the air. These combined pressures are utilized for the operation of the airspeed indicator (ASI), altimeter, and vertical speed indicator (VSI).

35. What instruments operate from the pitot-static system?
(FAA-H-8083-25)

The pitot/static system operates the altimeter, vertical speed indicator, and airspeed indicator.

36. How does the airspeed indicator operate?
(FAA-H-8083-25)

The airspeed indicator is a sensitive, differential pressure gauge which measures the difference between impact pressure from the pitot head and undisturbed atmospheric pressure from the static source. The difference is registered by the airspeed pointer on the face of the instrument.

37. What are the limitations of the airspeed indicator?
(FAA-H-8083-25)

The airspeed indicator is subject to proper flow of air in the pitot/static system.

38. How does the vertical speed indicator work?
(FAA-H-8083-15)

The vertical speed indicator is a pressure differential instrument. Inside the instrument case is an aneroid very much like the one in an airspeed indicator. Both the inside of this aneroid and the inside of the instrument case are vented to the static system, but the case is vented through a calibrated orifice that causes the pressure inside the case to change more slowly than the pressure inside the aneroid. As the aircraft ascends, the static pressure becomes lower and the pressure inside the case compresses the aneroid, moving the pointer upward, showing a climb and indicating the number of feet per minute the aircraft is ascending.

39. What are the limitations of the vertical speed indicator? (FAA-H-8083-25)

It is not accurate until the aircraft is stabilized. Sudden or abrupt changes in the aircraft attitude will cause erroneous instrument readings as airflow fluctuates over the static port. Both rough control technique and turbulent air result in unreliable needle indications.

40. Explain how the altimeter functions? (FAA-H-8083-15)

A sensitive altimeter is an aneroid barometer that measures the absolute pressure of the ambient air and displays it in terms of feet above a selected pressure level. The sensitive element in a sensitive altimeter is a stack of evacuated, corrugated bronze aneroid capsules. The air pressure acting on these aneroids tries to compress them against their natural springiness, which tries to expand them. The result is that their thickness changes as the air pressure changes. Stacking several aneroids increases the dimension change as the pressure varies over the usable range of the instrument.

41. A pressure altimeter is subject to what limitations? (FAA-H-8083-15)

Non-standard pressure and temperature:

a. Temperature variations expand or contract the atmosphere and raise or lower pressure levels that the altimeter senses.

On a warm day—The pressure level is higher than on a standard day. The altimeter indicates lower than actual altitude.

On a cold day—The pressure level is lower than on a standard day. The altimeter indicates higher than actual altitude.

(continued)

b. Changes in surface pressure also affect pressure levels at altitude.

Higher than standard pressure—The pressure level is higher than on a standard day. The altimeter indicates lower than actual altitude.

Lower than standard pressure—The pressure level is lower than on a standard day. The altimeter indicates higher than actual altitude.

42. Which instruments contain gyroscopes?
(FAA-H-8083-25)

The most common instruments containing gyroscopes are the turn coordinator, heading indicator, and attitude indicator.

43. What are the two fundamental properties of a gyroscope? (FAA-H-8083-25)

Rigidity in space—A gyroscope remains in a fixed position in the plane in which it is spinning.

Precession—The tilting or turning of a gyro in response to a deflective force. The reaction to this force does not occur at the point where it was applied; it occurs at a point 90 degrees later in the direction of rotation. The rate at which the gyro precesses is inversely proportional to the speed of the rotor and proportional to the deflective force.

44. What are the various sources that may be used to power the gyroscopic instruments in an airplane?
(FAA-H-8083-25)

In some airplanes, all the gyros are vacuum, pressure, or electrically operated; in others, vacuum or pressure systems provide the power for the heading and attitude indicators, while the electrical system provides the power for the turn coordinator. Most airplanes have at least two sources of power to ensure at least one source of bank information if one power source fails.

45. Explain how the vacuum system operates.
(FAA-H-8083-25)

Air is drawn into the vacuum system by the engine-driven vacuum pump. It first goes through a filter, which prevents foreign matter from entering the vacuum or pressure system. The air then moves through the attitude and heading indicators, where it causes the gyros to spin. A relief valve prevents the vacuum pressure, or suction, from exceeding prescribed limits. After that, the air is expelled overboard or used in other systems, such as for inflating pneumatic deicing boots.

46. How does the attitude indicator operate?
(FAA-H-8083-25)

The attitude indicator's gyro is mounted on a horizontal plane (a bar representing true horizon) and depends upon rigidity in space for its operation. The fixed gyro remains in a horizontal plane as the airplane is pitched or banked about its axis, indicating the attitude of the airplane relative to the true horizon.

47. Explain the limitations of an attitude indicator.
(FAA-H-8083-25)

Pitch and bank limits depend upon the make and model of the instrument. Limits in the banking plane are usually from 100 to 110 degrees; pitch limits are usually from 60 to 70 degrees. If either limit is exceeded, the instrument will tumble or spill giving incorrect indications until reset. Some modern attitude indicators will not tumble.

48. How does the heading indicator operate?
(FAA-H-8083-25)

It uses the principle of rigidity in space; the rotor turns in a vertical plane, and the compass card is fixed to the rotor. Since the rotor remains rigid in space, the points on the card hold the same position in space relative to the vertical plane. As the instrument case and the airplane revolve around the vertical axis, the card shows clear, accurate heading information.

49. What are the limitations of the heading indicator?
(FAA-H-8083-25)

The bank and pitch limits of the heading indicator vary with the particular design and make of instrument. On some heading indicators found in light aircraft, the limits are approximately 55 degrees of pitch and 55 degrees of bank. When either of these attitude limits is exceeded, the instrument "tumbles."

50. How does the turn coordinator operate? (FAA-H-8083-25)

The turn part of the instrument uses precession to indicate direction and approximate rate of turn. A gyro reacts by trying to move in reaction to the force applied, thus moving the needle or miniature aircraft in proportion to the rate of turn. The slip/skid indicator is a liquid-filled tube with a ball that reacts to centrifugal force and gravity.

51. What information does the turn coordinator provide? (FAA-H-8083-25)

It shows the yaw and roll of the aircraft around the vertical and longitudinal axes. The miniature airplane indicates the direction of the turn as well as rate of turn. When aligned with the turn index, it represents a standard rate of turn of 3° per second. The inclinometer of the turn coordinator indicates the coordination of aileron and rudder. The ball indicates whether the airplane is in coordinated flight or is in a slip or skid.

52. What will the turn indicator indicate when the aircraft is in a skidding or a slipping turn? (FAA-H-8083-25)

Skid—The ball in the tube will be to the outside of the turn; too much rate of turn for the amount of bank.

Slip—The ball in the tube will be on the inside of the turn; not enough rate of turn for the amount of bank.

53. How does an aircraft cabin heat system operate? (FAA-H-8083-25)

Outside air is drawn into the air inlet and is ducted through a shroud around the muffler. The muffler is heated by the exiting exhaust gases and, in turn, heats the air around the muffler. This heated air is then ducted to the cabin for heat and defrost applications. The heat and defrost are controlled in the flight deck and can be adjusted to the desired levels.

54. Explain the difference between a deice system and an anti-ice system. (FAA-H-8083-31)

A deice system is used to eliminate ice that has already formed. An anti-ice system is used to prevent the formation of ice. Most light aircraft have only a heated pitot tube and are not certified for flight in icing.

55. What aircraft equipment may be heated electrically? (FAA-H-8083-25)

Some aircraft may use electrical heating elements to provide heat to pitot and static ports, fuel vents, stall-warning sensors, and other optional equipment. Operational checks of the electrically heated systems are to be conducted in accordance with the AFM/POH.

56. Aircraft that are capable of high-altitude flight have what type of oxygen equipment installed? (FAA-H-8083-25)

Most high-altitude aircraft come equipped with some type of fixed oxygen installation. If the aircraft does not have a fixed installation, portable oxygen equipment must be readily accessible during flight. The portable equipment usually consists of a container, regulator, mask outlet, and pressure gauge.

F. Performance and Limitations

1. Explain the basic types of aircraft performance a pilot will be able to predict by using performance charts. (FAA-H-8083-25)

By using the aircraft manufacturer's performance charts, a pilot can determine the runway length needed to take off and land, the amount of fuel to be used during flight, and the time required to arrive at the destination.

2. What factors are most affected by aircraft performance? (FAA-H-8083-25)

The primary factors most affected by performance are the takeoff and landing distance, rate of climb, ceiling, payload, range, speed, maneuverability, stability, and fuel economy.

3. Aircraft flight manuals and operating handbooks provide a variety of performance charts to calculate aircraft performance. Briefly describe those charts and the information they offer. (FAA-H-8083-25)

a. *Takeoff charts*—These allow you to compute the takeoff distance of the airplane with no flaps or with a specific flap configuration. You can also compute distances for a no flap takeoff over a 50-foot obstacle scenario and for a takeoff

(continued)

with flaps over a 50-foot obstacle. The takeoff distance chart provides for various airplane weights, altitudes, temperatures, winds, and obstacle heights.

b. *Fuel, time, and distance-to-climb chart*—This chart gives the fuel amount used during the climb, the time it will take to accomplish the climb, and the ground distance that will be covered during the climb. To use this chart, obtain the information for the departing airport and for the cruise altitude.

c. *Cruise and range performance chart*—This chart is designed to give true airspeed, fuel consumption, endurance in hours, and range in miles at specific cruise configurations.

d. *Crosswind and headwind component chart*—This chart allows for calculating the headwind and crosswind component for any given wind direction and velocity.

e. *Landing charts*—These provide the normal landing distance as well as landing distance over a 50-foot obstacle.

f. *Stall speed performance charts*—These charts are designed to give an understanding of the speed at which the airplane will stall in a given configuration. They typically take into account the angle of bank, the position of the gear and flaps, and the throttle position.

4. Will the information provided by the performance charts always be accurate? (FAA-H-8083-25)

No. It is important to remember that the data from the charts will not be accurate if the aircraft is not in good working order or when operating under adverse conditions. Always consider the necessity to compensate for the performance numbers if the aircraft is not in good working order or piloting skills are below average.

5. What factors affect the performance of an aircraft during takeoffs and landings? (FAA-H-8083-25)

a. Air density (density altitude)
b. Surface wind
c. Runway surface
d. Upslope or downslope of runway
e. Weight
f. Powerplant thrust

6. Explain why the density of air has such a significant effect on an aircraft's performance. (FAA-H-8083-25)

As the air becomes less dense, it reduces:

a. Power, because the engine takes in less air.

b. Thrust, because the propeller is less efficient in thin air.

c. Lift, because the thin air exerts less force on the airfoils.

7. Explain the effect of wind on aircraft performance. (FAA-H-8083-25)

Takeoff—The effect of a headwind is that it allows the aircraft to reach the lift-off speed at a lower ground speed, which will increase airplane performance by shortening the takeoff distance and increasing the angle of climb. The effect of a tailwind is that the aircraft will need to achieve greater ground speed to get to lift-off speed. This decreases aircraft performance by increasing takeoff distance and reducing the angle of climb.

Landing—The effect of wind on landing distance is identical to its effect on takeoff distance. A headwind will lower ground speed and increase airplane performance by steepening the approach angle and reducing the landing distance. A tailwind will increase ground speed and decrease performance by decreasing the approach angle and increasing the landing distance.

Cruise flight—Winds aloft have a somewhat opposite effect on airplane performance. A headwind will decrease performance by reducing ground speed, which in turn increases the fuel requirement for the flight. A tailwind will increase performance by increasing the ground speed, which in turn reduces the fuel requirement for the flight.

8. Explain how the runway surface and gradient will affect performance. (FAA-H-8083-25)

a. *Runway surface*—Any surface that is not hard and smooth will increase the ground roll during takeoff. This is due to the inability of the tires to smoothly roll along the runway. Although muddy and wet surface conditions can reduce friction between the runway and the tires, they can also act as obstructions and reduce the landing distance.

(continued)

b. *Braking effectiveness*—The amount of power that is applied to the brakes without skidding the tires is referred to as braking effectiveness. Ensure that runways are adequate in length for takeoff acceleration and landing deceleration when less than ideal surface conditions are being reported, as it affects braking ability.

c. *Runway gradient or slope*—A positive gradient indicates that the runway height increases, and a negative gradient indicates that the runway decreases in height. An upsloping runway impedes acceleration and results in a longer ground run during takeoff. However, landing on an upsloping runway typically reduces the landing roll. A downsloping runway aids in acceleration on takeoff resulting in shorter takeoff distances. The opposite is true when landing, as landing on a downsloping runway increases landing distances.

9. **Define the following weight and balance terms: arm (moment arm); basic empty weight (GAMA); center of gravity (CG); CG limits; CG range; datum (reference datum); licensed empty weight; mean aerodynamic chord (MAC); moment; moment index (or index); standard empty weight (GAMA); station; useful load.** (FAA-H-8083-25)

Arm (moment arm)—The horizontal distance in inches from the reference datum line to the CG of an item. The algebraic sign is plus (+) if measured aft of the datum, and minus (−) if measured forward of the datum.

Basic empty weight (GAMA)—The standard empty weight plus the weight of optional and special equipment that have been installed.

Center of gravity (CG)—The point about which an aircraft would balance if it were possible to suspend it at that point. It is the mass center of the aircraft, or the theoretical point at which the entire weight of the aircraft is assumed to be concentrated. It may be expressed in inches from the reference datum, or in percent of MAC. The CG is a three-dimensional point with longitudinal, lateral, and vertical positioning in the aircraft.

CG limits—The specified forward and aft points within which the CG must be located during flight. These limits are indicated on pertinent aircraft specifications.

CG range—The distance between the forward and aft CG limits indicated on pertinent aircraft specifications.

Datum (reference datum)—An imaginary vertical plane or line from which all measurements of arm are taken. The datum is established by the manufacturer. Once the datum has been selected, all moment arms and the location of CG range are measured from this point.

Licensed empty weight—The empty weight that consists of the airframe, engine(s), unusable fuel, and undrainable oil plus standard and optional equipment as specified in the equipment list. Some manufacturers used this term prior to GAMA standardization.

Mean aerodynamic chord (MAC)—The average distance from the leading edge to the trailing edge of the wing.

Moment—The product of the weight of an item multiplied by its arm. Moments are expressed in pound-inches (lb-in). Total moment is the weight of the airplane multiplied by the distance between the datum and the CG.

Moment index (or index)—A moment divided by a constant such as 100, 1,000, or 10,000. The purpose of using a moment index is to simplify weight and balance computations of aircraft where heavy items and long arms result in large, unmanageable numbers.

Standard empty weight (GAMA)—Aircraft weight that consists of the airframe, engines, and all items of operating equipment that have fixed locations and are permanently installed in the aircraft, including fixed ballast, hydraulic fluid, unusable fuel, and full engine oil.

Station—A location in the aircraft that is identified by a number designating its distance in inches from the datum. The datum is, therefore, identified as station zero. An item located at station +50 would have an arm of 50 inches.

Useful load—The weight of the pilot, copilot, passengers, baggage, usable fuel, and drainable oil. It is the basic empty weight subtracted from the maximum allowable gross weight. This term applies to general aviation (GA) aircraft only.

10. What basic equation is used in all weight and balance problems to find the center of gravity location of an airplane and/or its components? (FAA-H-8083-25)

Weight × Arm = Moment

By rearrangement of this equation into the following forms, with any two known values, the third value can be found:

Weight = Moment ÷ Arm
Arm = Moment ÷ Weight
CG = Moment ÷ Weight

11. What are the different methods for determining loaded weight and CG of an aircraft? (FAA-H-8083-25)

Computational method—This method uses weights, arms, and moments. It relates the total weight and CG location to a CG limits chart similar to those included in the type certificate data sheet (TCDS) and the POH/AFM.

Graph method—Uses charts and graphs from the POH/AFM to simplify and speed up the preflight weight and balance computation. Some use a loading graph and moment indexes rather than the arms and moments. These charts eliminate the need for calculating the moments and thus make computations quicker and easier than the computational method.

Table method—This method applies the same principles as the computational and graph methods but uses a set of tables that use weight and moment indexes rather than weight, arm, and moments. This helps reduce errors by including tables of moment indexes for the various weights.

12. What performance characteristics will be adversely affected when an aircraft has been overloaded? (FAA-H-8083-31)

a. Higher takeoff speed
b. Longer takeoff run
c. Reduced rate and angle of climb
d. Lower maximum altitude
e. Shorter range
f. Reduced cruising speed
g. Reduced maneuverability

h. Higher stalling speed

i. Higher landing speed

j. Longer landing roll

k. Excessive weight on the nosewheel

13. What effect does a forward center of gravity have on an aircraft's flight characteristics? (FAA-H-8083-25)

Higher stall speed—Stalling angle of attack is reached at a higher speed due to increased wing loading.

Slower cruise speed—Increased drag, greater angle of attack required to maintain altitude.

More stable—When angle of attack is increased, the airplane tends to reduce angle of attack; longitudinal stability is improved.

Greater back elevator pressure required—Longer takeoff roll, higher approach speeds, and problems with the landing flare.

14. What effect does an aft center of gravity have on an aircraft's flight characteristics? (FAA-H-8083-25)

Lower stall speed—Less wing loading.

Higher cruise speed—Reduced drag, smaller angle of attack required to maintain altitude.

Less stable—Stall and spin recovery more difficult; when angle of attack is increased, it tends to result in additional increased angle of attack.

15. Identify the hazards a pilot should consider when assessing risk from the aircraft's performance and limitations. (FAA-S-ACS-25)

a. Inaccurate use of manufacturer's performance charts, tables, and data.

b. Exceeding airplane limitations.

c. Possible differences between calculated performance and actual performance.

G. National Airspace System

1. **Briefly describe the basic categories of airspace in the National Airspace System.** (FAA-H-8083-25)

   The two categories of airspace are regulatory and non-regulatory. Within these two categories there are four types: controlled, uncontrolled, special use, and other airspace.

   Controlled airspace is a generic term that covers the different classifications of airspace and defined dimensions within which air traffic control (ATC) service is provided in accordance with the airspace classification. Controlled airspace consists of Class A, Class B, Class C, Class D, and Class E.

   Uncontrolled airspace or Class G airspace is the portion of the airspace that has not been designated as Class A, B, C, D, or E. It is therefore designated uncontrolled airspace. Class G airspace extends from the surface to the base of the overlying Class E airspace. Although ATC has no authority or responsibility to control air traffic, pilots should remember there are visual flight rules (VFR) minimums that apply to Class G airspace.

2. **What is Class A airspace?** (AIM 3-2-2)

   Generally, that airspace from 18,000 feet MSL up to and including FL600, including that airspace overlying the waters within 12 nautical miles of the coast of the 48 contiguous states and Alaska; and designated international airspace beyond 12 nautical miles of the coast of the 48 contiguous states and Alaska within areas of domestic radio navigational signal or ATC radar coverage, and within which domestic procedures are applied.

3. **What is Class B airspace?** (AIM 3-2-3)

   Generally, that airspace from the surface to 10,000 feet MSL surrounding the nation's busiest airports in terms of IFR operations or passenger enplanements. The configuration of each Class B airspace area is individually tailored and consists of a surface area and two or more layers (some Class B airspace areas resemble upside down wedding cakes), and is designed to contain all published instrument procedures once an aircraft enters the airspace.

4. What is Class C airspace? (AIM 3-2-4)

Generally, that airspace from the surface to 4,000 feet above the airport elevation (charted in MSL) surrounding those airports that have an operational control tower, are serviced by a radar approach control, and that have a certain number of IFR operations or passenger enplanements.

5. What is Class D airspace? (AIM 3-2-5)

Generally, that airspace from the surface to 2,500 feet above the airport elevation (charted in MSL) surrounding those airports that have an operational control tower. The configuration of each Class D airspace area is individually tailored and when instrument procedures are published, the airspace will normally be designed to contain those procedures.

6. What is Class E (controlled) airspace? (AIM 3-2-6)

Generally, if the airspace is not Class A, Class B, Class C, or Class D, and it is controlled airspace, it is Class E airspace. Except for 18,000 feet MSL, Class E airspace has no defined vertical limit but rather it extends upward from either the surface or a designated altitude to the overlying or adjacent controlled airspace.

7. What is Class G (uncontrolled) airspace? (AIM 3-3-1)

Class G or uncontrolled airspace is that portion of the airspace that has not been designated as Class A, B, C, D, or E airspace. It is airspace in which air traffic control has no authority or responsibility to control air traffic; however, pilots should remember there are VFR minimums that apply to this airspace.

8. Define the following types of special use airspace: Prohibited Area; Restricted Area; Military Operations Area; Warning Area; Alert Area; Controlled Firing Area; National Security Areas, Special Air Traffic Rules (SATR); Special Flight Rules Area (SFRA). (AIM 3-4-2 through 3-4-8, 3-5-7)

Prohibited Area—For security or other reasons, aircraft flight is prohibited.

Restricted Area—Contains unusual, often invisible hazards to aircraft. Flights must have permission from the controlling agency if VFR. IFR flights will be cleared through or vectored around it.

(continued)

Military Operations Area—Designed to separate military training from IFR traffic. Permission is not required but VFR flights should exercise caution. IFR flights will be cleared through or vectored around it.

Warning Area—Same hazards as a restricted area; extends from 3 nautical miles outward from the coast of the United States and contains activity that may be hazardous to nonparticipating aircraft; may be located over domestic or international waters or both.

Alert Area—Airspace containing a high volume of pilot training or an unusual type of aerial activity. No permission required, but VFR flights should be particularly alert when flying in these areas. All activity shall be conducted in accordance with FARs, without waiver. All pilots will be equally responsible for collision avoidance.

Controlled Firing Areas—CFAs contain activities which, if not conducted in a controlled environment, could be hazardous to non-participating aircraft. Activities are suspended immediately when spotter aircraft, radar, or ground lookout positions indicate an aircraft might be approaching the area. CFAs are not charted.

National Security Areas—Airspace of defined vertical and lateral dimensions established at locations where there is a requirement for increased security and safety of ground facilities. Pilots are requested to voluntarily avoid flying through the depicted NSA. When it is necessary to provide a greater level of security and safety, flight in NSAs may be temporarily prohibited by regulation under the provisions of 14 CFR §99.7.

Special Air Traffic Rules (SATR)—Rules that govern procedures for conducting flights in certain areas listed in 14 CFR Part 93. The term SATR is used in the United States to describe the rules for operations in specific areas designated in the Code of Federal Regulations.

Special Flight Rules Area (SFRA)—Airspace of defined dimensions, above land areas or territorial waters, within which the flight of aircraft is subject to the rules set forth in Part 93, unless otherwise authorized by ATC. Not all areas listed in Part 93 are designated SFRA, but special air traffic rules apply to all areas described in Part 93.

9. What is a TFR? (AC 91-63)

Temporary Flight Restriction—a regulatory action issued via the U.S. Notice to Air Missions (NOTAM) system to restrict certain aircraft from operating within a defined area, on a temporary basis, to protect persons or property in the air or on the ground. A TFR may be issued when it is deemed necessary to restrict flight in the vicinity of a disaster or hazard area, an area being visited by the president or other public figure, space flight operations, aerial demonstrations or major sporting events, or for reasons of national security.

10. How do I determine if a TFR has been issued for a specific area? (AC 91-63)

You should contact a flight service station for TFR information; additionally, you can find information online at tfr.faa.gov or through automated pilot briefing services. In certain cases where the need for TFRs is known sufficiently in advance, the FAA might include it in NOTAMS or distribute TFR information to aviation user groups for further dissemination to their members.

11. When would a special VFR clearance be required? (AIM 4-4-6, 14 CFR 91.157)

An ATC special VFR clearance is required prior to operating within a Class B, Class C, Class D, or Class E surface area when the weather is less than that required for VFR flight. A VFR pilot may request and be given a clearance to enter, leave, or operate within most Class D and Class E surface areas and some Class B and Class C surface areas in special VFR conditions, traffic permitting, and providing such flight will not delay IFR operations. All special VFR flights must remain clear of clouds. A special VFR clearance at night requires that the pilot be instrument rated and that the aircraft be equipped for IFR flight.

12. What are the visibility requirements for special VFR aircraft? (AIM 4-4-6, 14 CFR 91.157)

a. At least 1 statute mile flight visibility for operations within Class B, Class C, Class D, and Class E surface areas.

b. At least 1 statute mile ground visibility if taking off or landing. If ground visibility is not reported at that airport, the flight visibility must be at least 1 statute mile.

13. Can a student pilot request a special VFR clearance? (14 CFR 61.89)

No. According to 14 CFR §61.89, a student pilot may not act as pilot-in-command of an aircraft when the flight or surface visibility is less than 3 statute miles during daylight hours or 5 statute miles at night.

14. How can a pilot determine that their printed aeronautical charts are current? (FAA AIS FAQ)

Aeronautical information changes rapidly, so it is important that pilots check the effective dates on each aeronautical chart and publication. To confirm that a chart or publication is current, refer to the next scheduled effective date printed on the cover. Between chart and publication cycles, pilots should also check NOTAMs for important updates that are essential for safe flight.

15. What publication provides pilots with updates to visual charts between edition dates? (AIM 9-1-4)

The *Chart Supplement U.S.* is published every 56 days while sectional aeronautical charts and VFR terminal area charts are generally revised every six months. Safety Alerts and Charting Notices are also available for free download at the Aeronautical Information Services website (www.faa.gov/air_traffic/flight_info/aeronav/).

16. What FAA publication should your learners reference for information on aeronautical charting symbols? (USRGD)

The FAA *Aeronautical Chart Users' Guide* is designed to be used as a teaching aid, reference document, and introduction to the wealth of information provided on FAA aeronautical charts and publications. It includes explanations of chart terms and a comprehensive display of aeronautical charting symbols organized by chart type.

H. Navigation Systems and Radar Services

1. What are the three radio navigation systems used for VFR navigation? (FAA-H-8083-25)

a. VHF omnidirectional range (VOR)

b. Non-directional radio beacon (NDB)

c. Global Positioning System (GPS)

2. What is a VOR or VORTAC? (FAA-H-8083-25)

VORs are VHF radio stations that project radials in all directions (360°) from the station like spokes from the hub of a wheel. Each radial is denoted by its outbound magnetic direction. Almost all VOR stations will also be VORTACs (VOR-Tactical Air Navigation), which provide the standard bearing information of a VOR plus distance information to pilots of airplanes with DME. VOR transmitting frequencies of omnirange stations are in the VHF (very high frequency) band between 108 and 117.95 MHz, which are immediately below aviation communication frequencies.

3. What is an NDB? (AIM 1-1-2)

A non-directional beacon (NDB) is a low–medium frequency radio beacon that transmits nondirectional signals whereby the pilot of a properly equipped aircraft can determine the aircraft's bearing and then *home* or *track* to the station. NDBs normally operate in the frequency band of 190 to 535 kHz (immediately below AM broadcast bands) and transmit a continuous carrier with either 400 or 1020 Hz modulation. All radio beacons, except compass locators, transmit a continuous three-letter identification code.

4. Explain *reverse sensing*. How will you teach your learner to avoid reverse sensing? (FAA-H-8083-25)

Reverse sensing occurs when the VOR needle indicates the reverse of normal operation. When an aircraft is flown toward a station with a "FROM" indication or away from a station with a "TO" indication, the course deviation needle will indicate in a direction opposite to that which it should indicate. For example, if the aircraft drifts to the right of a radial being flown, the needle moves to the right or points away from the radial. If the aircraft drifts to the left of the radial being flown, the needle moves left or in the direction opposite of the radial. When flying "TO" a station, always fly the selected course with a "TO" indication. When flying "FROM" a station, always fly the selected course with a "FROM" indication. If this is not done, the action of the course deviation needle is reversed.

5. What is DME? (FAA-H-8083-25)

Distance measuring equipment (DME) is an ultra-high frequency (UHF) navigational aid present with VOR/DMEs and VORTACs. It measures, in nautical miles (NM), the slant range distance of an airplane from a VOR/DME or VORTAC (both hereafter referred to as a VORTAC). DME operates on frequencies in the UHF spectrum between 960 MHz and 1215 MHz. Reliable signals may be received at distances up to 199 NM at line-of-sight altitude.

6. What is RNAV? (FAA-H-8083-15, FAA-H-8083-25)

Area navigation (RNAV) is a navigation technique that allows pilots to navigate directly between any two points on the globe. Using RNAV, any location on the map can be defined in terms of latitude and longitude and characterized as a waypoint. Onboard RNAV equipment can determine the present position of the aircraft and using this positional information, calculate the bearing and distance to or from any waypoint and permit navigation directly between any two waypoints. Present-day RNAV includes INS, VOR/DME, GPS, and WAAS.

7. Give a brief description of GPS. (AIM 1-1-17)

Global Positioning System (GPS) is a satellite-based radio navigation system that broadcasts a signal that is used by receivers to determine precise position anywhere in the world. The receiver tracks multiple satellites and determines a pseudo-range measurement that is then used to determine the user's location.

8. What is ADS-B? (P/CG)

Automatic Dependent Surveillance–Broadcast (ADS-B) is a surveillance system in which an aircraft to be detected is fitted with cooperative equipment in the form of a data link transmitter. The aircraft broadcasts its GPS-derived position and other information such as position, altitude, and velocity over the data link, which is received by a ground-based transmitter/receiver (transceiver) for processing and display at an ATC facility. In addition, aircraft equipped with ADS-B In capability can also receive these broadcasts and display the information to improve the pilot's situational awareness of other traffic. ADS-B is automatic because no external interrogation is required. It is dependent because it relies on onboard position sources and broadcast transmission systems to provide surveillance information to ATC and other users.

9. **What are the two basic types of radar systems?**
(FAA-H-8083-25)

Primary—A radar system in which a tiny portion of a radio pulse transmitted from a site is reflected by an object and then received back at the same site for processing and display at an ATC facility. In a primary system, large aircraft reflect better than small ones, and close aircraft reflect better than distant ones. Even the aircraft's structure (wood, fabric, aluminum, or composite) affects the strength of the reflected radio pulse.

Secondary—A system in which the aircraft responds to a radio pulse (an interrogation) from a site with a distinctive transmission from its transponder. This reply transmission, rather than the directly reflected signal, is received at the site for processing and display. Secondary radar is typically used in conjunction with primary radar at most locations, although some sites are equipped only with secondary radar. Sometimes referred to as the air traffic control radar beacon system (ATCRBS).

10. **Can a hand-held GPS receiver be used as the primary means of navigation on a VFR cross-country flight?**
(AIM 1-1-17)

The types of receivers used for GPS navigation under VFR are varied, from a full IFR installation used to support a VFR flight, to a VFR-only installation (in either a VFR or IFR capable aircraft), to a hand-held receiver. You need to understand the limitations of each type of installation in order to avoid misusing navigation information. In all cases, VFR pilots should never rely solely on one system of navigation. GPS navigation must be integrated with other forms of electronic navigation (when possible), as well as pilotage and dead reckoning. Only through the integration of these techniques can the VFR pilot ensure accuracy in navigation.

11. **When considering the use of a VFR GPS or hand-held GPS receiver for VFR navigation, what operational limitations should a pilot be aware of?** (AIM 1-1-17)

    a. *RAIM capability*—VFR GPS receivers and hand-held units have no RAIM alerting capability. This means that the pilot can't see information such as the loss of the required number of satellites in view or the detection of a position error.

    b. *Database currency*—In many receivers, an updatable database is used for navigation fixes, airports, and instrument procedures. These databases must be maintained to the current update for IFR operation, but no such requirement exists for VFR use.

    c. *Antenna location*—In many VFR installations of GPS receivers, antenna location is more a matter of convenience than performance. In IFR installations, care is exercised to ensure that an adequate clear view is provided for the antenna to see satellites. If an alternate location is used, some portion of the aircraft may block the view of the antenna, which means there is a chance you could lose navigation.

12. **What are the two different types of ATC radar facilities?** (FAA-H-8083-15)

    a. *Terminal Radar Approach Control (TRACON)*—Considered terminal facilities because they provide the link between the departure airport and the enroute structure of the NAS. Terminal airspace normally extends 30 nautical miles (NM) from the facility, with a vertical extent of 10,000 feet; however, dimensions vary widely. Class B and Class C airspace dimensions are provided on aeronautical charts. All terminal facilities are approach controls and should be addressed as "Approach" except when directed to do otherwise ("Contact departure on 120.4").

    b. *Air Route Traffic Control Center (ARTCC)*—Responsible for maintaining separation between IFR flights in the enroute structure. Center radars (Air Route Surveillance Radar) acquire and track transponder returns using the same basic technology as terminal radars. Center airspace is divided into sectors and additionally divided by altitudes (high and low sectors). Each sector has a dedicated team of controllers and a selection of radio frequencies, because each center has a network of remote transmitter/receiver sites. All center frequencies are listed in the *Chart Supplement U.S.* and on IFR enroute charts.

13. Describe the four types of radar services available. (P/CG)

a. *Basic radar service*—These services are provided for VFR aircraft by all commissioned terminal radar facilities. Basic radar service includes safety alerts, traffic advisories, limited radar vectoring when requested by the pilot, and sequencing at locations where procedures have been established for this purpose and/or when covered by a letter of agreement.

b. *TRSA service*—Provides, in addition to basic radar service, sequencing of all IFR and participating VFR aircraft to the primary airport and separation between all participating VFR aircraft. The purpose of this service is to provide separation between all participating VFR aircraft and all IFR aircraft operating within the area defined as a terminal radar service area (TRSA).

c. *Class C service*—Provides, in addition to basic radar service, approved separation between IFR and VFR aircraft, sequencing of VFR aircraft, and sequencing of VFR arrivals to the primary airport.

d. *Class B service*—Provides, in addition to basic radar service, approved separation of aircraft based on IFR, VFR, and/or weight, and sequencing of VFR arrivals to the primary airport(s).

14. Explain how radar assistance is provided to VFR aircraft. (FAA-H-8083-25)

Radar-equipped ATC facilities provide radar assistance to aircraft on IFR flight plans and VFR aircraft provided that the aircraft can communicate with the facility and are within radar coverage.

15. Explain how a transponder operates. (P/CG, FAA-H-8083-25)

A transponder is the airborne radar beacon receiver/transmitter portion of the Air Traffic Control Radar Beacon System (ATCRBS) that automatically receives radio signals from interrogators on the ground, and selectively replies with a specific reply pulse or pulse group only to those interrogations being received on the mode to which it is set to respond.

16. Explain the difference between Mode A, Mode C, and Mode S transponders. (AC 90-114, FAA-H-8083-25)

Mode A—transmits position as a four-digit identifying code only.

Mode C—transmits position and pressure altitude information automatically.

Mode S—transmits position and pressure altitude information and permits data exchange.

17. Explain the function of RAIM. (FAA-H-8083-15)

Receiver autonomous integrity monitoring (RAIM) is the self-monitoring function performed by a TSO-129 certified GPS receiver to ensure that adequate GPS signals are being received at all times. The GPS alerts the pilot whenever the integrity monitoring determines that the GPS signals do not meet the criteria for safe navigation use.

18. Identify the hazards a pilot should consider when assessing the risk associated with the use of navigation systems and radar services. (FAA-H-8083-15)

a. Management of automated navigation and autoflight systems.

b. Distractions, task prioritization, loss of situational awareness, or disorientation.

c. Limitations of the navigation system in use.

d. Loss of a navigation signal.

e. Use of an electronic flight bag (EFB), if used.

I. Navigation and Cross-Country Flight Planning

1. What are three common ways to navigate?
(FAA-H-8083-25)

To navigate successfully, a pilot must know their approximate position at all times or be able to determine it whenever they wish. Position may be determined by:

a. Pilotage (reference to visible landmarks);

b. Dead reckoning (computing direction and distance from a known position); or

c. Radio navigation (use of radio aids).

2. Define the following terms: isogonic line; magnetic variation; magnetic deviation; lines of latitude; lines of longitude; course; heading; track; drift angle; wind correction angle. (FAA-H-8083-25)

Isogonic line—connects points of equal magnetic variation; found on most aeronautical charts and shows amount and direction of variation.

Magnetic variation—the error induced by the difference in location of true north and magnetic north. Expressed in east or west variation.

Magnetic deviation—the amount of deflection of the compass needle caused by magnetic influences within the airplane (electrical circuits, radios, lights, tools, engine, magnetized metal parts, etc.).

Lines of latitude—circles parallel to the equator (lines running east and west); used to measure distance in degrees north or south of the equator.

Line of longitude—lines drawn from the North Pole to the South Pole at right angles to the equator. The Prime Meridian is used as the zero reference line from which measurement is made in degrees east or west to 180 degrees.

Course—the intended path of an aircraft over the earth; or the direction of a line drawn on a chart representing the intended aircraft path.

(continued)

Heading—the direction the nose of the airplane points during flight.

Track—the actual path made over the ground in flight.

Drift angle—the angle between heading and track.

Wind correction angle—correction applied to the course to establish a heading so track will coincide with course.

3. Explain what a wind triangle is and why it is important. (FAA-H-8083-25)

If there is no wind, the aircraft's ground track is the same as the heading and the ground speed is the same as the true airspeed. This condition rarely exists. A wind triangle, the pilot's version of vector analysis, is the basis of dead reckoning. The wind triangle is a graphic explanation of the effect of wind upon flight. Ground speed, heading, and time for any flight can be determined by using the wind triangle. It can be applied to the simplest kind of cross-country flight as well as the most complicated instrument flight.

4. Beginning with the true course, explain how to determine the final compass heading to be flown to reach your destination. (FAA-H-8083-25)

TC +/− WCA = TH +/− VAR = MH +/− DEV = CH

5. Describe the materials required for instruction in VFR cross-country flight planning. (FAA-H-8083-25)

Current VFR sectional(s), *Chart Supplement U.S.*, POH/AFM, weight and balance data, XC navigation log, flight computer or electronic calculator, navigation plotter, current and forecast weather, pencil.

6. Explain the hemispherical rule on VFR cruising altitudes. (14 CFR 91.159)

When operating above 3,000 feet AGL but less than 18,000 feet MSL on a *magnetic course* of 0° to 179°, fly at an odd-thousand-foot MSL altitude plus 500 feet. When on a *magnetic course* of 180° to 359°, fly at an even-thousand-foot MSL altitude plus 500 feet.

7. **Explain, as you would to a learner, the procedure for planning a VFR cross-country.** (FAA-H-8083-25)

   a. Get a preflight briefing consisting of the latest or most current weather, airport, and enroute NAVAID information.

   b. Draw course lines and mark checkpoints on the chart.

   c. Enter checkpoints on the log. Measure distances between checkpoints and total leg length.

   d. Enter NAVAIDs on the log.

   e. Enter VOR courses on the log.

   f. Enter altitude on the log—consider hemispherical rule, winds aloft, airspace, terrain elevation.

   g. Enter the wind (direction/velocity) and temperature on the log.

   h. Measure the true course on the chart and enter it on the log.

   i. Compute the true airspeed and enter it on the log.

   j. Compute the WCA and ground speed and enter them on the log.

   k. Determine variation from chart and enter it on the log.

   l. Determine deviation from compass correction card and enter it on the log.

   m. Enter compass heading on the log.

   n. Measure distances on the chart and enter them on the log.

   o. Figure ETE and ETA and enter them on the log.

   p. Calculate fuel burn and usage; enter them on the log.

   q. Compute weight and balance.

   r. Compute takeoff and landing performance.

   s. Complete a flight plan form.

   t. File the flight plan with FSS.

8. **While en route on a cross-country flight, weather has deteriorated and it has become necessary to divert to an alternate airport. Assuming no GPS or DME capability, describe how you will teach a learner to navigate to an alternate.** (FAA-H-8083-25)

   - After selecting the alternate, I will approximate the magnetic course to the alternate using a straight edge and a compass rose from a nearby VOR or an airway that closely parallels my direction to the alternate:

   - I can use the straight edge and scale at the bottom of the chart to approximate a distance to the alternate. I can fine-tune this course and distance later, as time permits, with a plotter.

   - If time permits, I'll start my diversion over a prominent ground feature. However, in an emergency, I will divert promptly toward my alternate.

   Note: Attempting to complete all plotting, measuring, and computations involved before diverting to the alternate destination may only aggravate an actual emergency.

   - Once established on course, I'll note the time, and then use the winds aloft nearest to my diversion point to calculate a heading and GS. Once I have my GS, I'll determine my ETA and fuel consumption to the alternate.

   - I'll give priority to flying the aircraft while dividing attention between navigation and planning.

   - When determining my altitude to use while diverting, I'll consider cloud heights, winds, terrain, and radio reception.

9. **During the preflight planning phase of a cross-country flight, what hazards should a pilot consider when assessing the potential risk of the planned flight?** (FAA-S-ACS-25)

   Pilot-in-command—general health, physical/mental/emotional state, proficiency, currency.

   Aircraft—airworthiness, equipment, performance capability, fuel.

   enVironment—weather hazards, terrain, airports/runways to be used, conditions.

   External pressures—meetings, people waiting at destination, desire to impress someone, etc.

10. **Are electronic flight bags (EFBs) approved for use as a replacement for paper reference material (POH and supplements, charts, etc.) in the cockpit?** (AC 91-78)

    Yes. EFBs can be used during all phases of flight operations in lieu of paper reference material when the information displayed is the functional equivalent of the paper reference material replaced and is current, up-to-date, and valid. It is recommended that a secondary or back-up source of aeronautical information necessary for the flight be available.

J. 14 CFR and Publications

1. **Describe the general content of the following parts of the Code of Federal Regulations: 14 CFR Parts 1, 61, 91, and 141.**

    14 CFR Part 1—Definitions and Abbreviations

    14 CFR Part 61—Certification: Pilots, Flight Instructors, and Ground Instructors

    14 CFR Part 91—General Operating and Flight Rules

    14 CFR Part 141—Pilot Schools

2. **Explain what requirements 14 CFR Part 61 prescribes.** (14 CFR 61.1)

    Part 61 prescribes the requirements for issuing pilot, flight instructor, and ground instructor certificates and ratings, the conditions under which those certificates and ratings are necessary, and their associated privileges and limitations.

3. **What are the various certificates issued under Part 61?** (14 CFR 61.5)

    a. Pilot certificates—student pilot, sport pilot, recreational pilot, private pilot, commercial pilot, airline transport pilot.

    b. Flight instructor certificates.

    c. Ground instructor certificates.

4. What is the purpose and general content of NTSB 49 CFR Part 830?

Notification and reporting of aircraft accidents or incidents and overdue aircraft and preservation of aircraft wreckage, mail, cargo, and records.

5. Describe the contents of a typical airplane flight manual (AFM)/pilot's operating handbook (POH). (FAA-H-8083-25)

The typical AFM/POH contains the following nine sections: General; Limitations; Emergency Procedures; Normal Procedures; Performance; Weight and Balance/Equipment List; Systems Description; Handling, Service, and Maintenance; and Supplements. Manufacturers also have the option of including additional sections, such as one on safety and operational tips or an alphabetical index at the end of the POH.

6. What are advisory circulars? (AIM General Information)

Advisory circulars (ACs) are issued by the FAA to inform the aviation public in a systematic way of non-regulatory material. Unless incorporated into a regulation by reference, the contents of an advisory circular are not binding on the public. Advisory circulars are issued in a numbered-subject system corresponding to the subject areas of 14 CFR Chapter 1. An AC is issued to provide guidance and information in a designated subject area or to show a method acceptable to the FAA.

7. What are SAFOs and InFOs? (AIM 7-7-5)

SAFOs and InFOs are issued by the FAA to communicate important information to the aviation community:

Safety Alerts For Operators (SAFO) contain important safety information that is often time-critical. A SAFO may contain information and/or recommended (non-regulatory) action to be taken by the respective operators or parties identified in the SAFO.

Information For Operators (InFO) are similar to SAFOs, but contain valuable information for operators that should help them meet administrative requirements or certain regulatory requirements with relatively low urgency or impact on safety.

8. **Explain the purpose and general content of the Airman Certification Standards and Practical Test Standards.** (FAA-H-8083-3)

Practical tests for FAA pilot certificates and associated ratings are administered by FAA inspectors and DPEs in accordance with FAA-developed Practical Test Standards (PTS) and Airman Certification Standards (ACS). 14 CFR Part 61 specifies the areas of operation in which knowledge and skill must be demonstrated by the applicant. The CFRs provide the flexibility to permit the FAA to publish PTS and ACS containing the areas of operation and specific tasks in which competence must be demonstrated. The FAA requires that all practical tests be conducted in accordance with the appropriate PTS and ACS and the policies set forth in the introduction section of the PTS and ACS.

9. **Explain the availability, purpose, and general content of the *Chart Supplement U.S.*** (AIM 9-1-4)

It is a seven-volume booklet series containing data on airports, seaplane bases, heliports, NAVAIDs, communications data, weather data sources, airspace, special notices, and operational procedures. Coverage includes the conterminous U.S., Puerto Rico, and the Virgin Islands. The *Chart Supplement U.S.* shows data that cannot be readily depicted in graphic form (e.g., airport hours of operations, types of fuel available, runway widths, lighting codes, etc.). It also provides a means for pilots to update visual charts between edition dates—it is published every 56 days while sectional and Terminal Area Charts are generally revised every six months.

10. **What do the regulations indicate about carrying and using expired charts?** (FAA AIS FAQ)

The specific FAA regulation, 14 CFR §91.103, Preflight Action, states that each pilot-in-command shall, before beginning a flight, become familiar with all available information concerning that flight. Although the regulation does not specifically require it, you should always carry a current chart with you in flight. Expired charts may not show frequency changes or newly constructed obstructions, both of which when unknown could be a hazard.

K. Endorsements and Logbook Entries

1. **What FAA advisory circular provides guidance to pilots, flight instructors, and examiners on the certification standards, knowledge test procedures, logbook endorsements and other requirements of 14 CFR Part 61?**

   FAA AC 61-65—Certification: Pilots and Flight and Ground Instructors.

2. **Briefly describe the different endorsements you will provide for student pilots training for the Private Pilot Certificate.** (14 CFR Part 61; AC 61-65)

   a. Pre-solo aeronautical knowledge—14 CFR §61.87(b).

   b. Pre-solo flight training, make and model—14 CFR §61.87(c).

   c. Pre-solo flight training at night—14 CFR §§61.87(c) and 61.87(o).

   d. Solo flight (first 90-day period), make and model—14 CFR §61.87(n).

   e. Solo flight (each additional 90-day period)—14 CFR §61.87(p).

   f. Solo takeoffs and landings at another airport within 25 NM—14 CFR §61.93(b)(1).

   g. Solo cross-country flight, category—14 CFR §61.93(c)(1) and make and model, §61.93(c)(2).

   h. Solo cross-country flight, review of cross-country flight planning—14 CFR §61.93(c)(3).

   i. Repeated solo cross-country flights not more than 50 NM from the point of departure—14 CFR §61.93(b)(2).

   j. Solo flight in Class B airspace—14 CFR §61.95(a).

   k. Solo flight to, from, or at an airport located in Class B airspace—14 CFR §§61.95(a) and 91.131(b)(1).

   l. Endorsement of a U.S. citizenship recommended by the TSA—49 CFR §1552.3(h).

3. **What are the endorsements required of a flight instructor before allowing a student pilot to conduct their first solo flight?** (14 CFR 61.87; AC 61-65)

   a. An endorsement in the student's logbook for satisfactory completion of a pre-solo aeronautical exam (14 CFR §61.87(b)).

   b. An endorsement in the student's logbook for the specific make and model aircraft to be flown by an authorized instructor who gave the training within the 90 days preceding the date of the flight (14 CFR §61.87(c)).

4. **What are the endorsements required of a flight instructor before allowing a student pilot to conduct the initial solo cross-country flight?** (14 CFR 61.93; AC 61-65)

   Prior to the initial solo cross-country flight, the learner is required to receive:

   a. A solo cross-country endorsement from the authorized instructor who conducted the training that is placed in that person's logbook for the specific category of aircraft to be flown (14 CFR §61.93(c)(1)).

   b. A solo cross-country endorsement from an authorized instructor that is placed in that person's logbook for the specific make and model of aircraft to be flown (14 CFR §61.93(c)(2)).

   c. An endorsement in that person's logbook for each cross-country flight from an authorized instructor who reviews the cross-country planning and states that the planning and preparation is correct (14 CFR §61.93(c)(3)).

   Note: The instructor should also make sure the student's initial solo flight endorsement is current for the make and model to be flown.

5. **Your student is making the final preparations for a solo cross-country flight you have instructed them to make. You are not available to review the planning and preparation as required. Can another flight instructor conduct the review and provide the necessary endorsement?** (AC 61-65)

   Yes. This endorsement does not need to be made by the instructor who normally provides training to the student. However, the flight instructor would have the responsibility to ensure that all other required endorsements have been previously provided, such as the endorsement required by §61.93(b)(2)(ii) for conducting solo cross-country flights.

6. **Give examples of additional endorsements you may give as a flight instructor.** (AC 61-65)

   Within the limitations of your flight instructor certificate and ratings, and your pilot certificate and ratings, you may give the following training and endorsements:

   a. For completion of a flight review.

   b. For completion of a phase of an FAA-sponsored pilot proficiency award program.

   c. For completion of an instrument proficiency check.

   d. To act as PIC in a complex airplane.

   e. To act as PIC in a high-performance airplane.

   f. To act as PIC in a pressurized aircraft capable of high-altitude operations.

   g. To act as PIC in a tailwheel airplane.

   h. To act as PIC of an aircraft in solo operation when the pilot does not hold an appropriate category and class rating.

   i. For retesting after failure of a knowledge or practical test.

   j. For additional aircraft category or class rating (other than ATP).

7. **Do the regulations require flight instructors to endorse the logbook of a person they have given ground training to?** (14 CFR 61.189)

   Yes. 14 CFR §61.189(a) states, "A flight instructor must sign the logbook of each person to whom that instructor has given flight training or ground training."

8. **Your student is ready for the Private Pilot practical test. What are the required logbook endorsements you must make to recommend your student for the test?** (14 CFR Part 61; AC 61-65)

Prerequisites for the practical test endorsements:

- Aeronautical knowledge test—14 CFR §§61.35(a)(1), 61.103(d), and 61.105.
- Flight proficiency/practical test—14 CFR §§61.103(f), 61.107(b), and 61.109.
- Prerequisites for practical test—14 CFR Part 61, §61.39(a)(6) (i) and (ii).
- Review of deficiencies identified on airman knowledge test—14 CFR §61.39(a)(6)(iii) as required.

Exam Tip: Before recommending a pilot for the practical check, make sure that they have *all* of the required endorsements. A commonly forgotten endorsement to check is the 90 day solo endorsement. Make sure that it is still valid. It's entirely possible that it has expired, and if so, your student will not be eligible to take the practical test.

9. **What type of flight time must be documented and recorded by all pilots?** (14 CFR 61.51)

   a. Training and aeronautical experience used to meet the requirements for a certificate, rating, or flight review.

   b. The aeronautical experience required for meeting the recency of flight experience requirements of Part 61.

10. **What time is considered "training" time and how should this be logged?** (14 CFR 61.51)

    a. A person may log training time when that person receives training from an authorized instructor in an aircraft, flight simulator, or flight training device.

    b. The training time must be logged in a logbook and must be endorsed in a legible manner by the authorized instructor; it must include a description of the training given, the length of the training lesson, and the authorized instructor's signature, certificate number, and certificate expiration date.

11. For instructional flights with both an authorized flight instructor and a certificated private pilot on board, which person is allowed to log pilot-in-command time? (14 CFR 61.51)

Both the flight instructor and private pilot will log PIC time. Provided the private pilot is the sole manipulator of the controls of an aircraft for which the pilot is rated, that pilot may log the time as PIC.

12. What regulatory guidelines are established concerning the logging of instrument time? (14 CFR 61.51)

a. A person may log instrument flight time only for that flight time when the person operates the aircraft solely by reference to instruments under actual or simulated instrument flight conditions.

b. An authorized instructor may log instrument flight time when conducting instrument flight instruction in actual instrument flight conditions.

c. For the purposes of logging instrument flight time to meet the recent instrument experience requirements of §61.57(c), the following information must be recorded in the person's logbook: the location and type of each instrument approach accomplished; and the name of the safety pilot, if required.

d. A flight simulator, flight training device, or ATD may be used for acquiring instrument aeronautical experience for a pilot certificate, rating, or instrument recency experience, provided an authorized instructor is present to observe that time and signs the person's logbook or training record to verify the time and the content of the training session.

13. What logbook entries should be made by the flight instructor if a pilot demonstrates unsatisfactory performance during a flight review? (AC 61-98)

The FAA does not intend the flight review to be a checkride. If the review is not satisfactory, the flight instructor should log the flight as "dual instruction given" and not as a "failure." The flight instructor should then recommend additional training in the areas of the review that were unsatisfactory.

14. What are the required records a flight instructor must retain? (14 CFR 61.189)

a. A flight instructor must sign the logbook of each person to whom that instructor has given flight training or ground training.

b. A flight instructor must maintain a record in a logbook or a separate document that contains the name of each person whose logbook that instructor has endorsed for solo flight privileges, the date of the endorsement, the name of each person that instructor has endorsed for a knowledge test or practical test, the kind of test, the date, and the results.

c. Each flight instructor must retain the required records for at least 3 years.

15. How can a flight instructor certificate be renewed? (14 CFR 61.197)

A person who holds a flight instructor certificate that has not expired may renew that flight instructor certificate for an additional 24 calendar months if the holder:

a. Has passed a practical test for one of the ratings listed on the current flight instructor certificate, or an additional flight instructor rating; or

b. Has submitted a completed and signed application to the FAA and satisfactorily completed one of the following renewal requirements:

  • A record of training showing that, during the preceding 24 calendar months, the flight instructor has endorsed at least 5 students for a practical test for a certificate or rating and at least 80 percent of those students passed that test on the first attempt.

  • A record showing that, within the preceding 24 calendar months, the flight instructor has served as a company check pilot, chief flight instructor, company check airman, or flight instructor in a Part 121 or Part 135 operation, or in a position involving the regular evaluation of pilots.

  • A graduation certificate showing that, within the preceding 3 calendar months, the person has successfully completed an approved flight instructor refresher course (FIRC) consisting of ground training or flight training, or a combination of both.

- A record showing that, within the preceding 24 months from the month of application, the flight instructor passed an official U.S. Armed Forces military instructor pilot or pilot examiner proficiency check in an aircraft for which the military instructor already holds a rating or in an aircraft for an additional rating.

16. What is the duration of a flight instructor certificate? (14 CFR 61.19, 61.199)

A flight instructor certificate expires 24 calendar months from the month in which it was issued, renewed, or reinstated, as appropriate. If the certificate has not expired, several options exist for renewing it. However, once it is allowed to expire, the only option for renewal is a checkride with the FAA or a designated pilot examiner.

L. Night Operations

1. What is the function of the rods and cones, and where are they located in the eye? (FAA-H-8083-3)

Rods—concentrated in a ring around the cones; primary function is peripheral vision. The process of night vision is placed almost entirely on the rods; about 30 minutes is needed for the rods to become adjusted to darkness; when adjusted they are about 100,000 times more sensitive to light.

Cones—located in the center of the retina and their function is to detect color, details, and faraway objects; after approximately 5 to 10 minutes, cones become adjusted to the dim light and the eyes become 100 times more sensitive.

2. What can a pilot do to improve the effectiveness of vision at night? (FAA-H-8083-3)

a. Adapt the eyes to darkness prior to flight and keep them adapted; usually 30 minutes is needed to adjust the eyes to maximum efficiency.

b. If oxygen is available, use it during night flying; a significant deterioration in night vision can occur at cabin altitudes as low as 5,000 feet.

    c. Close one eye when exposed to bright light to help avoid the blinding effect.

    d. Move the eyes more slowly than in daylight.

    e. Force the eyes to view off center.

3. During preflight, what things should be done to adequately prepare for a night flight? (FAA-H-8083-3)

    a. Study all weather reports and forecasts. Pay particular attention to temperature/dew point spreads to detect the possibility of fog formation.

    b. Calculate wind directions and speeds along the proposed route of flight to ensure accurate drift calculations, as night visual perception of drift is generally inaccurate.

    c. Obtain applicable aeronautical charts for both the proposed route as well as adjacent charts and clearly mark lighted checkpoints.

    d. Review all radio navigational aids for correct frequencies and availability.

    e. Check all personal equipment such as flashlights and portable transceivers for proper operation.

    f. Do a thorough preflight inspection of the aircraft.

    g. Check all aircraft position lights, as well as the landing light and rotating beacon, for proper operation.

    h. Check ground areas for obstructions that may not be readily visible from the cockpit.

4. What are the different types of rotating beacons used to identify airports? (AIM 2-1-9)

    a. White and green—lighted land airport.

    b. Green alone*—lighted land airport.

    c. White and yellow—lighted water airport.

    d. Yellow alone*—lighted water airport.

    e. Green, yellow, and white—lighted heliport.

    f. White (dual peaked) and green—military airport.

* "Green alone" and "yellow alone" beacons are used only in connection with a white-and-green, or white-and-yellow beacon display, respectively.

5. **Describe the following airport lights: runway edge, lights marking end of runway, REIL, taxiway edge, taxiway centerline.** (AIM 2-1-3, 2-1-4, 2-1-10)

   Runway edge lights—used to outline the edges of runways during periods of darkness or restricted visibility conditions. These lights are white, except on instrument runways, yellow replaces white on the last 2,000 feet or half the runway length (whichever is less), to form a caution zone for landings.

   Lights marking the ends of the runway—emit red light toward the runway to indicate the end of the runway to a departing aircraft, and emit green light outward from the runway end to indicate the threshold to landing aircraft.

   Runway end identifier lights (REIL)—provide rapid and positive identification of the approach end of a particular runway. They consist of a pair of synchronized flashing lights located laterally on each side of the runway threshold. REILs may be either omnidirectional or unidirectional facing the approach area.

   Taxiway edge lights—emit blue light and are used to outline the edges of taxiways during periods of darkness or restricted visibility conditions.

   Taxiway centerline lights—emit steady-burning, green light and are used to facilitate ground traffic under low-visibility conditions.

6. **How does a pilot determine the status of a light system at a particular airport?** (FAA-H-8083-3)

   The pilot needs to check the *Chart Supplements U.S.* and any NOTAMs to find out about available lighting systems, light intensities, and radio-controlled light system frequencies, and also call Flight Service for updates.

7. **Explain the arrangement and interpretation of the position lights on an aircraft.** (FAA-H-8083-3)

   A red light is positioned on the left wingtip, a green light on the right wingtip, and a white light on the tail. If both a red and green light of another aircraft are observed, and the red light is on the left and the green to the right, the airplane is flying in the same direction. Care must be taken not to overtake the other aircraft and to maintain clearance. If a red light is observed on the right and a green light to the left on another aircraft, then the airplane could be on a collision course.

8. Position lights are required to be on during what period of time? (14 CFR 91.209)

No person may operate an aircraft during the period from sunset to sunrise unless the aircraft has lighted position lights.

9. When operating an aircraft in, or in close proximity to, a night operations area, what is required of the aircraft? (14 CFR 91.209)

The aircraft must:

- Be clearly illuminated;
- Have lighted position lights; or
- Be in an area marked by obstruction lights.

10. When are aircraft that are equipped with an anti-collision light system required to operate that light system? (AIM 4-3-23; 14 CFR 91.209)

Aircraft equipped with an anti-collision light system are required to operate that light system during all types of operations (day and night). However, the anti-collision lights need not be lighted when the PIC determines that, because of operating conditions, it would be in the interest of safety to turn the lights off.

11. Describe several visual illusions that can occur at night. (FAA-H-8083-25)

a. On a clear night, distant stationary lights can be mistaken for stars or other aircraft.

b. Cloud layers can confuse a pilot and indicate a false visual horizon.

c. Certain geometrical patterns of ground lights, such as a freeway, runway, approach, or even lights on a moving train, can cause confusion.

d. Visual autokinesis can occur when staring at a single light source for several seconds, resulting in the light appearing to move.

e. Flickering light in the flightdeck, such as light from anti-collision light or other aircraft lights, can cause flicker vertigo resulting in nausea, dizziness, etc.

(continued)

f. A black-hole approach occurs when a landing is made from over water or non-lighted terrain where the runway lights are the only source of light. The runway can seem out of position (downsloping or upsloping) and in the worst case, can result in landing short of the runway.

g. Bright runway and approach lighting systems, especially where few lights illuminate the surrounding terrain, may create the illusion of being lower or having less distance to the runway, resulting in a tendency to fly a higher approach.

12. What are some guidelines to follow during the starting, taxiing, and run-up phases of a night flight? (FAA-H-8083-3)

a. The pilot should exercise extra caution on clearing the propeller arc area. The use of lights prior to engine startup can also alert persons in the area to the presence of the active aircraft.

b. During taxiing, avoid unnecessary use of electrical equipment that would put an abnormal load on the electrical system, such as the landing light.

c. Taxi slowly and follow any taxi lines.

13. What are some guidelines to follow during the takeoff and departure phases of a night flight? (FAA-H-8083-3)

During takeoff the pilot should, on initial takeoff roll, use the distant runway edge lights as well as the landing light area to keep the aircraft straight and parallel with the runway on the initial takeoff roll. Upon liftoff, the pilot should keep a positive climb by referencing the attitude indicator along with positive rate of climb on the vertical speed indicator. During climbout, the pilot should not initiate any turns until reaching a safe maneuvering altitude and should turn the landing light off as soon as possible.

14. Identify the hazards a pilot should consider when conducting night flight operations. (FAA-S-ACS-25)

a. Inoperative equipment.

b. Weather considerations specific to night operations.

c. Collision hazards.

d. Distractions, task prioritization, loss of situational awareness, or disorientation.

e. Effect of visual illusions and night adaptation during all phases of night flying.

f. Runway incursion.

g. Night currency versus proficiency.

M. High Altitude Operations— Supplemental Oxygen

1. What are the regulations concerning use of supplemental oxygen on board an aircraft? (14 CFR 91.211)

No person may operate a civil aircraft of U.S. registry:

a. At cabin pressure altitudes above 12,500 feet MSL up to and including 14,000 feet MSL, unless, for that part of the flight at those altitudes that is more than 30 minutes, the required minimum flight crew is provided with and uses supplemental oxygen.

b. At cabin pressure altitudes above 14,000 feet MSL, unless the required flight crew is provided with and uses supplemental oxygen for the entire flight time at those altitudes.

c. At cabin pressure altitudes above 15,000 feet MSL, unless each occupant is provided with supplemental oxygen.

2. What are the regulations pertaining to the use of supplemental oxygen on board a pressurized aircraft? (14 CFR 91.211)

Above flight level 250—At least a 10-minute supply of supplemental oxygen, in addition to any oxygen required to satisfy 14 CFR §91.211(a), is available for each occupant of the aircraft for use in the event that a descent is necessitated by loss of cabin pressurization.

Above flight level 350—At least one pilot at the controls of the airplane is wearing and using an oxygen mask that is secured and sealed that either supplies oxygen at all times or automatically supplies oxygen whenever the cabin pressure altitude of the airplane exceeds 14,000 feet MSL.

3. **What are the four major physiological problems a pilot would experience if the cabin suddenly decompressed from a cabin altitude of 7,000 feet to an aircraft's cruise altitude of 35,000 feet in 30 seconds?** (AC 61-107, CAMI OK-21-0375)

   Hypoxia, decompression sickness, hypothermia, and spatial disorientation.

4. **Define the term *time of useful consciousness* (TUC).** (FAA-H-8083-25)

   TUC describes the maximum time the pilot has to make rational, life-saving decisions and carry them out at a given altitude without supplemental oxygen. As altitude increases above 10,000 feet, the symptoms of hypoxia increase in severity, and the TUC rapidly decreases. The TUC varies from 1 to 2 minutes at 30,000 feet MSL to only 9 to 15 seconds at 40,000 feet MSL.

5. **What are several types of oxygen systems in use?** (FAA-H-8083-25, FAA-H-8083-31)

   Systems are often characterized by the type of regulator used to dispense the oxygen:

   a. Diluter-demand
   b. Pressure-demand
   c. Continuous-flow
   d. Electrical pulse-demand

6. **How does a continuous-flow oxygen system operate?** (FAA-H-8083-25)

   Continuous-flow oxygen systems are usually provided for passengers. The passenger mask typically has a reservoir bag that collects oxygen from the continuous-flow oxygen system during the time when the mask user is exhaling. The oxygen collected in the bag allows a higher inspiratory flow rate during the inhalation cycle, which reduces the amount of air dilution. Ambient air is added to the supplied oxygen during inhalation after the reservoir bag oxygen supply is depleted. The exhaled air is released to the cabin.

7. How does a pressure-demand oxygen system operate? (FAA-H-8083-25)

Pressure-demand oxygen systems are similar to diluter-demand oxygen equipment, except that oxygen is supplied to the mask under pressure at cabin altitudes above 34,000 feet. Pressure-demand regulators create airtight and oxygen-tight seals, but they also provide a positive pressure application of oxygen to the mask face piece that allows the user's lungs to be pressurized with oxygen; this makes them safe at altitudes above 40,000 feet. Some systems may have a pressure-demand mask with the regulator attached directly to the mask, rather than mounted on the instrument panel or other area within the flight deck.

8. Explain how a diluter-demand oxygen system operates. (FAA-H-8083-25)

Diluter-demand oxygen systems supply oxygen only when the user inhales through the mask. An automix lever allows the regulators to automatically mix cabin air and oxygen or supply 100 percent oxygen, depending on the altitude. The demand mask provides a tight seal over the face to prevent dilution with outside air and can be used safely up to 40,000 feet.

9. Can any kind of oxygen be used for aviator's breathing oxygen? (FAA-H-8083-25)

No; oxygen used for medical purposes or welding normally should not be used because it may contain too much water. The excess water could condense and freeze in the oxygen lines when flying at high altitudes. Specifications for aviator's breathing oxygen are 99.5% pure oxygen with not more than two milliliters of water per liter of oxygen.

10. Describe operational precautions when using supplemental oxygen systems. (CAMI OK-21-0375)

a. Keep your equipment clean—the interaction of oil-based products and oxygen creates a fire hazard. Additionally, oil attracts dirt particles, which can contaminate storage containers, regulators, masks, and valves.

b. Protect your oxygen mask from direct sunlight and dust. Store in proper containers.

(continued)

c. Inspect oxygen storage containers. Ensure they are securely fastened in the aircraft.

d. Proper inspections are important. Have oxygen equipment inspected regularly at an authorized FAA inspection station.

e. No smoking! Although oxygen itself is not flammable, it can cause other materials to ignite more easily and will make existing fires burn hotter and faster.

f. Ensure that the aircraft is properly grounded before loading oxygen.

g. Mix and match components with caution. When interchanging oxygen system components, ensure compatibility of the components (e.g., storage containers, regulators, and masks).

11. Identify the hazards a pilot should consider when conducting high-altitude operations using supplemental oxygen. (FAA-S-ACS-25)

a. High-altitude flight operations—hypoxia, decompression, weather etc.

b. Use of supplemental oxygen.

c. Management of compressed gas containers.

d. Combustion hazards in an oxygen-rich environment.

N. High Altitude Operations— Pressurization

1. What is a pressurized aircraft? (FAA-H-8083-25)

In a pressurized aircraft, the cabin, flight compartment, and baggage compartments are incorporated into a sealed unit that is capable of containing air under a pressure higher than outside atmospheric pressure. On aircraft powered by turbine engines, bleed air from the engine compressor section is used to pressurize the cabin, and piston-powered aircraft may use air supplied from each engine turbocharger through a sonic venturi (flow limiter). Air is released from the fuselage by a device called an outflow valve. Since the superchargers provide a constant inflow of air to the pressurized area, the outflow valve, by regulating the air exit, is the major controlling element in the pressurization system.

2. What operational advantages are there in flying pressurized aircraft? (FAA-H-8083-25)

A cabin pressurization system performs several functions:

a. It allows an aircraft to fly higher, which can result in better fuel economy, higher speeds, and the capability to avoid bad weather and turbulence.

b. It will typically maintain a cabin pressure altitude of 8,000 feet at the maximum designed cruising altitude of the airplane.

c. It prevents rapid changes of cabin altitude that may be uncomfortable or injurious to passengers and crew.

d. It permits a reasonably fast exchange of air from inside to outside of the cabin. This is necessary to eliminate odors and to remove stale air.

3. Describe a typical cabin pressure control system. (FAA-H-8083-25)

The cabin pressure control system provides cabin pressure regulation, pressure relief, vacuum relief, and the means for selecting the desired cabin altitude in the isobaric and differential range. In addition, dumping of the cabin pressure is a function of the pressure control system. A cabin pressure regulator, an outflow valve, and a safety valve are used to accomplish these functions.

4. What are the components of a cabin pressure control system? (FAA-H-8083-25)

a. *Cabin pressure regulator*—Controls cabin pressure to a selected value in the isobaric range and limits cabin pressure to a preset differential value in the differential range.

b. *Cabin air pressure safety valve*—A combination pressure relief, vacuum relief, and dump valve.

• *Pressure relief valve*—prevents cabin pressure from exceeding a predetermined differential pressure above ambient pressure.

• *Vacuum relief valve*—prevents ambient pressure from exceeding cabin pressure by allowing external air to enter the cabin when the ambient pressure exceeds cabin pressure.

• *Dump valve*—actuated by a cockpit control, which will cause the cabin air to be dumped to the atmosphere.

(continued)

c. *Instrumentation*—Several instruments used in conjunction with the pressurization controller are:
- *Cabin differential pressure gauge*—indicates difference between inside and outside pressure; should be monitored to ensure the cabin does not exceed maximum allowable differential pressure.
- *Cabin altimeter*—this is a check on system performance. Sometimes differential pressure and cabin altimeter are combined into one.
- *Cabin rate-of-climb*—indicates cabin rate-of-climb or descent.

5. What is meant by *decompression*? (FAA-H-8083-25)

Decompression is the inability of the aircraft's pressurization system to maintain the designed aircraft cabin pressure. For example, an aircraft is flying at an altitude of 29,000 feet but the aircraft cabin is pressurized to an altitude equivalent to 8,000 feet. If decompression occurs, the cabin pressure may become equivalent to that of the aircraft's altitude of 29,000 feet. The rate at which this occurs determines the severity of decompression.

6. What are the three types of decompression?
(FAA-H-8083-25, AC 61-107)

Explosive decompression—Cabin pressure decreases faster than the lungs can decompress. Most authorities consider any kind of decompression that occurs in less than ½ second as explosive and potentially dangerous. This type of decompression could only be caused by structural damage, material failure, or by a door popping open.

Rapid decompression—A change in cabin pressure where the lungs decompress faster than the cabin. Rapid decompression decreases the period of useful consciousness because oxygen in the lungs is exhaled rapidly. The pilot's effective performance time is reduced by one-third to one-fourth its normal time.

Gradual or slow decompression—Can be the most dangerous and occurs when the cabin pressure decreases at a rate so slow that it may not be detected by the flight crew. If not corrected, the insidious effects of hypoxia take effect and eventually result in crew incapacitation. Possible causes of a slow decompression include cracked windows, pressure seal leaks, and pressurization system component failures. Automatic visual and aural warning systems generally provide an indication of a slow decompression.

7. What are the dangers of decompression?
(FAA-H-8083-25)

a. Proper use of oxygen equipment must be accomplished quickly to avoid hypoxia. Unconsciousness may occur in a very short time. The time of useful consciousness (TUC) is considerably shortened when a person is subjected to a rapid decompression, which causes a rapid reduction of pressure on the body leading to a quick exhalation of the oxygen in the lungs.

b. At higher altitudes where the pressure differential is greater, being tossed or blown out of the airplane is a danger if one is near an opening during a decompression. Those who must be near an opening should always wear safety harnesses or seatbelts when in pressurized aircraft.

c. Evolved gas decompression sickness (the bends).

d. Exposure to windblast and extreme cold.

8. Describe the general procedures required after experiencing a decompression at a high altitude.
(AC 61-107)

Immediately don oxygen masks and breathe 100 percent oxygen slowly. Descend to a safe altitude. If supplemental oxygen is not available, initiate an emergency descent to an altitude below 10,000 feet MSL. If symptoms of hypoxia are experienced and persist, land as soon as possible.

9. Why is slow decompression as dangerous as or more dangerous than a rapid or explosive decompression?
(AC 61-107)

During a slow decompression, the typical indications of a decompression (noise, flying debris, etc.) may not be evident. Furthermore, the insidious nature of hypoxia and depression of mental function decreases the ability to recognize the emergency and undertake appropriate recovery procedures. For those reasons, a slow decompression is the most dangerous, and the aviator must always be on guard against this insidious threat.

Preflight
Preparation

3

A. Pilot Qualifications

General

1. **To act as a required pilot flight crewmember of a civil aircraft, what must a pilot have in his/her physical possession or readily accessible in the aircraft?** (14 CFR 61.3)

   a. A pilot certificate (including any special purpose pilot authorization or temporary certificate).

   b. A photo identification (driver's license, government or state ID, passport, etc.).

   c. An appropriate medical certificate or BasicMed requirements.

2. **What are the various certificates issued under Part 61?** (14 CFR 61.5)

   a. Pilot certificates—student pilot, sport pilot, recreational pilot, private pilot, commercial pilot, airline transport pilot;

   b. Flight instructor certificates; and

   c. Ground instructor certificates.

3. **What are the various ratings that may be placed on a pilot certificate (other than student pilot)?** (14 CFR 61.5)

   These ratings are placed on a pilot certificate (other than student pilot) when an applicant satisfactorily accomplishes the training and certification requirements for the rating sought:

   a. *Aircraft category ratings*—Airplane; Rotorcraft; Glider; Lighter-than-Air; Powered-Lift; Powered Parachute; Weight-Shift Control Aircraft.

   b. *Airplane class ratings*—Single-Engine Land; Multi-Engine Land; Single-Engine Sea; Multi-Engine Sea.

   c. *Rotorcraft class ratings*—Helicopter; Gyroplane.

   d. *Lighter-than-air class ratings*—Airship; Balloon.

   e. *Weight-shift-control aircraft class ratings*—Weight-Shift Control Aircraft Land; Weight-Shift Control Aircraft Sea.

   f. *Powered parachute class ratings*—Powered Parachute Land; Powered Parachute Sea.

g. *Aircraft type ratings*—Large aircraft other than lighter-than-air; turbojet-powered airplanes; other aircraft type ratings specified by the Administrator through the aircraft type certification procedures; second-in-command pilot type rating for aircraft that is certificated for operations with a minimum crew of at least two pilots.

h. *Instrument ratings* (on Private and Commercial Pilot Certificates only)—Instrument–Airplane; Instrument–Helicopter; Instrument–Powered-Lift.

4. What are the various ratings that may be placed on a Flight Instructor Certificate? (14 CFR 61.5)

These ratings are placed on a Flight Instructor Certificate when an applicant satisfactorily accomplishes the training and certification requirements for the rating sought:

a. *Aircraft category ratings*—Airplane; Rotorcraft; Glider; Powered-Lift.

b. *Airplane class ratings*—Single-Engine; Multi-Engine.

c. *Rotorcraft class ratings*—Helicopter; Gyroplane.

d. *Instrument ratings*—Instrument–Airplane; Instrument–Helicopter; Instrument–Powered-Lift.

5. A temporary pilot certificate that has been recently issued will remain effective for what length of time? (14 CFR 61.17)

120 days.

6. What is the duration of a Flight Instructor Certificate? (14 CFR 61.19, 61.199)

A Flight Instructor Certificate expires 24 calendar months from the month in which it was issued, renewed, or reinstated, as appropriate. If the certificate has not expired, several options exist for renewing it. However, once it is allowed to expire, the only option for renewal is a checkride with the FAA or a designated pilot examiner.

7. What are the required medical certificates for the various pilot certificates? (14 CFR 61.23)

a. Must hold a First-Class Medical Certificate when exercising the PIC privileges of an Airline Transport Pilot Certificate;

b. Must hold at least a Second-Class Medical Certificate when exercising the privileges of a Commercial Pilot Certificate; or

c. Must hold at least a Third-Class Medical Certificate when

- exercising the privileges of a Private Pilot Certificate, Recreational Pilot Certificate, or Student Pilot Certificate, except when operating under the conditions and limitations set forth in §61.113(i);

- exercising the privileges of a Flight Instructor Certificate and acting as the pilot-in-command or as a required flightcrew member, except when operating under the conditions and limitations set forth in §61.113(i);

- taking a practical test in an aircraft for a Recreational Pilot, Private Pilot, Commercial Pilot, or Airline Transport Pilot Certificate, or for a Flight Instructor Certificate, except when operating under the conditions and limitations set forth in §61.113(i); or

- performing the duties as an Examiner in an aircraft when administering a practical test or proficiency check for an airman certificate, rating, or authorization.

8. Give several examples of operations that do not require a medical certificate. (14 CFR 61.23)

a. When exercising the privileges of a Flight Instructor Certificate if not acting as pilot-in-command or serving as a required crewmember.

b. When exercising the privileges of a Ground Instructor Certificate.

c. When serving as an examiner or check airman and administering a practical test or proficiency check for an airman certificate, rating, or authorization conducted in a glider, balloon, flight simulator, or flight training device.

d. When taking a practical test or a proficiency check for a certificate, rating, authorization or operating privilege conducted in a glider, balloon, flight simulator, or flight training device.

9. **Does a Student Pilot Certificate have an expiration date?**
(14 CFR 61.19)

If issued after April 1, 2016, a Student Pilot Certificate will not expire; the certificate will be surrendered and superseded upon successful completion of a higher certification. If a Student Pilot Certificate was issued prior to April 1, 2016, it will expire either 24 or 60 months from the date of issuance.

10. **What is a *Statement of Demonstrated Ability* (SODA)?**
(14 CFR 67.401)

At the discretion of the Federal Air Surgeon, a Statement of Demonstrated Ability (SODA) may be granted, instead of an Authorization, to a person whose disqualifying condition is static or nonprogressive and who has been found capable of performing airman duties without endangering public safety. A SODA does not expire and authorizes a designated aviation medical examiner to issue a medical certificate of a specified class if the examiner finds that the condition described on its face has not adversely changed.

11. **What are several medical conditions that could delay or prevent the issuance of a medical certificate?**
(FAA-H-8083-25, 14 CFR Part 67)

a. Clinical diabetes
b. Coronary heart disease/heart attack
c. Epilepsy
d. Disturbance of consciousness
e. Alcoholism
f. Drug dependence
g. Psychosis

12. **What should learners know about flight operations conducted while suffering from a medical deficiency?**
(14 CFR 61.53)

No person may act as pilot-in-command, or in any other capacity as a required flight crewmember, while having a known medical deficiency that would make him/her unable to meet the requirements for his/her current medical certificate.

13. A pilot holds a Commercial Pilot Certificate with ASEL and Instrument Ratings. The pilot would like to add an AMEL Rating to his/her certificate. To be eligible for the practical test, what class of medical certificate is required? (14 CFR 61.39)

The applicant must hold at least a Third-Class Medical Certificate.

14. What is BasicMed? (AC 68-1, 14 CFR Part 68)

BasicMed is an alternate way for pilots to fly without holding an FAA medical certificate as long as they meet certain requirements. The regulation permits pilots to operate as PIC of certain covered aircraft without having to undergo the medical certification process under 14 CFR Part 67. The pilot and aircraft must meet certain prescribed conditions to operate under BasicMed.

15. Explain the requirements to fly under the BasicMed regulations. (14 CFR 61.23, AC 68-1)

A pilot must:

a. Hold a U.S. driver's license.

b. Hold or have held a medical certificate issued by the FAA at any point after July 15, 2006.

c. Answer the health questions on the Comprehensive Medical Examination Checklist (CMEC).

d. Get a physical examination by any state-licensed physician, and have that physician complete the CMEC; keep the signed CMEC document.

e. Take an online medical education course and complete the attestations/consent to the National Driver Register (NDR) check. Keep the course completion document.

16. Explain the privileges and limitations of a pilot flying under BasicMed. (14 CFR 61.113, AC 68-1)

Pilots can conduct any operation that they would otherwise be able to conduct using their pilot certificate and a Third-Class Medical Certificate, except they are limited to:

a. Fly with no more than five passengers.

b. Fly an aircraft under 6,000 pounds maximum certificated takeoff weight.

c. Fly an aircraft that is authorized to carry no more than six occupants.

d. Flights within the United States, at an indicated airspeed of 250 knots or less, and at an altitude at or below 18,000 feet mean sea level (MSL).

e. May not fly for compensation or hire.

17. In the event an airman certificate, medical certificate, or knowledge test report is lost or destroyed, what procedure should be followed? (14 CFR 61.29)

a. An application for the replacement of a lost or destroyed certificate or report must be made by letter to the Department of Transportation, FAA.

b. A person who has lost a certificate or report may obtain, in a form or manner approved by the FAA, a document conveying temporary authority to exercise the certificate privileges. The document may be carried as a certificate for up to 60 days pending receipt of a duplicate certificate.

18. When is a type rating required? (14 CFR 61.31)

A type rating is required when acting as pilot-in-command of any of the following:

a. Large aircraft (except lighter-than-air).

b. Turbojet-powered airplanes.

c. Other aircraft (specified through aircraft type certificate procedures).

19. According to regulations, what additional training is required to act as pilot-in-command of a complex airplane? (14 CFR 61.31)

No person may act as pilot-in-command of a complex airplane (an airplane with retractable landing gear, flaps, and controllable-pitch propeller, or in the case of a seaplane, flaps, and controllable-pitch propeller), unless the person has:

a. Received and logged ground and flight training from an authorized instructor in a complex airplane, or in a flight simulator or flight training device (representative of a complex airplane), and has been found proficient in its operation and systems; and

b. Received a one-time logbook endorsement from an authorized instructor certifying the person is proficient to operate a complex airplane.

Note: This is not required if the person has logged flight time as pilot-in-command of a complex airplane, or in a flight simulator or flight training device that is representative of a complex airplane prior to August 4, 1997.

20. According to regulations, what additional training is required to act as pilot-in-command of a high-performance airplane? (14 CFR 61.31)

No person may act as pilot-in-command of a high-performance airplane (an engine of more than 200 horsepower), unless the person has:

a. Received and logged ground and flight training from an authorized instructor in a high-performance airplane, or in a flight simulator or flight training device (representative of a high-performance airplane), and has been found proficient in its operation and systems; and

b. Received a one-time logbook endorsement from an authorized instructor certifying the person is proficient to operate a high-performance airplane.

Note: This is not required if the person has logged flight time as pilot-in-command of a high-performance airplane, or in a flight simulator or flight training device representative of a high-performance airplane prior to August 4, 1997.

21. Describe the minimum required elements of instruction for transition to a tailwheel aircraft. (14 CFR 61.31)

No person may act as pilot-in-command of a tailwheel airplane unless that person has received and logged flight training from an authorized instructor in a tailwheel airplane, and has received a logbook endorsement from an authorized instructor who found the person proficient in the operation of a tailwheel airplane, to include at least the following maneuvers and procedures: normal and crosswind takeoffs and landings, wheel landings (unless the manufacturer has recommended against such landings), and go-around procedures. This is not required if the person logged pilot-in-command time in a tailwheel airplane before April 15, 1991.

22. To be eligible to take an FAA knowledge test (other than ATP), what must an applicant accomplish? (14 CFR 61.35)

An applicant must have received an endorsement from an authorized instructor certifying that the applicant accomplished a required ground-training or a home-study course for the certificate or rating sought and is prepared for the knowledge test; and must have proper identification at the time of application that contains the applicant's photograph, signature, date of birth (which shows the applicant meets or will meet the age requirements of Part 61 for the certificate sought before the expiration date of the airman knowledge test report), and current residential address (if the permanent mailing address is a P.O. box number).

23. What various methods may be used by a student to show evidence of ground school or home study course completion? (AC 61-65)

a. A certificate of graduation from a pilot training course conducted by an FAA-certificated pilot school.

b. An endorsement from an authorized instructor who has certified that the applicant has satisfactorily completed the ground training required for the certificate or rating sought and is prepared for the test.

c. A certificate of graduation or statement of accomplishment from a ground school course (e.g., high school, college, adult education program, etc.).

d. A certificate of graduation from an industry-provided aviation home study course.

e. An endorsement from an appropriately rated FAA-certificated ground or flight instructor for completion of an individually developed home study course.

24. **What actions is an applicant (other than ATP) required to have accomplished in order to be eligible for a practical test for a certificate or rating issued under 14 CFR Part 61?** (14 CFR 61.39)

a. Pass the required knowledge test within the 24-calendar-month period preceding the month the applicant completes the practical test, if a knowledge test is required;

b. Present the knowledge test report at the time of application for the practical test, if a knowledge test is required;

c. Have satisfactorily accomplished the required training and obtained the aeronautical experience prescribed by 14 CFR Part 61 for the certificate or rating sought;

d. Hold at least a current Third-Class Medical Certificate, if a medical certificate is required;

e. Meet the prescribed age requirement of Part 61 for the issuance of the certificate or rating sought;

f. Have a logbook or training record endorsement, if required by Part 61, signed by an authorized instructor who certifies that the applicant has received and logged training time within 2 calendar months preceding the month of application in preparation for the practical test; is prepared for the required practical test; and has demonstrated satisfactory knowledge of subject areas in which the applicant was deficient on the knowledge test; and

g. Have a completed and signed application form.

25. **Other than the Airman Certification Standards or Practical Test Standards (as applicable), what general guidelines will an examiner follow when judging the ability of an applicant for a pilot certificate or rating?** (14 CFR 61.43)

The examiner will judge based on that applicant's ability to safely:

a. Perform the tasks specified in the areas of operation for the airman certificate or rating sought;

b. Demonstrate mastery of the aircraft by performing each task successfully;

c. Demonstrate proficiency and competency within the approved standards;

    d. Demonstrate sound judgment; and

    e. Demonstrate single-pilot proficiency if the aircraft's FAA-approved flight manual or type certification data sheet requires the pilot flight crew complement be a single pilot.

26. An applicant for a knowledge or practical test who fails that test may only reapply when what actions have been accomplished? (14 CFR 61.49)

An applicant who fails may only reapply for the test after the applicant has received:

    a. The necessary training from an authorized instructor, who has determined that the applicant is proficient to pass the test; and

    b. An endorsement from an authorized instructor who gave the applicant the additional training.

27. What requirements must be met when conducting a flight review? (14 CFR 61.56)

A flight review consists of a minimum of 1 hour of flight training and 1 hour of ground training, including a review of the current general operating and flight rules of Part 91 and a review of those maneuvers and procedures that, at the discretion of the person giving the review, are necessary for the pilot to demonstrate the safe exercise of the privileges of the pilot certificate.

28. Before conducting a flight review, the flight instructor should interview the pilot to determine the nature of his or her flying and operating requirements. What are several areas to consider? (AC 61-98)

    a. *Type of equipment flown*—The pilot may hold multiple categories and/or ratings; the reviewed maneuvers and procedures will vary depending on the category, class, and make and model of the aircraft used.

    b. *Nature of flight operations*—The flight instructor should consider the type of flying usually done by the pilot before establishing the plan for conducting the review, and also consider the need for an in-depth review of certain subjects or procedures if the type of flight operation is likely to change.

(continued)

c. *Amount and recency of flight experience*—the flight instructor should review the pilot's logbook to determine total flight time, time-in-type, and recency of experience in order to evaluate the need for particular maneuvers and procedures in the review.

29. When is a flight review not required? (14 CFR 61.56)

A flight review is not required for pilots who have satisfactorily completed, within the preceding 24 calendar months before the month in which they act as pilot-in-command, any of the following:

a. A pilot proficiency check or practical test conducted by an examiner, an approved pilot check airman, or a U.S. armed force, for a pilot certificate, rating, or operating privilege.

b. A practical test conducted by an examiner for the issuance of a Flight Instructor Certificate, an additional rating on a Flight Instructor Certificate, renewal of a Flight Instructor Certificate, or reinstatement of a Flight Instructor Certificate.

c. One or more phases of an FAA-sponsored pilot proficiency award program.

A flight instructor who has, within the preceding 24 calendar months before the month in which they act as PIC, satisfactorily completed a renewal of a Flight Instructor Certificate under the provisions in §61.197 need not accomplish the one hour of ground training.

A student pilot need not accomplish the flight review provided they are undergoing training for a certificate and have a current solo flight endorsement as required by §61.87.

Note: The flight review may be accomplished in combination with the requirements of §61.57 and other applicable recency-of-experience requirements at the discretion of the instructor.

30. What are the recency-of-experience requirements for acting as pilot-in-command of an aircraft carrying passengers? (14 CFR 61.57)

No person may act as a pilot-in-command of an aircraft carrying passengers, or as a required pilot on board an aircraft that requires more than one pilot flight crewmember, unless that person has made at least three takeoffs and three landings within the preceding 90 days, and:

a. The person acted as the sole manipulator of the flight controls; and

b. The required takeoffs and landings were performed in an aircraft of the same category, class, and type (if a type rating is required), and if the aircraft to be flown is an airplane with a tailwheel, the takeoffs and landings must have been made to a full stop in an airplane with a tailwheel.

For the purpose of meeting these requirements, a person may act as a pilot-in-command of an aircraft under day VFR or day IFR, provided no persons or property are carried onboard the aircraft, other than those necessary for the conduct of the flight.

31. When acting as PIC of an aircraft carrying passengers at night, what recent night experience must the pilot have accomplished? (14 CFR 61.57)

No person may act as pilot-in-command of an aircraft carrying passengers during the period beginning 1 hour after sunset and ending 1 hour before sunrise, unless within the preceding 90 days that person:

a. Has made at least three takeoffs and three landings to a full stop during the period beginning 1 hour after sunset and ending 1 hour before sunrise;

b. Has acted as sole manipulator of the flight controls;

c. Has performed the required takeoffs and landings in an aircraft of the same category, class, and type (if a type rating is required).

32. Explain the difference between being current and being proficient. (FAA-H-8083-2, FAA-P-8740-36)

Being *current* means that a pilot has accomplished the minimum FAA regulatory requirements within a specific time period to exercise the privileges of their certificate. It means that the pilot is legal to make a flight, but it does not necessarily mean that the pilot is proficient or competent to make that flight.

Being *proficient* means that a pilot is capable of conducting a flight with a high degree of competence or skill, and it requires that the pilot have a wide range of knowledge and skills. Being proficient is not about just being legal in terms of the regulations, but about being smart and safe in terms of pilot experience and proficiency.

33. How can flying an unfamiliar aircraft or an aircraft with unfamiliar avionics or flight display systems increase the total risk of a flight? (FAA-H-8083-25)

Pilot familiarity with all equipment is critical in optimizing both safety and efficiency. If a pilot is unfamiliar with any aircraft systems, this will add to workload and may contribute to a loss of situational awareness. This level of proficiency is critical and should be looked upon as a requirement, not unlike carrying an adequate supply of fuel. As a result, pilots should consider unfamiliarity with the aircraft and its systems a hazard with high risk potential. Discipline is key to success.

Aircraft Rating and Special Certification

1. If a pilot wants to add an additional category rating to his or her pilot certificate, what is required? (14 CFR 61.63)

This person must:

a. Have completed the training and have the applicable aeronautical experience.

b. Have a logbook or training record endorsement from an authorized instructor attesting that the person was found competent in the appropriate aeronautical knowledge areas and proficient in the appropriate areas of operation.

c. Pass the practical test. This person need not take an additional knowledge test provided the applicant holds an Airplane, Rotorcraft, Powered-Lift, Weight-Shift-Control Aircraft, Powered Parachute, or Airship Rating at that pilot certificate level.

2. If a pilot wants to add on an additional class rating to his or her pilot certificate, what is required? (14 CFR 61.63)

This person:

a. Must have a logbook or training record endorsement from an authorized instructor attesting that the person was found competent in the appropriate aeronautical knowledge areas and proficient in the appropriate areas of operation.

b. Must pass the practical test.

c. Need not meet the specified training time requirements that apply to the pilot certificate for the aircraft class rating sought, unless the person only holds a Lighter-than-Air category rating with a Balloon class rating and is seeking an Airship class rating, then that person must receive the specified training time requirements and possess the appropriate aeronautical experience.

d. Need not take an additional knowledge test provided the person holds an Airplane, Rotorcraft, Powered-Lift, Weight-Shift-Control Aircraft, Powered Parachute, or Airship rating at that pilot certificate level.

3. **For an applicant training under Part 61, what minimum aeronautical experience is required before application for an Instrument Rating may take place?** (14 CFR 61.65)

A person who applies for an Instrument–Airplane Rating must have logged the following:

a. 50 hours of cross-country flight time as PIC, of which 10 hours must have been in an airplane;

b. 40 hours of actual or simulated instrument time in the Part 61 areas of operation, of which 15 hours must have been received from an authorized instructor who holds an Instrument–Airplane Rating, and the instrument time includes:

• 3 hours of instrument flight training from an authorized instructor in an airplane that is appropriate to the Instrument–Airplane Rating within 2 calendar months before the date of the practical test;

• Instrument flight training on cross-country flight procedures, including one cross-country flight in an airplane with an authorized instructor, that is performed under IFR, when a flight plan has been filed with an ATC facility, and that involves a flight of 250 NM along airways or direct routing from ATC, an instrument approach at each airport, and 3 different kinds of approaches with the use of navigation systems.

4. **In what minimum aeronautical knowledge areas must a person who applies for an Instrument Rating have received instruction from an authorized instructor or home-study course?** (14 CFR 61.65)

   a. Federal Aviation Regulations that apply to flight operations under IFR.

   b. Appropriate information from the *AIM* that applies to flight operations under IFR.

   c. Air traffic control system and procedures for instrument flight operations.

   d. IFR navigation and approaches by use of navigation systems.

   e. Use of IFR enroute and instrument approach procedure charts.

   f. Procurement and use of aviation weather reports and forecasts and the elements of forecasting weather trends based on that information and personal observation of weather conditions.

   g. Safe and efficient operation of aircraft under instrument flight rules and conditions.

   h. Recognition of critical weather situations and wind shear avoidance.

   i. Aeronautical decision-making and judgment.

   j. Crew resource management, including crew communication and coordination.

5. **To be eligible for an Instrument Rating, in what minimum areas of operation must the applicant have received training?** (14 CFR 61.65)

   A person who applies for an Instrument Rating must receive and log training from an authorized instructor in an aircraft, or in a full flight simulator or flight training device, that includes the following areas of operation:

   a. Preflight preparation;
   b. Preflight procedures;
   c. Air traffic control clearances and procedures;
   d. Flight by reference to instruments;
   e. Navigation systems;
   f. Instrument approach procedures;
   g. Emergency operations; and
   h. Postflight procedures.

Student Pilots

1. **What are the eligibility requirements for a Student Pilot Certificate?** (14 CFR 61.83)

   An applicant must:

   a. Be at least 16 years of age for other than the operation of a glider or balloon.

   b. Be at least 14 years of age for the operation of a glider or balloon.

   c. Be able to read, speak, write, and understand the English language. If the applicant is unable to meet one of these requirements due to medical reasons, then the Administrator may place such operating limitations on that applicant's pilot certificate as are necessary for the safe operation of the aircraft.

2. **Explain the procedure a student should follow to obtain a Student Pilot Certificate.** (FAA-H-8083-25)

   a. The student will complete an application through the IACRA website or by paper using FAA Form 8710-1.

   b. Submit the application to a FSDO, an FAA-designated pilot examiner, an airman certification representative associated with a Part 141 flight school, or a flight instructor.

   c. The authorized individual will process the application and submit the required documents to the Airmen Certification Branch.

   d. Once reviewed by the Airman Certification Branch, the Student Pilot Certificate will be mailed to the address provided by the student on the application.

3. **Does a Student Pilot Certificate have an expiration date?** (14 CFR 61.19)

   If issued after April 1, 2016, a Student Pilot Certificate will not expire; the certificate will be surrendered and superseded upon successful completion of a higher certification. If a Student Pilot Certificate was issued prior to April 1, 2016, it will expire either 24 or 60 months from the date of issuance.

4. When should a student pilot obtain a medical certificate? (FAA-H-8083-25)

The FAA suggests the individual get a medical certificate before beginning flight training to avoid the expense of flight training that cannot be continued due to a medical condition. The student must have a medical certificate before they can fly solo but they don't need it to begin taking flying lessons.

5. Explain how the learner can obtain a medical certificate. (FAA-H-8083-25)

A medical certificate is obtained by passing a physical examination administered by a doctor who is an FAA-authorized Aviation Medical Examiner (AME). A list of AMEs for a given area can be found at www.faa.gov/licenses_certificates/medical_certification.

6. What minimum aeronautical knowledge must be demonstrated by a student pilot before solo privileges are permitted? (14 CFR 61.87)

A student pilot must demonstrate satisfactory aeronautical knowledge on a knowledge test.

a. The test must address the student pilot's knowledge of:
   - Applicable sections of 14 CFR Parts 61 and 91;
   - Airspace rules and procedures for the airport where the solo flight will be performed; and
   - Flight characteristics and operational limitations for the make and model of aircraft to be flown.

b. The student's authorized instructor must:
   - Administer the test; and
   - At the conclusion of the test, review all incorrect answers with the student before authorizing that student to conduct a solo flight.

7. What minimum flight training must a student pilot receive before solo privileges are permitted? (14 CFR 61.87)

Prior to conducting a solo flight, a student pilot must have:

a. Received and logged flight training for the Part 61 maneuvers and procedures appropriate to the make and model of aircraft to be flown; and

b. Demonstrated satisfactory proficiency and safety, as judged by an authorized instructor, on the Part 61 maneuvers and procedures in the make and model of aircraft or similar make and model of aircraft to be flown.

A student pilot training for a Single-Engine Airplane Rating must receive and log flight training for the following maneuvers and procedures:

a. Proper flight preparation procedures, including preflight planning and preparation, powerplant operation, and aircraft systems;

b. Taxiing or surface operations, including runups;

c. Takeoffs and landings, including normal and crosswind;

d. Straight-and-level flight, and turns in both directions;

e. Climbs and climbing turns;

f. Airport traffic patterns, including entry and departure procedures;

g. Collision avoidance, wind shear avoidance, and wake turbulence avoidance;

h. Descents, with and without turns, using high and low drag configurations;

i. Flight at various airspeeds from cruise to slow flight;

j. Stall entries from various flight attitudes and power combinations with recovery initiated at the first indication of a stall, and recovery from a full stall;

k. Emergency procedures and equipment malfunctions;

l. Ground reference maneuvers;

m. Approaches to a landing area with simulated engine malfunctions;

n. Slips to a landing; and

o. Go-arounds.

8. **What basic requirements must a student pilot meet before being allowed to conduct solo flight at night?** (14 CFR 61.87)

   a. Flight training at night on night-flying procedures, including takeoffs, approaches, landings, and go-arounds at night at the airport where the solo flight will be conducted;

   b. Navigation training at night in the vicinity of the airport where the solo flight will be conducted;

   c. An endorsement in the student's logbook for the specific make and model of aircraft to be flown for night solo flight, by an authorized instructor who gave the training within the 90-day period preceding the date of the flight.

9. **What limitations are imposed upon student pilots operating an aircraft in solo flight?** (14 CFR 61.87)

   A student pilot may not operate an aircraft in solo flight unless that student pilot has received an endorsement in the student's logbook for the specific make and model of aircraft to be flown by an authorized instructor who gave the training within the 90 days preceding the date of the flight.

10. **What limitations are imposed upon flight instructors authorizing student pilot solo flights?** (14 CFR 61.87)

    No instructor may authorize a student pilot to perform a solo flight unless that instructor has:

    a. Given that student pilot training in the make and model of aircraft or a similar make and model of aircraft in which the solo flight is to be flown;

    b. Determined the student pilot is proficient in the Part 61 prescribed maneuvers and procedures;

    c. Determined the student pilot is proficient in the make and model of aircraft to be flown; and

    d. Endorsed the student pilot's logbook for the specific make and model of aircraft to be flown, and that endorsement remains current for solo flight privileges, provided an authorized instructor updates the student's logbook every 90 days thereafter.

11. State the general limitations that apply to all student pilots. (14 CFR 61.89)

A student pilot may not act as pilot-in-command of an aircraft:

a. Carrying a passenger;

b. Carrying property for compensation or hire;

c. For compensation or hire;

d. In furtherance of a business;

e. On an international flight (with exceptions; see §61.89);

f. With a flight or surface visibility of less than 3 statute miles during daylight hours or 5 statute miles at night;

g. When the flight cannot be made with visual reference to the surface; or

h. In a manner contrary to any limitations placed in the pilot's logbook by an authorized instructor.

A student pilot may not act as a required pilot flight crewmember on any aircraft for which more than one pilot is required by the type certificate of the aircraft or regulations under which the flight is conducted, except when receiving flight training from an authorized instructor onboard an airship, and no person other than a required flight crewmember is carried on the aircraft.

12. What requirements must be met before a flight instructor can allow a student pilot to make repeated specific solo cross-country flights without each flight being logbook endorsed? (14 CFR 61.93)

Repeated specific solo cross-country flights may be made to another airport within 50 NM of the airport from which the flight originated, provided:

a. The authorized instructor has given the student pilot flight training at the other airport(s), and that training includes flight in both directions over the route, entering and exiting the traffic patterns, and takeoffs and landings at the other airport(s);

b. The authorized instructor who gave the training has endorsed the student's logbook certifying the student is proficient to make such flights;

(continued)

    c. The student has a solo flight endorsement in accordance with §61.87; and

    d. The student has a solo cross-country flight endorsement in accordance with §61.93(c); however, for repeated solo cross-country flights to another airport within 50 NM from which the flight originated, separate endorsements are not required to be made for each flight.

13. Before a student pilot is permitted solo cross-country privileges, the student must have received several endorsements. What are they? (14 CFR 61.63, 61.93)

    a. A student pilot must have a solo cross-country endorsement from the authorized instructor who conducted the training that is placed in that person's logbook for the specific *category* of aircraft to be flown. (14 CFR 61.93(c)(1))

    b. A student pilot must have a solo cross-country endorsement from an authorized instructor that is placed in that person's logbook for the specific *make and model* of aircraft to be flown. (14 CFR 61.93(c)(2))

    c. For each cross-country flight, the authorized instructor who reviews the cross-country planning must make an endorsement in the person's logbook after reviewing that person's cross-country planning, as specified in 14 CFR 61.93(d). The endorsement must specify the make and model of aircraft to be flown, state that the student's preflight planning and preparation is correct and that the student is prepared to make the flight safely under the known conditions, and state that any limitations required by the student's authorized instructor are met. (14 CFR 61.93(c)(3))

Note: A certificated pilot who is receiving training for an additional aircraft category or class rating on a pilot certificate (other than for an ATP Certificate) must have a logbook or training record endorsement from an authorized instructor attesting that the person was found competent in the appropriate aeronautical knowledge areas and proficient in the appropriate areas of operation. (14 CFR 61.63(b)(2))

14. **Before solo cross-country privileges are permitted, what minimum cross-country flight training requirements must a student pilot satisfy?** (14 CFR 61.93)

The student pilot must receive and log flight training in the following maneuvers and procedures:

a. Use of aeronautical charts for VFR navigation using pilotage and dead reckoning with aid of a magnetic compass;

b. Use of aircraft performance charts for cross-country flight;

c. Procurement and analysis of aeronautical weather reports and forecasts, recognizing critical weather situations and estimating visibility while in flight;

d. Emergency procedures;

e. Traffic pattern procedures that include area departure, area arrival, entry into the traffic pattern, and approach;

f. Collision avoidance, wake turbulence precautions, and wind shear avoidance;

g. Recognition, avoidance, and operational restrictions of hazardous terrain features in the geographical area where the cross-country flight will be flown;

h. Proper operation of the instruments and equipment installed in the aircraft to be flown;

i. Use of radios for VFR navigation and two-way communications;

j. Takeoff, approach, and landing procedures, including short-field, soft-field, and crosswind takeoffs, approaches, and landings;

k. Climbs at best angle and best rate; and

l. Control and maneuvering solely by reference to flight instruments, including straight-and-level flight, turns, descents, climbs, use of radio aids, and ATC directives.

15. **Before a flight instructor can authorize a student pilot to conduct a solo cross-country flight, what requirements must be met?** (14 CFR 61.93)

    The instructor must have determined that:

    a. The student's cross-country planning is correct for the flight;

    b. Upon review, the current and forecast weather conditions show that the flight can be completed under VFR;

    c. The student is proficient to conduct the flight safely;

    d. The student has the appropriate solo cross-country endorsement for the make and model of aircraft to be flown; and

    e. The student's solo flight endorsement is current for the make and model of aircraft to be flown.

16. **What actions must a flight instructor take to allow a student pilot to operate an aircraft on a solo flight within Class B airspace?** (14 CFR 61.95)

    A student pilot may not operate an aircraft on a solo flight in Class B airspace unless:

    a. The student pilot has received both ground and flight training from an authorized instructor on that Class B airspace area, and the flight training was received in the specific Class B airspace area for which solo flight is authorized;

    b. The logbook of that student pilot has been endorsed by the authorized instructor who gave the student pilot flight training, and the endorsement is dated within the 90-day period preceding the date of the flight in that Class B airspace area; and

    c. The logbook endorsement specifies that the student pilot has received the required ground and flight training and has been found proficient to conduct solo flight in that specific Class B airspace area.

17. **What action must a flight instructor take to allow a student pilot to operate an aircraft on a solo flight to, from, or at an airport located within Class B airspace?** (14 CFR 61.95)

A student pilot may not operate an aircraft on a solo flight to, from, or at an airport located within Class B airspace unless:

a. The student pilot has received both ground and flight training from an instructor authorized to provide training to operate at that airport, and the flight and ground training has been received at the specific airport for which the solo flight is authorized;

b. The logbook of that student pilot has been endorsed by an authorized instructor who gave the student pilot flight training, and the endorsement is dated within the 90-day period preceding the date of the flight at that airport; and

c. The logbook endorsement specifies that the student pilot has received the required ground and flight training and has been found proficient to conduct solo flight operations at that specific airport.

Recreational Pilots

1. **What are the eligibility requirements for a Recreational Pilot Certificate?** (14 CFR 61.96)

a. Be at least 17 years of age;

b. Be able to read, speak, write, and understand the English language;

c. Receive a logbook endorsement from an authorized instructor who conducted the training or reviewed the applicant's home study on the required aeronautical knowledge areas and who certified that the applicant is prepared for the required knowledge test;

d. Pass the required knowledge test on the aeronautical knowledge areas;

e. Receive flight training and a logbook endorsement from an authorized instructor who conducted the training on the required areas of operation and certified that the applicant is prepared for the required practical test;

(continued)

    f. Meet the required aeronautical experience;

    g. Pass the practical test on the areas of operation listed in §61.98 that apply to the aircraft category and class rating;

    h. Comply with the sections of Part 61 that apply to the aircraft category and class rating; and

    i. Hold either a Student Pilot Certificate or Sport Pilot Certificate.

2. What aeronautical experience must an applicant for a Recreational Pilot Certificate have accomplished?
(14 CFR 61.99)

An applicant must receive and log at least 30 hours of flight time that includes at least:

a. 15 hours of flight training from an authorized instructor on the required areas of operation that consists of at least 2 hours of flight training en route to an airport more than 25 NM from the airport where the applicant normally trains, which includes at least three takeoffs and three landings at the airport, and 3 hours of flight training in the aircraft for the rating sought in preparation for the practical test within the preceding 2 calendar months from the month of the test; and

b. 3 hours of solo flying in the aircraft for the rating sought on the areas of operation listed in 14 CFR §61.98 that apply to the aircraft category and class rating sought.

3. What are the privileges that apply to recreational pilots?
(14 CFR 61.101)

A recreational pilot may:

a. Carry no more than one passenger; and

b. Not pay less than the pro rata share of the operating expenses of a flight with a passenger, provided the expenses involve only fuel, oil, airport expenses, or aircraft rental fees.

c. Act as pilot-in-command of an aircraft on a flight within 50 NM from the departure airport, provided that person has:

    • Received ground and flight training for takeoff, departure, arrival, and landing procedures at the departure airport;

- Received ground and flight training for the area, terrain, and aids to navigation that are in the vicinity of the departure airport;
- Been found proficient to operate the aircraft at the departure airport and the area within 50 NM from that airport; and
- Received from an authorized instructor a logbook endorsement, which is carried in the person's possession in the aircraft, that permits flight within 50 NM from the departure airport.

d. Act as pilot-in-command of an aircraft on a flight that exceeds 50 NM from the departure airport, provided that person has:

- Received ground and flight training from an authorized instructor on the required cross-country training that applies to the aircraft rating held;
- Been found proficient in cross-country flying; and
- Received from an authorized instructor a logbook endorsement, which is in the person's possession in the aircraft, that certifies the person has received and been found proficient in the required cross-country training that applies to the aircraft rating held.

4. What are the limitations that apply to all recreational pilots? (14 CFR 61.101)

A recreational pilot may not act as pilot-in-command of an aircraft:

a. That is certificated for more than four occupants, with more than one powerplant, with a powerplant of more than 180 horsepower (except aircraft certificated in the rotorcraft category), or with retractable landing gear;

b. That is classified as a multi-engine airplane, powered-lift, glider, airship, balloon, powered parachute, or weight-shift control aircraft;

c. That is carrying a passenger or property for compensation or hire;

d. For compensation or hire;

e. In furtherance of a business;

f. Between sunset and sunrise;

(continued)

g. In Class A, B, C, and D airspace, at an airport located in Class B, C, or D airspace, or to, from, through, or at an airport having an operational control tower; unless that person has received and logged ground and flight training, been found proficient, and received an endorsement covering the appropriate aeronautical knowledge areas and areas of operation;

h. At an altitude of more than 10,000 feet MSL or 2,000 feet AGL, whichever is higher;

i. When the flight or surface visibility is less than 3 statute miles;

j. Without visual reference to the surface;

k. On a flight outside the United States, unless authorized by the country in which the flight is conducted;

l. To demonstrate that aircraft in flight as an aircraft salesperson to a prospective buyer;

m. That is used in a passenger-carrying airlift and sponsored by a charitable organization; and

n. That is towing any object.

A recreational pilot may not act as a pilot flight crewmember on any aircraft for which more than one pilot is required by the type certificate of the aircraft or the regulations under which the flight is conducted, except when receiving flight training from a person authorized to provide flight training on board an airship, and no person other than a required flight crewmember is carried on the aircraft.

Private Pilots

1. What are the general eligibility requirements for a Private Pilot Certificate? (14 CFR 61.103)

To be eligible for a Private Pilot Certificate, a person must:

a. Be at least 17 years of age for a rating in other than a glider or balloon.

b. Be at least 16 years of age for a rating in a glider or balloon.

c. Be able to read, speak, write, and understand the English language.

d. Receive a logbook endorsement from an authorized instructor who conducted the training or reviewed the person's home study on the required aeronautical knowledge areas and certified that the person is prepared for the required knowledge test.

e. Pass the required knowledge test on the aeronautical knowledge areas.

f. Receive flight training and a logbook endorsement from an authorized instructor who conducted the training in the required areas of operation and certified that the person is prepared for the required practical test.

g. Meet the aeronautical experience requirements that apply to the aircraft rating sought before applying for the practical test.

h. Pass a practical test on the required areas of operation that apply to the aircraft rating sought;

i. Comply with the appropriate sections of Part 61 that apply to the category and class rating sought.

j. Hold a U.S. Student Pilot Certificate, Sport Pilot Certificate, or Recreational Pilot Certificate.

2. In what areas of aeronautical knowledge must an applicant for a Private Pilot Certificate have received instruction? (14 CFR 61.105)

a. Federal Aviation Regulations that relate to private pilot privileges, limitations, and flight operations;

b. NTSB accident reporting requirements;

c. Use of the *Aeronautical Information Manual* and FAA ACs;

d. Aeronautical charts for VFR navigation using pilotage, dead reckoning, and navigation systems;

e. Radio communication procedures;

f. Recognition of critical weather situations from the ground and in flight, wind shear avoidance, and the procurement and use of aeronautical weather reports and forecasts;

g. Safe and efficient operation of aircraft, including collision avoidance, and recognition and avoidance of wake turbulence;

(continued)

  h. Effects of density altitude on takeoff and climb performance;

  i. Weight and balance computations;

  j. Principles of aerodynamics, powerplants, and aircraft systems;

  k. Stall awareness, spin entry, spins, and spin recovery techniques for the airplane and glider category ratings;

  l. Aeronautical decision making and judgment; and

  m. Preflight action that includes how to obtain information on runway lengths at airports of intended use, data on takeoff and landing distances, weather reports and forecasts, and fuel requirements, and how to plan for alternatives if the planned flight cannot be completed or delays are encountered.

3. **In what pilot operations must an applicant for a Private Pilot Certificate have received instruction?** (14 CFR 61.107)

  a. Preflight preparation
  b. Preflight procedures
  c. Airport and seaplane base operations
  d. Takeoffs, landings, and go-arounds
  e. Performance maneuvers
  f. Ground reference maneuvers
  g. Navigation
  h. Slow flight and stalls
  i. Basic instrument maneuvers
  j. Emergency operations
  k. Night operations
  l. Postflight procedures

4. **What minimum aeronautical experience must be accumulated by a student pilot before application for a Private Pilot Certificate?** (14 CFR 61.109)

Total Time: 40 hours of flight time that consists of at least the following:

Dual: 20 hours of flight training with an authorized instructor on the Private Pilot areas of operation that includes:

  a. 3 hours of cross-country flight training in a single-engine airplane;

b. 3 hours of night flight training in a single-engine airplane that includes at least:
  - 1 cross-country flight of over 100 NM total distance; and
  - 10 takeoffs and 10 landings to a full stop, each involving a flight in the traffic pattern.

c. 3 hours of flight training by reference to instruments in a single-engine airplane; and

d. 3 hours of flight training with an authorized instructor in a single-engine airplane in preparation for the practical test within the preceding 2 calendar months from the month of the test.

Solo: 10 hours of solo flying in a single-engine airplane on the Private Pilot areas of operation that includes:

a. 5 hours of solo cross-country flying;

b. 1 solo cross-country flight of 150 NM total distance, with full-stop landings at 3 points, and one segment consisting of a straight-line distance of more than 50 NM between the takeoff and landing locations; and

c. 3 takeoffs and landings to a full stop (with each landing involving a flight in the traffic pattern) at an airport with an operating control tower.

5. How much time in a flight simulator or flight training device may be credited toward the flight training required for a Private Pilot Certificate? (14 CFR 61.109)

A maximum of 2.5 hours of training (5 hours if under Part 142) in a flight simulator or flight training device representing the category, class, and type, if applicable, of aircraft appropriate to the rating sought, may be credited toward the flight training time required by §61.109, if received from an authorized instructor.

6. May a student pilot take the Private Pilot practical test without completing the 3 hours of night flying instruction? (14 CFR 61.110)

No, with one exception: student pilots who receive flight training in and reside in the state of Alaska are not required to comply with the night flight training requirements.

7. What privileges and limitations apply to private pilots? (14 CFR 61.113)

a. No person who holds a Private Pilot Certificate may act as pilot-in-command of an aircraft that is carrying passengers or property for compensation or hire; nor may that person, for compensation or hire, act as pilot-in-command of an aircraft.

b. A private pilot may, for compensation or hire, act as pilot-in-command of an aircraft in connection with any business or employment if the flight is only incidental to that business or employment, and the aircraft does not carry passengers or property for compensation or hire.

c. A private pilot may not pay less than the pro rata share of operating expenses of a flight with passengers, provided the expenses involve only fuel, oil, airport expenditures, or rental fees.

d. A private pilot may act as PIC of a charitable, nonprofit, or community event flight described in §91.146, if the sponsor and pilot comply with the requirements of §91.146.

e. A private pilot may be reimbursed for aircraft operating expenses directly related to search and location operations, provided the expenses involve only fuel, oil, airport expenditures, or rental fees, and the operation is sanctioned and under the direction and control of a local, state, or federal agency or an organization that conducts search and location operations.

f. A private pilot who is an aircraft salesperson and who has at least 200 hours of logged flight time may demonstrate an aircraft in flight to a prospective buyer.

g. A private pilot who meets the requirements of §61.69 may act as PIC of an aircraft towing a glider or unpowered ultralight vehicle.

h. A private pilot may act as PIC for the purpose of conducting a production flight test in a light-sport aircraft intended for certification in the light-sport category.

Commercial Pilots

1. What are the general eligibility requirements for a Commercial Pilot Certificate? (14 CFR 61.123)

a. Be at least 18 years of age;

b. Be able to read, speak, write, and understand the English language;

c. Receive a logbook endorsement from an authorized instructor who conducted the required ground training or reviewed the person's home study on the required aeronautical knowledge areas that apply to the aircraft category and class rating sought, and certified that the person is prepared for the required knowledge test;

d. Pass the required knowledge test on the aeronautical knowledge areas;

e. Receive the required training and a logbook endorsement from an authorized instructor who conducted the training on the required areas of operation that apply to the aircraft category and class rating sought and certified that the person is prepared for the required practical test;

f. Meet the required aeronautical experience before applying for the practical test;

g. Pass the required practical test on the required areas of operation;

h. Hold at least a Private Pilot Certificate; and

i. Comply with the sections of Part 61 that apply to the aircraft category and class rating sought.

2. In what areas of aeronautical knowledge must an applicant for a Commercial Pilot Certificate have received instruction? (14 CFR 61.125)

a. Federal Aviation Regulations that relate to commercial pilot privileges, limitations, and flight operations;

b. NTSB accident reporting requirements;

c. Basic aerodynamics and the principles of flight;

(continued)

    d. Meteorology (recognition of critical weather situations, wind shear recognition and avoidance, and the use of aeronautical weather reports and forecasts);

    e. Safe and efficient operation of aircraft;

    f. Weight and balance computations;

    g. Use of performance charts;

    h. Significance and effects of exceeding aircraft performance limitations;

    i. Use of aeronautical charts and a magnetic compass for pilotage and dead reckoning;

    j. Use of air navigation facilities;

    k. Aeronautical decision making and judgment;

    l. Principles and functions of aircraft systems;

    m. Maneuvers, procedures, and emergency operations appropriate to the aircraft;

    n. Night and high-altitude operations;

    o. Procedures for operating within the National Airspace System; and

    p. Procedures for flight and ground training for lighter-than-air ratings.

3. **In what areas of operation must an applicant for a Commercial Pilot Certificate have received instruction?** (14 CFR 61.127)

    a. Preflight preparation

    b. Preflight procedures

    c. Airport and seaplane base operations

    d. Takeoffs, landings, and go-arounds

    e. Performance maneuvers

    f. Ground reference maneuvers

    g. Navigation

    h. Slow flight and stalls

    i. Emergency operations

    j. High-altitude operations

    k. Postflight procedures

4. **What minimum aeronautical experience must be accumulated by a private pilot training under Part 61 before application for a Commercial Pilot Certificate?** (14 CFR 61.129)

Total Time: 250 hours of flight time as a pilot that consists of at least:

a. 100 hours in powered aircraft, of which 50 hours must be in airplanes.

b. 100 hours of pilot-in-command flight time that includes at least:
   - 50 hours in airplanes; and
   - 50 hours in cross-country flying of which at least 10 hours must be in airplanes.

Dual: 20 hours of flight training on the Commercial Pilot areas of operation that includes at least:

a. 10 hours of instrument training using a view-limiting device including attitude instrument flying, partial panel skills, recovery from unusual flight attitudes, and intercepting and tracking navigational systems. Five of the 10 hours required must be in a single-engine airplane;

b. 10 hours of training in a complex airplane, a turbine-powered airplane, or a technically advanced airplane (TAA);

c. One 2-hour cross-country flight in a single-engine airplane in daytime conditions of a total straight-line distance of more than 100 NM from the original departure point;

d. One 2-hour cross-country flight in a single-engine airplane in nighttime conditions that consists of a total straight-line distance of more than 100 NM from the original point of departure; and

e. 3 hours in a single-engine airplane with an authorized instructor within the preceding 2 calendar months from the month of the test.

Solo: 10 hours of solo flight time in a single-engine airplane or 10 hours of flight time performing PIC duties in a single-engine airplane with an authorized instructor on board (either of which may be credited toward the 100-hour PIC flight time requirement) on the Commercial Pilot areas of operation, including:

(continued)

    a. One cross-country flight of not less than 300 NM with landings at a minimum of 3 points, one of which is a straight-line distance of at least 250 NM; and

    b. 5 hours in night VFR conditions with 10 takeoffs and 10 landings (each landing must involve flight in the traffic pattern) at an airport with an operating control tower.

5. What privileges and limitations apply to commercial pilots? (14 CFR 61.133)

Commercial pilot general privileges are as follows: a person who holds a Commercial Pilot Certificate may act as pilot-in-command of an aircraft carrying persons or property for compensation or hire, provided the person is qualified in accordance with 14 CFR Part 61, and for compensation or hire, provided the person is qualified in accordance with Part 61 and applicable parts of the regulations that apply to the operation.

As for limitations, a person who applies for a Commercial Pilot Certificate with an Airplane category or Powered-Lift category rating and does not hold an Instrument Rating in the same category and class will be issued a Commercial Pilot Certificate that contains the limitation, "The carriage of passengers for hire in (airplanes) (powered-lifts) on cross-country flights in excess of 50 nautical miles or at night is prohibited." The limitation may be removed when the person satisfactorily accomplishes the requirements listed in §61.65 for an Instrument Rating in the same category and class of aircraft listed on the person's Commercial Pilot Certificate.

6. As a commercial pilot, certain operations are allowed without being in possession of an operating certificate. What are examples of those operations? (14 CFR 119.1)

Student instruction, certain nonstop commercial air tours, ferry or training flights, and aerial work operations including crop dusting, banner towing, aerial photography or survey, powerline or pipeline patrol, etc.

Airline Transport Pilots

1. What are the general eligibility requirements for an Airline Transport Pilot Certificate? (14 CFR 61.153)

a. For an ATP Certificate obtained under the aeronautical experience requirements of §§61.159, 61.161, or 61.163, be at least 23 years of age; or for an ATP Certificate obtained under the aeronautical experience requirements of §61.160, be at least 21 years of age;

b. Be able to read, speak, write, and understand the English language;

c. Be of good moral character;

d. Meet at least one of the following requirements:
   - Hold a Commercial Pilot Certificate with an Instrument Rating issued under Part 61;
   - Meet the military experience requirements under §61.73 to qualify for a Commercial Pilot Certificate, and an Instrument Rating if the person is a rated military pilot or former rated military pilot of a U.S. armed force; or
   - Hold either a foreign ATP license with instrument privileges, or a foreign commercial pilot license with an Instrument Rating, that was issued by a contracting state to the Convention on International Civil Aviation, and contains no geographical limitations;

e. For an ATP Certificate with an Airplane category Multi-Engine class rating or an ATP Certificate obtained concurrently with a Multi-Engine Airplane type rating, receive a graduation certificate from an ATP-CTP program specified in §61.156 before applying for the required knowledge test;

f. Meet the aeronautical experience requirements of Part 61 Subpart G that apply to the aircraft category and class rating sought before applying for the practical test;

g. Pass a knowledge test on the aeronautical knowledge areas of §61.155(c) that apply to the aircraft category and class rating sought;

h. Pass the practical test on the areas of operation listed in §61.157(e) that apply to the aircraft category and class rating sought; and

(continued)

    i.   Comply with the sections of Part 61 Subpart G that apply to the aircraft category and class rating sought.

2. What minimum aeronautical experience must be accumulated by a person applying for an Airline Transport Pilot Certificate with an Airplane category and class rating? (14 CFR 61.159)

    a.   500 hours of cross-country flight time.

    b.   100 hours of night flight time.

    c.   50 hours of flight time in the class of airplane for the rating sought.

    d.   75 hours of instrument flight time, in actual or simulated instrument conditions.

    e.   250 hours of flight time in an airplane as a PIC, or as SIC performing the duties of PIC while under the supervision of a PIC, or any combination thereof, that includes at least:

- 100 hours of cross-country flight time; and
- 25 hours of night flight time.

Flight Instructors

1. In what areas of aeronautical knowledge must an applicant for a Flight Instructor Certificate have received instruction? (14 CFR 61.185)

The fundamentals of instructing, including:

    a.   The learning process;

    b.   Elements of effective teaching;

    c.   Student evaluation and testing;

    d.   Course development;

    e.   Lesson planning; and

    f.   Classroom training techniques.

Also, the aeronautical knowledge areas for a Recreational, Private, and Commercial Pilot Certificate applicable to the aircraft category for which flight instructor privileges are sought; and the aeronautical knowledge areas for the instrument rating applicable to the category for which instrument flight instructor privileges are sought.

2. In what areas of operation must an applicant for a Flight Instructor Certificate have received instruction? (14 CFR 61.187)

a. Fundamentals of instructing
b. Technical subject areas
c. Preflight preparation
d. Preflight lesson on a maneuver to be performed in flight
e. Preflight procedures
f. Airport and seaplane base operations
g. Takeoffs, landings, and go-arounds
h. Fundamentals of flight
i. Performance maneuvers
j. Ground reference maneuvers
k. Slow flight, stalls, and spins
l. Basic instrument maneuvers
m. Emergency operations
n. Postflight procedures

3. What are the required records a flight instructor must retain? (14 CFR 61.189)

a. A flight instructor must sign the logbook of each person to whom that instructor has given flight training or ground training.

b. A flight instructor must maintain a record in a logbook or a separate document that contains the name of each person whose logbook that instructor has endorsed for solo flight privileges, the date of the endorsement, the name of each person that instructor has endorsed for a knowledge test or practical test, the kind of test, the date, and the results.

c. Each flight instructor must retain the required records for at least 3 years.

4. **What are the various endorsements a flight instructor is authorized to give?** (14 CFR 61.193)

   A person who holds a Flight Instructor Certificate is authorized within the limitations of that person's Flight Instructor Certificate and ratings to give training and endorsements that are required for:

   a. A student pilot certificate;

   b. A pilot certificate;

   c. A flight instructor certificate;

   d. A ground instructor certificate;

   e. An aircraft rating;

   f. An instrument rating;

   g. A flight review, operating privilege, or recency of experience requirement;

   h. A practical test; and

   i. A knowledge test.

   Note: A person who holds a Flight Instructor Certificate is authorized to:

   - Accept an application for a Student Pilot Certificate; or, for an applicant who holds a pilot certificate (other than a Student Pilot Certificate) issued under Part 61 and meets the flight review requirements specified in §61.56, a Remote Pilot Certificate with a small UAS Rating;

   - Verify the identity of the applicant; and

   - Verify the applicant meets the eligibility requirements in §61.83.

5. **What limitations on endorsements apply to all flight instructors?** (14 CFR 61.195)

   A flight instructor may *not* endorse:

   a. A student pilot's logbook for solo flight privileges, unless that flight instructor has given that student the flight training required for solo flight privileges and has determined that the student is prepared to conduct the flight safely under known circumstances, subject to any limitations listed in the student's logbook that the instructor considers necessary for the safety of the flight;

b. A student pilot's logbook for a solo cross-country flight, unless that flight instructor has determined the student's flight preparation, planning, equipment, and proposed procedures are adequate for the proposed flight under the existing conditions and within any limitations listed in the logbook that the instructor considers necessary for the safety of the flight;

c. A student pilot's logbook for solo flight in a Class B airspace area or at an airport within Class B airspace unless that flight instructor has given that student ground and flight training in that Class B airspace or at that airport, and determined that the student is proficient to operate the aircraft safely;

d. The logbook of a recreational pilot, unless that flight instructor has given that pilot the required ground and flight training; and determined that the recreational pilot is proficient to operate the aircraft safely;

e. The logbook of a pilot for a flight review, unless that instructor has conducted a review of that pilot in accordance with the requirements of §61.56(a); or

f. The logbook of a pilot for an instrument proficiency check, unless that instructor has tested that pilot in accordance with the requirements of §61.57(d).

6. **How many hours of flight training is a flight instructor limited to?** (14 CFR 61.195)

In any 24-consecutive-hour period, a flight instructor may not conduct more than 8 hours of flight training.

7. **What qualifications must a flight instructor possess before instrument training may be given for the issuance of an Instrument Rating, a type rating not limited to VFR, or the instrument training required for Commercial Pilot and Airline Transport Pilot Certificates?** (14 CFR 61.195)

The flight instructor must hold an Instrument Rating on his or her Flight Instructor Certificate and pilot certificate that is appropriate to the category and class of aircraft in which instrument training is being provided.

8. What is the minimum pilot-in-command time requirement for a flight instructor with multi-engine privileges to give instruction to a student for a Multi-Engine Rating? (14 CFR 61.195)

That flight instructor must have at least 5 flight hours of pilot-in-command time in the specific make and model of multi-engine airplane, helicopter, or powered-lift, as appropriate.

9. How can a Flight Instructor Certificate be renewed? (14 CFR 61.197)

A person who holds a Flight Instructor Certificate that has not expired may renew that Flight Instructor Certificate for an additional 24 calendar months if the holder:

a. Has passed a practical test for one of the ratings listed on the current Flight Instructor Certificate or an additional flight instructor rating; or

b. Has submitted a completed and signed application to the FAA and satisfactorily completed one of the following renewal requirements:

   • A record of training showing that, during the preceding 24 calendar months, the flight instructor has endorsed at least 5 students for a practical test for a certificate or rating and at least 80 percent of those students passed that test on the first attempt.

   • A record showing that, within the preceding 24 calendar months, the flight instructor has served as a company check pilot, chief flight instructor, company check airman, or flight instructor in a Part 121 or part 135 operation, or in a position involving the regular evaluation of pilots.

   • A graduation certificate showing that, within the preceding 3 calendar months, the person has successfully completed an approved flight instructor refresher course (FIRC) consisting of ground training or flight training, or a combination of both.

   • A record showing that, within the preceding 24 months from the month of application, the flight instructor passed an official U.S. Armed Forces military instructor pilot proficiency check.

B. Airworthiness Requirements

1. What documents are required on board an aircraft prior to flight? (14 CFR 91.203, 91.9)

Airworthiness certificate (14 CFR §91.203)

Registration certificate (14 CFR §91.203)

Radio station license—if operating outside of U.S.; FCC regulation (47 CFR §87.18)

Operating limitations—AFM/POH and supplements, placards, markings (14 CFR §91.9)

Weight and balance data—current (14 CFR §23.2620)

Compass deviation card—if required by aircraft's TCDS/AFM (14 CFR §23.1547)

External data plate/serial number (14 CFR §45.11)

Exam Tip: During the practical test, your evaluator may wish to examine the various required aircraft documents (ARROW) during the preflight inspection, as well as the currency of any aeronautical charts, EFB data, etc., on board the aircraft. Prior to the test, verify that all of the necessary aircraft documentation, onboard databases, charts, etc., are current and available.

2. What is an airworthiness certificate? (FAA-H-8083-25)

An airworthiness certificate is issued by the FAA to all aircraft that have been proven to meet the minimum requirements of Part 21 and that are in condition for safe operation. Under any circumstances, the aircraft must meet the requirements of the original type certificate or it is no longer airworthy. Airworthiness certificates come in two different classifications: standard airworthiness and special airworthiness.

3. Describe what the following indications on an aircraft's airworthiness certificate would signify: *normal category* and *utility category*. (14 CFR Part 23)

a. *Normal category*—Aircraft structure capable of withstanding a load factor of 3.8 Gs without structural failure. Applicable to aircraft intended for non-aerobatic operation.

b. *Utility category*—Aircraft structure must be capable of withstanding a load factor of 4.4 Gs. This would usually permit limited aerobatics, including spins (if approved for the aircraft).

4. Does an airworthiness certificate have an expiration date? (FAA-H-8083-25)

No. A standard airworthiness certificate remains valid for as long as the aircraft meets its approved type design, is in a condition for safe operation, and the maintenance, preventative maintenance, and alterations are performed in accordance with Parts 21, 43, and 91.

5. Where must the airworthiness certificate be located? (14 CFR 91.203)

The certificate must be displayed at the cabin or cockpit entrance so that it is legible to passengers or crew.

6. For an aircraft to be considered airworthy, what two conditions must be met? (14 CFR 3.5, FAA-H-8083-25)

a. The aircraft must conform to its type design (type certificate). Conformity to type design is attained when the required and proper components are installed to be consistent with the drawings, specifications, and other data that are part of the type certificate. Conformity includes applicable STCs and field-approval alterations.

b. The aircraft must be in a condition for safe operation, referring to the condition of the aircraft with relation to wear and deterioration.

7. Explain how a pilot determines if an aircraft conforms to its approved type design and is in a condition for safe operation. (14 CFR Parts 21, 43 and 91)

a. To determine that the aircraft conforms to its type design, a pilot must determine that the maintenance, preventive maintenance, and alterations have been performed in accordance with Parts 21, 43, and 91 and that the aircraft is registered in the United States. The pilot does this by ensuring that all required inspections, maintenance, preventive maintenance, repairs, and alterations have been appropriately documented in the aircraft's maintenance records.

b. To determine that the aircraft is in condition for safe operation, the pilot conducts a thorough preflight inspection of the aircraft for wear and deterioration, structural damage, fluid leaks, tire wear, inoperative instruments and equipment, etc. If an unsafe condition exists or inoperative instruments or equipment are found, the pilot uses the guidance in 14 CFR §91.213 for handling the inoperative equipment.

8. **Who is responsible for ensuring that an aircraft is maintained in an airworthy condition?** (14 CFR 91.403)

   The owner or operator of an aircraft is primarily responsible for maintaining an aircraft in an airworthy condition.

9. **What are *airworthiness directives*?** (FAA-H-8083-25)

   An airworthiness directive (AD) is the medium the FAA uses to notify aircraft owners and other potentially interested persons of unsafe conditions that may exist because of design defects, maintenance, or other causes, and to specify the conditions under which the product may continue to be operated. Airworthiness directives are regulatory in nature, and compliance is mandatory. It is the aircraft owner's or operator's responsibility to ensure compliance with all pertinent ADs. Airworthiness directives may be found on the FAA's website at drs.faa.gov/browse.

10. **What are the two types of ADs?** (FAA-H-8083-25)

    Airworthiness directives are divided into two categories: Those of an emergency nature requiring immediate compliance prior to further flight, and those of a less urgent nature requiring compliance within a specified period of time.

11. **When are emergency ADs issued?** (FAA-H-8083-25)

    An emergency AD is issued when an unsafe condition exists that requires immediate action by an owner/operator. The intent of an emergency AD is to rapidly correct an urgent safety-of flight situation. All known owners and operators of affected U.S.-registered aircraft or those aircraft that are known to have an affected product installed will be sent a copy of an emergency AD.

    Exam Tip: ADs and recurring ADs—be capable of finding and explaining the status of all ADs and recurring ADs that exist for your aircraft (locate and tab prior to the practical test).

12. **While reviewing the aircraft logbooks, you discover that your aircraft is not in compliance with an AD's specified time or date. Are you allowed to continue to operate that aircraft until the next required maintenance inspection? Do the regulations allow any kind of buffer?** (AC 39-7)

    The belief that AD compliance is only required at the time of a required inspection (e.g., at a 100-hour or annual inspection) is not correct. The required compliance time/date is specified in each AD, and no person may operate the affected product after expiration of that stated compliance time without an alternative method of compliance (AMOC) approval for a change in compliance time.

13. **What are *special airworthiness information bulletins*? Are they regulatory?**

    A special airworthiness information bulletin (SAIB) is an information tool that alerts, educates, and makes recommendations to the aviation community. An SAIB contains non-regulatory information and guidance that does not meet the criteria for an AD. Guidance on when to use a SAIB and how to develop and issue a SAIB is provided in FAA Order 8110.100B. Additional information can be found at www.faa.gov/aircraft/safety/alerts/saib.

14. **What is a *type certificate data sheet*?** (FAA-H-8083-30)

    The FAA issues a type certificate when a new aircraft, engine, propeller, etc., is found to meet safety standards set forth by the FAA. The type certificate data sheet (TCDS) lists the specifications, conditions, and limitations under which airworthiness requirements were met for the specified product, such as engine make and model, fuel type, engine limits, airspeed limits, maximum weight, minimum crew, etc. Information on the TCDS by make and model can be found on the FAA website at drs.faa.gov/search.

15. **What is a *supplemental type certificate* (STC)?** (FAA-H-8083-3, FAA-H-8083-30, AC 21-40)

    An STC is the FAA's approval of a major change in the type design of a previously approved type-certificated product. The certificate authorizes an alteration to an airframe, engine, or component that has been granted an approved type certificate. Sometimes alterations are made that are not specified or authorized in the TCDS. When that condition exists, an STC will be issued. STCs are considered a part of the permanent records of an aircraft and should be maintained as part of that aircraft's logs.

16. What is an aircraft registration certificate?
(FAA-H-8083-25)

Before an aircraft can be flown legally, it must be registered with the FAA Aircraft Registry. The certificate of aircraft registration, which is issued to the owner as evidence of the registration, must be carried in the aircraft at all times.

17. Does an aircraft's registration certificate have an expiration date? (14 CFR 47.31, 47.40)

Yes. A certificate of aircraft registration issued in accordance with §47.31 on or after January 23, 2023, expires seven years after the last day of the month in which it was issued notwithstanding the expiration date on the valid certificate of aircraft registration.

18. Where can you find information on the placards and marking information required to be in the airplane?
(FAA-H-8083-25, AC 60-6, 14 CFR 91.9, 14 CFR 23.1541)

The principal source of information for identifying the required airplane flight manuals, approved manual materials, markings, and placards is the TCDS or aircraft specification issued for each airplane eligible for an airworthiness certificate. The required placards are also reproduced in the "Limitations" section of the AFM or as directed by an AD.

19. Are airplane flight manuals (AFM) required to be on board all aircraft? (AC 60-6)

14 CFR §91.9 requires that all U.S.-registered aircraft have available in the aircraft a current, approved AFM, or if applicable, any combination of approved manual materials, markings, and placards. Generally, all aircraft manufactured after March 1, 1979, must have an AFM. For airplanes type-certificated at gross weights of 6,000 pounds or under which were not required to have an AFM, the required information may be an AFM or any combination of approved manual material, markings, and placards. These materials must be current and available in the airplane during operation.

Aircraft Maintenance Requirements

1. **What are the required tests and inspections to be performed on an aircraft? Include inspections for IFR.** (14 CFR 91.171, 91.207, 91.403, 91.409, 91.411, 91.413, 91.417)

   Annual inspection within the preceding 12 calendar months (14 CFR §91.409).

   Airworthiness directives and life-limited parts complied with as required (14 CFR §§91.403, 91.417).

   VOR equipment check every 30 days (for IFR ops) (14 CFR §91.171).

   100-hour inspection, if used for hire or flight instruction in aircraft flight instructor provides (14 CFR §91.409).

   Altimeter, altitude reporting equipment, and static pressure systems tested and inspected (for IFR ops) every 24 calendar months (14 CFR §91.411).

   Transponder tests and inspections, every 24 calendar months (14 CFR §91.413).

   Emergency locator transmitter, operation and battery condition (1 cumulative hour use or 50% useful life) inspected every 12 calendar months (14 CFR §91.207).

2. **What is an annual inspection, and which aircraft are required to have annual inspections?** (FAA-H-8083-25)

   An annual inspection is a complete inspection of an aircraft and engine required by the regulations to be accomplished every 12 calendar months on all certificated aircraft. Only an Aviation Mechanic holding an Inspection Authorization (IA) can conduct an annual inspection.

3. **What aircraft are required to have 100-hour inspections?** (FAA-H-8083-25, 14 CFR 91.409)

   a. All aircraft under 12,500 pounds (except turbojet/ turbopropeller-powered multi-engine airplanes and turbine-powered rotorcraft) used to carry passengers for hire.

   b. Aircraft used for flight instruction for hire, when provided by the person giving the flight instruction.

4. If an aircraft is operated for hire, is it required to have a 100-hour inspection as well as an annual inspection? (14 CFR 91.409)

Yes; if an aircraft is operated for hire, it must have a 100-hour inspection as well as an annual inspection when due. If not operated for hire, it must have an annual inspection only.

5. If an aircraft has been on a schedule of inspection every 100 hours, under what condition may it continue to operate beyond the 100 hours without a new inspection? (14 CFR 91.409)

The 100-hour limitation may be exceeded by not more than 10 hours while en route to a place where the inspection can be done. The excess time used to reach a place where the inspection can be done must be included in computing the next 100 hours of time in service.

6. If the annual inspection date has passed, can an aircraft be operated to a location where the inspection can be performed? (FAA-H-8083-25)

An aircraft overdue for an annual inspection may be operated under a special flight permit issued by the FAA for the purpose of flying the aircraft to a location where the annual inspection can be performed. However, all applicable ADs that are due must be complied with before the flight.

7. While inspecting the engine logbook of the aircraft you are planning to fly, you notice that the engine has exceeded its TBO. Is it legal to fly this aircraft? (AC 20-105)

Time between overhaul (TBO) is computed by the engine manufacturer and is a reliable estimate of the number of hours the engine could perform reliably within the established engine parameters and still not exceed the service wear limits for overhaul for major component parts such as the crankshaft, cam shaft, cylinders, connecting rods, and pistons. TBO times are make and model specific, and the recommended overhaul times are usually identified in the engine manufacturer's service bulletin or letter. For 14 CFR Part 91 operations, compliance to the TBO time is not a mandatory maintenance requirement; however, for engines in 14 CFR Part 121 or 135 service, TBO compliance is mandatory.

8. **What are *special flight permits*, and when are they necessary?** (14 CFR 91.213, 14 CFR 21.197)

   A special flight permit may be issued for an aircraft that may not currently meet applicable airworthiness requirements but is capable of safe flight. These permits are typically issued for the following purposes:

   a. Flying an aircraft to a base where repairs, alterations, or maintenance are to be performed, or to a point of storage.

   b. Delivering or exporting an aircraft.

   c. Production flight testing new-production aircraft.

   d. Evacuating aircraft from areas of impending danger.

   e. Conducting customer demonstration flights in new-production aircraft that have satisfactorily completed production flight tests.

9. **How are special flight permits obtained?** (FAA-H-8083-25)

   If a special flight permit is needed, assistance and the necessary forms may be obtained from the local FSDO or Designated Airworthiness Representative (DAR).

10. **After aircraft inspections have been made and defects have been repaired, who is responsible for determining that the aircraft is in an airworthy condition?** (14 CFR 91.7)

    The PIC of a civil aircraft is responsible for determining whether that aircraft is in a condition for safe flight. The PIC shall discontinue the flight when unairworthy, mechanical, electrical, or structural conditions occur.

11. **What regulations apply concerning the operation of an aircraft that has had alterations or repairs that may substantially affect its operation in flight?** (14 CFR 91.407)

    No person may operate or carry passengers in any aircraft that has undergone maintenance, preventative maintenance, rebuilding, or alteration that may have appreciably changed its flight characteristics or substantially affected its operation in flight until an appropriately rated pilot with at least a Private Pilot Certificate

a. Flies the aircraft;

b. Makes an operational check of the maintenance performed or alteration made; and

c. Logs the flight in the aircraft records.

12. Can a pilot conduct flight operations in an aircraft with known inoperative equipment? (14 CFR 91.213)

14 CFR Part 91 describes acceptable methods for the operation of an aircraft with certain inoperative instruments and equipment which are not essential for safe flight:

a. Operation of aircraft with a Minimum Equipment List (MEL), as authorized by 14 CFR §91.213(a), or

b. Operation of an aircraft without a MEL under 14 CFR §91.213(d)

13. What limitations apply to aircraft operations conducted using the deferral provision of 14 CFR §91.213(d)? (FAA-H-8083-25)

When inoperative equipment is found during preflight or prior to departure, the decision should be to cancel the flight, obtain maintenance prior to flight, or defer the item or equipment. Maintenance deferrals are not used for inflight discrepancies. The manufacturer's AFM/POH procedures are to be used in those situations.

14. During the preflight inspection in an aircraft that does not have a MEL, you notice that an instrument or equipment item is inoperative. Describe how you will determine if the aircraft is still airworthy for flight. (14 CFR 91.213(d), FAA-H-8083-25)

I will ask myself the following questions to determine if I can legally fly the airplane with the inoperative equipment item:

a. Are the inoperative instruments or equipment part of the VFR-day type certification?

b. Are the inoperative instruments or equipment listed as "Required" on the aircraft's equipment list or Kinds of Operations Equipment List (KOEL) for the kind of flight operation being conducted?

(continued)

    c. Are the inoperative instruments or equipment required by 14 CFR §91.205, §91.207, or any other rule of Part 91 for the specific kind of flight operation being conducted (e.g., VFR, IFR, day, night)?

    d. Are the inoperative instruments or equipment required to be operational by an AD?

If the answer is "Yes" to any of these questions, the aircraft is not airworthy, and maintenance is required before I can fly. If the answer is "No" to all of these questions, then the inoperative instruments or equipment must be removed (by an A&P) from the aircraft or be deactivated and placarded "Inoperative."

15. What is a Kinds of Operations Equipment List (KOEL)?
(AC 23-8)

A KOEL identifies the systems and equipment upon which type certification for each kind of operation was predicated (i.e., day or night VFR, day or night IFR, icing conditions) and which must be installed and operable for the particular kind of operation indicated. The KOEL is located in the Limitations section of the FAA-approved AFM.

16. What is a Minimum Equipment List (MEL)?
(FAA-H-8083-25)

An MEL is a precise listing of instruments, equipment, and procedures allowing an aircraft to be operated under specific conditions with inoperative equipment. The MEL is the specific inoperative equipment document for a particular make and model of aircraft by serial and registration numbers (e.g., BE-200, N12345). The FAA-approved MEL includes only those items of equipment that the FAA finds may be inoperative and still maintain an acceptable level of safety.

17. For an aircraft with an approved MEL, explain the decision sequence a pilot would use after discovering the position lights are inoperative. (FAA-H-8083-25)

With an approved MEL, if the position lights were discovered inoperative prior to a daytime flight, the pilot would make an entry in the maintenance record or discrepancy record provided for that purpose. The item is then either repaired or deferred in accordance with the MEL. Upon confirming that daytime flight with inoperative position lights is acceptable in accordance with the provisions of the MEL, the pilot would leave the position lights switch OFF, open the circuit breaker (or whatever action is called for in the procedures document), and placard the position light switch as INOPERATIVE.

18. What limitations apply to aircraft operations being conducted using an MEL? (FAA-H-8083-25)

The FAA considers an approved MEL to be a supplemental type certificate (STC) issued to an aircraft by serial number and registration number. It therefore becomes the authority to operate that aircraft in a condition other than originally type certificated. Once an operator requests an MEL, a letter of authorization (LOA) is issued by the FAA; then the use of the MEL becomes mandatory for that airplane. All maintenance deferrals must be accomplished in accordance with the terms and conditions of the MEL and the operator-generated procedures document.

19. What instruments and equipment are required for VFR day flight? (14 CFR 91.205)

For VFR flight during the day, the following instruments and equipment are required:

Anticollision light system—aviation red or white for small airplanes certificated after March 11, 1996.

Tachometer for each engine.

Oil pressure gauge for each engine.

Manifold pressure gauge (for each altitude engine, i.e., turbocharged).

Altimeter.

Temperature gauge for each liquid-cooled engine.

(continued)

Oil temperature gauge for each air-cooled engine.

Fuel gauge indicating the quantity in each tank.

Flotation gear—if operated for hire over water beyond power-off gliding distance from shore.

Landing gear position indicator, if the airplane has retractable gear.

Airspeed indicator.

Magnetic direction indicator.

Emergency locator transmitter (if required by 14 CFR §91.207).

Safety belts (and shoulder harnesses for each front seat in aircraft manufactured after 1978).

20. What instruments and equipment are required for VFR night flight? (14 CFR 91.205)

For VFR flight at night, all the instruments and equipment for VFR day flight are required, plus the following:

Fuses—one spare set or three fuses of each kind required accessible to the pilot in flight.

Landing light—if the aircraft is operated for hire.

Anticollision light system—approved aviation red or white.

Position lights—(navigation lights).

Source of electrical energy—adequate for all installed electrical and radio equipment.

C. Weather Information

1. What service does the FAA provide for pilots to obtain a weather briefing? (AIM 7-1-2)

The FAA provides the Flight Service program, which provides weather briefings to pilots through its flight service stations (FSS) by phone at 1-800-WX-BRIEF and online (through Leidos Flight Service) at 1800wxbrief.com.

2. Explain the three types of weather information available to pilots. (AIM 7-1-3)

The FAA has identified three distinct types of weather information available to pilots and operators:

a. *Observations*—Raw weather data collected by some type of sensor suite including surface and airborne observations, radar, lightning, satellite imagery, and profilers.

b. *Analysis*—Enhanced depiction and/or interpretation of observed weather data.

c. *Forecasts*—Predictions of the development and/or movement of weather phenomena based on meteorological observations and various mathematical models.

3. What are the three main categories of FAA-approved sources of aviation weather information? (AIM 7-1-3)

Federal government—The FAA and National Weather Service (NWS) collect weather observations. The NWS analyzes the observations and produces forecasts, and the FAA and NWS disseminate observations, analyses, and forecasts through a variety of systems. The federal government is the only approval authority for sources of weather observations (e.g., contract towers and airport operators).

Enhanced Weather Information System (EWINS)—An EWINS is an FAA-authorized, proprietary system for tracking, evaluating, reporting, and forecasting the presence or lack of adverse weather phenomena. The FAA authorizes a certificate holder to use an EWINS to produce flight movement forecasts, adverse weather phenomena forecasts, and other meteorological advisories.

Commercial weather information providers—These entities repackage proprietary weather products based on NWS information with formatting and layout modifications but make no material changes to the weather information. Other commercial providers produce forecasts, analyses, and other proprietary weather products that may substantially differ from the information contained in NWS products.

4. Does the weather data provided by commercial and/or third-party vendors satisfy the preflight action required by 14 CFR §91.103? (AIM 7-1-3)

Pilots and operators should be aware that weather services provided by entities other than the FAA, NWS, or their contractors may not meet FAA/NWS quality control standards. Operators and pilots contemplating using such services should request and/or review an appropriate description of services and provider disclosure. This should include, but is not limited to, the type of weather product (e.g., current weather or forecast weather), the currency of the product (product issue and valid times), and the relevance of the product. When in doubt, consult with an FAA Flight Service Specialist.

Note: Commercial weather information providers *contracted* by the FAA to provide weather observations, analyses, and forecasts (e.g., contract towers) are included in the federal government category of approved sources by virtue of maintaining required technical and quality assurance standards under federal government oversight.

5. Does the FAA consider weather self-briefings compliant with the regulations? (AC 91-92)

For many GA pilots, Flight Service remains an important source of comprehensive weather and aeronautical information. However, most pilots have become more accustomed to performing a self-briefing than calling Flight Service. The FAA considers that a self-briefing may be compliant with current Federal Aviation Regulations. By self-briefing, pilots can often improve their knowledge of weather and aeronautical information. Flight Service personnel are available should a pilot need assistance.

6. What types of weather briefings are available from Flight Service? (AIM 7-1-5)

Standard briefing—Request anytime you are planning a flight and you have not received a previous briefing or have not received preliminary information through online resources.

Abbreviated briefing—Request when you need information to supplement mass-disseminated data or update a previous briefing, or when you need only one or two items.

Outlook briefing—Request whenever your proposed time of departure is six or more hours from the time of the briefing. This is for planning purposes only.

Inflight briefing—Request when needed to update a preflight briefing.

7. What pertinent information should a weather briefing include? (AIM 7-1-5)

For a standard briefing, the briefing will automatically provide the following information in this sequence: adverse conditions, VFR flight not recommended, synopsis, current conditions, en route forecast, destination forecast, winds aloft, Notices to Air Missions (NOTAMs), ATC delays, and any additional information upon request.

8. What is a Flight Information Services–Broadcast (FIS-B)? (FAA-H-8083-25, AIM 7-1-9)

Flight Information Services–Broadcast (FIS-B) is a ground-based broadcast service provided through the ADS-B Universal Access Transceiver (UAT) network. The service provides users with a 978 MHz data link capability when operating within range and line-of-sight of a transmitting ground station. FIS-B enables users of properly equipped aircraft to receive and display a suite of broadcast weather and aeronautical information products.

9. Can onboard datalink weather (FIS-B) be useful in navigating an aircraft safely around an area of thunderstorms? (FAA-H-8083-28, AIM 7-1-9)

FIS aviation weather products (for example, graphical ground-based radar precipitation depictions) are not appropriate for tactical (typical timeframe of less than 3 minutes) avoidance of severe weather such as negotiating a path through a weather hazard area. FIS supports strategic (typical timeframe of 20 minutes or more) weather decision-making such as route selection to avoid a weather hazard area in its entirety. The misuse of information beyond its applicability may place the pilot and aircraft in jeopardy. In addition, FIS should never be used in lieu of an individual preflight weather and flight planning briefing.

10. **While en route, how can a pilot obtain updated weather information?** (FAA-H-8083-25)

    a. Flight Service on 122.2 and appropriate remote communication outlet (RCO) frequencies.

    b. ATIS, Automated Surface Observing System (ASOS), or Automated Weather Observing System (AWOS) broadcasts along the route of flight.

    c. Air Route Traffic Control Center (ARTCC) broadcasts—AWW, Convective SIGMET, SIGMET, AIRMET, Urgent PIREP, and CWA alerts are broadcast once on all frequencies, except emergency.

    d. Datalink weather—cockpit display of FIS-B information.

    e. ATC (workload permitting).

11. **What is a METAR?** (FAA-H-8083-28)

    The aviation routine weather report (METAR) is the weather observer's interpretation of the weather conditions at a given site and time. There are two types of METARs: a routine METAR that is transmitted every hour and an aviation selected special weather report (SPECI). This is a special report that can be given at any time to update the METAR for rapidly changing weather conditions, aircraft mishaps, or other critical information

    Example:
    METAR KOKC 011955Z AUTO 22015G25KT 180V250 3/4SM R17L/2600FT +TSRA BR OVC010CB 18/16 A2992 RMK AO2 TSB25 TS OHD MOV E SLP132

12. **What are PIREPs and where are they usually found?** (FAA-H-8083-28)

    A pilot report (PIREP) provides valuable information regarding the conditions as they actually exist in the air—information which cannot be gathered from any other source. Pilots can confirm the height of bases and tops of clouds, locations of wind shear and turbulence, and the location of inflight icing. There are two types of PIREPs: routine (UA) and urgent (UUA). PIREPs should be given to the ground facility with which communications are established (i.e., FSS, ARTCC, or terminal ATC). Altitudes are MSL, visibilities in SM, and distances in NM. PIREPs are available from ATC, FSS, and on the internet.

13. What is an AIREP and how does it differ from a PIREP? (FAA-H-8083-28)

An aircraft report (AIREP) is a report of actual weather conditions encountered by an aircraft while in flight. There are two types of reports. An AIREP is a routine, often automated report of in-flight weather conditions such as wind and temperature. A PIREP is reported by a pilot to indicate encounters of hazardous weather such as icing or turbulence. Both are transmitted in real-time via radio to a ground station.

14. What are terminal aerodrome forecasts (TAFs)? (FAA-H-8083-28)

A TAF is a concise statement of the expected meteorological conditions significant to aviation for a specified time period within 5 SM of the center of the airport's runway complex (terminal). The TAFs use the same weather codes found in METAR weather reports, in the following format:

a. *Type of reports*—A routine forecast (TAF); an amended forecast (TAF AMD), or a corrected forecast (TAF COR).

b. *ICAO station identifier*—4-letter station identifier.

c. *Date and time of origin*—The date/time of the forecast showing the day of the month in two digits, and the time in which the forecast is completed and ready for transmission in four digits, appended with a Z to denote UTC. *Example:* 061737Z—the TAF was issued on the 6th day of the month at 1737 UTC.

d. *Valid period date and time*—The first two digits are the day of the month for the start of the TAF, followed by two digits that indicate the starting hour (UTC). The next two digits indicate the day of the month for the end of the TAF, and the last two digits are the ending hour (UTC) of the valid period. Scheduled 24- and 30-hour TAFs are issued four times per day at 0000, 0600, 1200, and 1800Z. *Example:* A 00Z TAF issued on the 9th of the month and valid for 24 hours would have a valid period of 0900/0924.

e. *Forecasts*—Wind, visibility, significant and vicinity weather, cloud and vertical obscuration, non-convective low-level wind shear, and forecast change indicators (FM, TEMPO, and PROB).

15. From which primary source should information be obtained regarding expected weather at the ETA if your destination airport does not have a TAF? (FAA-H-8083-28)

The Graphical Forecasts for Aviation (GFA).

16. Describe the GFA. (AIM 7-1-4, FAA-H-8083-28)

The GFA is a set of web-based graphics that provide observations, forecasts, and warnings that can be viewed from 14 hours in the past to 15 hours in the future. The GFA covers the continental United States (CONUS) from the surface up to Flight Level 480 (FL480). Wind, icing, and turbulence forecasts are available in 3,000-foot increments from the surface up to 30,000 feet MSL, and in 6,000-foot increments from 30,000 feet MSL to 48,000 feet MSL. Turbulence forecasts are also broken into LO (below FL180) and HI (at or above FL180) graphics. A maximum icing graphic and maximum wind velocity graphic (regardless of altitude) are also available. The GFA can be viewed at aviationweather.gov/gfa.

17. What are the four types of inflight aviation weather advisories? (AIM 7-1-6, FAA-H-8083-28)

Inflight aviation weather advisories are forecasts to advise enroute aircraft of the development of potentially hazardous weather. The four types are the SIGMET (WS), the convective SIGMET (WST), the AIRMET (WA; text or graphical product), and the center weather advisory (CWA). All heights are referenced MSL, except in the case of ceilings (CIG) which indicate AGL.

18. What is a convective SIGMET? (FAA-H-8083-28)

Convective SIGMETs (WST) imply severe or greater turbulence, severe icing, and low-level wind shear. They may be issued for any convective situation that the forecaster feels is hazardous to all categories of aircraft. Bulletins are issued hourly at H+55, and special bulletins are issued at any time as required and updated at H+55. The text of the bulletin consists of either an observation and a forecast, or just a forecast (valid for up to 2 hours):

a. Severe thunderstorms due to:
   - Surface winds greater than or equal to 50 knots.
   - Hail at the surface greater than or equal to ¾ inches in diameter.
   - Tornadoes.

b. Embedded thunderstorms.

c. A line of thunderstorms.

d. Thunderstorms that produce precipitation levels greater than or equal to heavy-intensity precipitation, affecting 40 percent or more of an area at least 3,000 square miles.

19. What is a SIGMET (WS)? (AIM 7-1-6)

A SIGMET (WS) advises of weather that is potentially hazardous to all aircraft. SIGMETs are unscheduled products that are valid for 4 hours. However, SIGMETs associated with tropical cyclones and volcanic ash clouds are valid for 6 hours. Unscheduled updates and corrections are issued as necessary. In the conterminous United States, SIGMETs are issued when the following phenomena occur or are expected to occur:

a. Severe icing not associated with thunderstorms.

b. Severe or extreme turbulence or clear air turbulence (CAT) not associated with thunderstorms.

c. Widespread dust storms or sandstorms lowering surface visibilities to below 3 miles.

d. Volcanic ash.

20. What is an AIRMET (WA or G-AIRMET)? (AIM 7-1-6)

An AIRMET is an advisory of significant weather phenomena that describes conditions at intensities lower than those which require the issuance of SIGMETs. They are issued every 6 hours beginning at 0245 UTC. Pilots should use AIRMETs in the preflight and enroute phase of flight to enhance safety. AIRMET information is available in two formats: text bulletins (WA) and graphics (G-AIRMET). Unscheduled updates and corrections are issued as necessary. AIRMETs contain details about IFR, extensive mountain obscuration, turbulence, strong surface winds, icing, and freezing levels.

21. **What are the different types of AIRMETs?** (AIM 7-1-6)

    There are three types of AIRMETs: Sierra, Tango, and Zulu:

    a. AIRMET Sierra describes IFR conditions and/or extensive mountain obscurations.

    b. AIRMET Tango describes moderate turbulence, sustained surface winds of 30 knots or greater, and/or nonconvective low-level wind shear.

    c. AIRMET Zulu describes moderate icing and provides freezing level heights.

22. **What is a winds and temperatures aloft forecast (FB)?** (FAA-H-8083-28)

    Winds and temperatures aloft are forecast for specific locations in the contiguous U.S. and also for a network of locations in Alaska and Hawaii. These forecasts, called FBs, are issued 4 times daily. In an FB, a 4-digit code group shows wind direction in reference to true north, and wind speed in knots, with an additional 2-digit code group showing forecast temperatures in degrees Celsius. Wind forecasts are not issued for altitudes within 1,500 feet of a location's elevation.

    Note: The AWC's website provides a graphical depiction of the FB Winds/Temps forecasts as well as a text version at aviationweather. gov/windtemp.

23. **What valuable information can be determined from an FB?** (FAA-H-8083-28)

    Most favorable altitude—based on winds and direction of flight.

    Areas of possible icing—by noting air temperatures of +2°C to −20°C.

    Temperature inversions—a temperature increase with altitude can mean a stable layer aloft reducing the chance for convective activity.

    Turbulence—by observing abrupt changes in wind direction and speed at different altitudes.

24. What is a Center Weather Advisory (CWA)?
(FAA-H-8083-28)

Issued by a Center Weather Service Unit (CWSU), this is an aviation warning for use by aircrews to anticipate and avoid adverse weather conditions in the enroute and terminal environments. The CWA is a short-term "nowcast," pinpointing hazardous weather already causing an impact or expected to cause an impact within a 2-hour period; therefore, it is an inflight advisory rather than a flight planning tool. CWAs are valid for a maximum of 2 hours; if conditions are expected to continue beyond the 2-hour valid period, a statement will be included in the CWA.

25. What is a Convective Outlook (AC)? (FAA-H-8083-28)

The AC is a narrative and graphical outlook of the potential for severe (tornado, wind gusts 50 knots or greater, or hail 1 inch or greater in diameter) and non-severe (general) convection and specific severe weather threats during the following 8 days. It defines areas of marginal risk (MRGL), slight risk (SLGT), enhanced risk (ENH), moderate risk (MDT), or high risk (HIGH) of severe weather based on a percentage probability.

Aviation Weather Charts

1. What is a surface analysis chart? (FAA-H-8083-28)

A surface analysis chart is an analyzed chart of surface weather observations. It depicts the distribution of multiple items, including sea level pressure; the positions of highs, lows, ridges, and troughs; the location and character of fronts; and the various boundaries such as drylines, outflow boundaries, sea-breeze fronts, and convergence lines. The chart is produced eight times daily.

2. **Define the terms LIFR, IFR, MVFR, and VFR.** (AIM 7-1-7)

   LIFR—Low IFR; ceiling less than 500 feet and/or visibility less than 1 mile.

   IFR—Ceiling 500 to less than 1,000 feet and/or visibility 1 to less than 3 miles.

   MVFR—Marginal VFR; ceiling 1,000 to 3,000 feet and/or visibility 3 to 5 miles inclusive.

   VFR—Ceiling greater than 3,000 feet and visibility greater than 5 miles; includes sky clear.

   Note: Ceiling is defined as the height above the earth's surface of the lowest layer of clouds, which is reported as broken or overcast, or the vertical visibility into an obscuration.

3. **What information do short-range surface prognostic charts provide?** (FAA-H-8083-28)

   Short-range surface prognostic (prog) charts provide a forecast of surface pressure systems, fronts, and precipitation for a two-and-a-half-day period. They cover a forecast area of the 48 contiguous states and coastal waters. Predicted conditions are divided into five forecast periods: 12, 18, 24, 48, and 60 hours. Each chart depicts a snapshot of weather elements expected at the specified valid time. Charts are issued four times a day and can be used to obtain an overview of the progression of surface weather features during the included periods.

4. **Describe a low-level significant weather chart.** (FAA-H-8083-28)

   The low-level significant weather (SIGWX) charts provide a forecast of aviation weather hazards and are primarily intended to be used as guidance products for preflight briefings. The forecast domain covers the CONUS and the coastal waters for altitudes flight level 240 and below. The chart depicts weather flying categories, turbulence, and freezing levels and provides a snapshot of weather expected at the specified valid time. The charts are issued four times per day by the NWS AWC. Two charts are issued: a 12-hour and a 24-hour prog. Both are available at: aviationweather.gov.

5. **When flying an airplane without onboard thunderstorm detection equipment, describe procedures a pilot can take to avoid thunderstorms and/or the turbulence associated with them.** (AIM 7-1-27)

   a. Remember that the data-linked NEXRAD mosaic imagery shows where the weather was, not where the weather is. The weather conditions may be 15 to 20 minutes older than the age indicated on the display.

   b. Listen to chatter on the ATC frequency for PIREPs and other aircraft requesting to deviate or divert.

   c. Ask ATC for radar navigation guidance or to approve deviations around thunderstorms, if needed.

   d. Use data-linked weather NEXRAD mosaic imagery (i.e., FIS-B) for route selection to avoid thunderstorms entirely (strategic maneuvering).

   e. Advise ATC, when switched to another controller, that you are deviating for thunderstorms before accepting to rejoin the original route.

   f. Always ensure that after an authorized weather deviation, before accepting to rejoin the original route, that the route of flight is clear of thunderstorms.

   g. Avoid by at least 20 miles any thunderstorm identified as severe or giving an intense radar echo. This is especially true under the anvil of a large cumulonimbus.

   h. Circumnavigate the entire area if the area has 6/10 thunderstorm coverage.

   i. Remember that vivid and frequent lightning indicates the probability of a severe thunderstorm.

6. **Can ATC provide inflight assistance in avoiding thunderstorms and severe weather?** (AIM 7-1-12)

   Yes, to the extent possible, controllers will issue pertinent information on weather or chaff areas and assist pilots in avoiding such areas when requested. Pilots should respond to a weather advisory by either acknowledging the advisory or by requesting an alternate course of action as appropriate. However, the controller's primary responsibility is to provide safe separation between

   (continued)

aircraft. Additional services such as weather avoidance assistance can only be provided to the extent that it doesn't interfere with their primary function. ATC radar limitations and frequency congestion may also limit the controller's capability to assist.

7. **Give some examples of charts and reports useful in determining the potential for and location of thunderstorms along your route.** (FAA-H-8083-28)

   a. *Convective Outlook (AC)*—A narrative and graphical outlook of areas of slight, moderate, or high risk of severe thunderstorms for a 24-hour period.

   b. *Significant Weather Chart (SIGWX)*—Provides a forecast of aviation weather hazards; depicts a snapshot of weather expected at the specified valid time.

   c. *Weather radar observations* (and their resultant images)— Graphical displays of precipitation and non-precipitation targets detected by weather radars (NEXRAD). Regional and national radar mosaics can be found on the websites of the NWS, AWC, all NWS weather forecast offices (WFOs), and commercial aviation weather providers.

   d. *Convective SIGMETs (WST)*—Issued for any convective situation involving severe, embedded, and lines of thunderstorms.

   e. *Pilot reports (PIREPs)*—Help determine actual conditions along your planned route of flight.

   f. *Supplementary weather products*—Can be used for enhanced situational awareness; must only be used in conjunction with one or more NWS primary weather products.

8. **What types of weather information will you examine to determine if microburst/wind shear conditions might affect your flight?** (FAA-H-8083-28)

   The following should be examined for clues of potential microburst/wind shear conditions affecting the flight:

   TAFs—Examine the terminal forecast for convective activity.

   METARs—Inspect for wind shear clues (thunderstorms, rain showers, blowing dust).

Severe weather watch reports—Check for issuance since severe convective weather is a prime source for microbursts and wind shear.

LLWAS reports—Low Level Windshear Alert System is designed to detect wind shifts between outlying stations and a reference station.

TDWR—Terminal Doppler Weather Radar, deployed at 45 airports across the United States; detects microbursts, gust fronts, wind shifts, and precipitation intensities and provides severe weather alerts and warnings to ATC and pilots.

SIGMETs and convective SIGMETs—May provide essential clues.

Visual clues from the cockpit—Heavy rain (in a dry or moist environment) which can be accompanied by curling outflow, a ring of blowing dust or localized dust in general, flying debris, virga, a rain core with rain diverging away horizontally from the core, or tornadic features (funnel clouds, tornadoes). At night, lightning may be the only visual clue.

PIREPs—Reports of sudden airspeed changes in the airport approach or landing corridors provide indication of the presence of wind shear.

Airborne weather radar—To detect convective cells.

Meteorology

1. Briefly describe the composition of the Earth's atmosphere. (FAA-H-8083-28)

The Earth's atmosphere consists of numerous gases with nitrogen, oxygen, argon, and carbon dioxide making up 99.998 percent of all gases.

2. Most of the Earth's weather occurs in what region of the atmosphere? (FAA-H-8083-28)

Most of the Earth's weather occurs in the troposphere, which begins at the Earth's surface and extends up to approximately 36,000 feet. As the gases in this layer decrease with height, the air becomes thinner and the temperature decreases from about 15°C (59°F) to −56.5°C (−70°F).

3. **What are standard atmosphere temperature and pressure lapse rates?** (FAA-H-8083-25)

   A standard temperature lapse rate is one in which the temperature decreases at the rate of approximately 3.5°F (2°C) per 1,000 feet up to 36,000 feet. Above this point, the temperature is considered constant up to 80,000 feet. A standard pressure lapse rate is one in which pressure decreases at a rate of approximately 1 "Hg per 1,000 feet of altitude gain to 10,000 feet.

4. **Explain the difference between a stable atmosphere and an unstable atmosphere. Why is the stability of the atmosphere important?** (FAA-H-8083-28)

   The stability of the atmosphere depends on its ability to resist vertical motion. A stable atmosphere makes vertical movement difficult, and small vertical disturbances dampen out and disappear. In an unstable atmosphere, small vertical air movements tend to become larger, resulting in turbulent airflow and convective activity. Instability can lead to significant turbulence, extensive vertical clouds, and severe weather.

5. **How can you determine the stability of the atmosphere?** (FAA-H-8083-28)

   When temperature decreases uniformly and rapidly as you climb (approaching 3°C per 1,000 feet), you have an indication of unstable air. If the temperature remains unchanged or decreases only slightly with altitude, the air tends to be stable. When air near the surface is warm and moist, suspect instability.

6. **List the effects of stable and unstable air on clouds, turbulence, precipitation, and visibility.** (FAA-H-8083-28)

	Stable	Unstable
Clouds	Stratiform	Cumuliform
Turbulence	Smooth	Rough
Precipitation	Steady	Showery
Visibility	Fair to poor	Good

7. What causes the wind? (FAA-H-8083-25)

Differences in air density caused by changes in temperature result in a change in pressure. This, in turn, creates motion in the atmosphere, both vertically and horizontally, in the form of wind and convective currents.

8. What are the three forces that affect the wind? (FAA-H-8083-28)

Pressure gradient force (PGF), Coriolis force, and friction.

9. Explain how the pressure gradient force affects the wind. (FAA-H-8083-28)

Wind is driven by pressure differences, which create a force called the pressure gradient force (PGF). Whenever a pressure difference develops over an area, the PGF makes the wind blow in an attempt to equalize pressure differences. This force is identified by height contour gradients on constant pressure charts and by isobar gradients on surface charts. PGF is directed from higher height/pressure to lower height/pressure and is perpendicular to contours/isobars. Whenever a pressure difference develops over an area, the PGF begins moving the air directly across the contours/isobars.

10. What are several examples of local winds that may affect an aircraft in flight? (FAA-H-8083-28)

Local winds include a sea breeze, land breeze, lake breeze, lake effect, valley breeze, mountain-plains wind circulation, and mountain breeze.

11. Explain the term *wind shear* and state the areas it is likely to occur. (FAA-H-8083-28)

Wind shear is the sudden, drastic change in wind speed and/or direction over a small area, from one level or point to another, usually in the vertical. Wind shear occurs in all directions, but for convenience, it is measured along vertical and horizontal axes, thus becoming horizontal and vertical wind shear. Wind shear can affect any flight at any altitude (e.g., at upper levels near jet steams or near the ground due to convection).

12. While on a cross-country flight, you notice a lens-shaped cloud over a mountainous area along your route of flight. What does the presence of this type of cloud indicate? (FAA-H-8083-28)

It indicates the presence of a mountain wave, which is an atmospheric wave disturbance formed when stable air flow passes over a mountain or mountain ridge. Mountain waves are a form of mechanical turbulence that develops above and downwind of mountains and frequently produces severe to extreme turbulence. When sufficient moisture is present in the upstream flow, mountain waves produce cloud formations, including cap clouds, cirrocumulus standing lenticular (CCSL), altocumulus standing lenticular (ACSL), and rotor clouds. These clouds provide visual proof that mountain waves exist; however, the clouds may be absent if the air is too dry.

13. The amount of moisture in the air is dependent on what factor? (FAA-H-8083-28)

The temperature of the air. Every 20°F increase in temperature doubles the amount of moisture the air can hold. Conversely, a decrease of 20°F cuts the capacity in half.

14. Define the terms *relative humidity* and *dew point*. (FAA-H-8083-28)

Relative humidity—The ratio, usually expressed as a percentage, of water vapor actually in the air parcel compared to the amount of water vapor the air parcel could hold at a particular temperature and pressure.

Dew point—The temperature to which an air parcel must be cooled at constant pressure and constant water vapor pressure to allow the water vapor in the parcel to condense into water (dew).

15. What are the different precipitation types? (FAA-H-8083-28)

Precipitation types include drizzle, rain, freezing rain, freezing drizzle, snow, snow grains, ice crystals, ice pellets, hail, and small hail and/or snow pellets.

16. **What are the three ingredients necessary for precipitation to form?** (FAA-H-8083-28)

Precipitation formation requires three ingredients: water vapor, sufficient lift to condense the water vapor into clouds, and a growth process that allows cloud droplets to grow large and heavy enough to fall as precipitation. Significant precipitation usually requires clouds to be at least 4,000 feet thick.

17. **Explain the general characteristics in regard to the flow of air around high-pressure and low-pressure systems in the Northern Hemisphere.** (FAA-H-8083-28)

Low pressure—inward, upward, and counterclockwise.

High pressure—outward, downward, and clockwise.

18. **If your route of flight takes you toward a low-pressure system, in general what kind of weather can you expect? What if you were flying toward a high-pressure system?** (FAA-H-8083-28)

A low-pressure system is characterized by rising air, which is conducive to cloudiness, precipitation, and bad weather. A high-pressure system is an area of descending air, which tends to favor dissipation of cloudiness and good weather.

19. **Describe the different types of fronts.** (FAA-H-8083-28)

Cold front—Occurs when a mass of cold, dense, and stable air advances and replaces a body of warmer air.

Occluded front—A frontal occlusion occurs when a fast-moving cold front catches up with a slow-moving warm front. The two types are the cold front occlusion and warm front occlusion.

Warm front—The boundary area formed when a warm air mass contacts and flows over a colder air mass.

Stationary front—When the forces of two air masses are relatively equal, the boundary or front that separates them remains stationary and influences the local weather for days. The weather is typically a mixture of both warm and cold fronts.

20. What are the general characteristics of the weather a pilot would encounter when operating near a cold front? A warm front? (FAA-H-8083-28)

Cold front—As the front passes, expected weather can include towering cumulus or cumulonimbus, heavy rain accompanied by lightning, thunder, and/or hail; tornadoes possible; during passage, poor visibility, winds variable and gusting; temperature/dew point and barometric pressure drop rapidly.

Warm front—As the front passes, expected weather can include stratiform clouds, drizzle, low ceilings, and poor visibility; variable winds; rise in temperature.

Note: The weather associated with a front depends on the amount of moisture available, the degree of stability of the air that is forced upward, the slope of the front, the speed of frontal movement, and the upper wind flow.

21. What is a trough? (FAA-H-8083-28)

A trough (also called a trough line) is an elongated area of relatively low atmospheric pressure. At the surface, when air converges into a low, it cannot go outward against the pressure gradient, and it cannot go downward into the ground; it must go upward. Therefore, a low or trough is an area of rising air. Rising air is conducive to cloudiness and precipitation; hence the general association of low pressure and bad weather.

22. What is a ridge? (FAA-H-8083-28)

A ridge (also called a ridge line) is an elongated area of relatively high atmospheric pressure. Air moving out of a high or ridge depletes the quantity of air; therefore, these are areas of descending air. Descending air favors dissipation of cloudiness; hence the association of high pressure and good weather.

23. What does a cloud consist of, and why do clouds form?
(FAA-H-8083-28)

A cloud is a visible aggregate of minute water droplets and/or ice particles in the atmosphere above the Earth's surface. Clouds form in the atmosphere as a result of condensation of water vapor in rising currents of air, or by the evaporation of the lowest layer of fog. Rising currents of air are necessary for the formation of vertically deep clouds capable of producing precipitation heavier than light intensity.

24. Describe the four basic cloud forms observed in the Earth's atmosphere. (FAA-H-8083-28)

Cirri-form—High-level clouds that form above 20,000 feet and are usually composed of ice crystals; they are typically thin and white in appearance.

Nimbo-form—Nimbus is Latin meaning "rain." These clouds form between 7,000 and 15,000 feet and bring steady precipitation. As clouds thicken and precipitation begins, the cloud bases tend to lower toward the ground.

Cumuli-form—Clouds that show the vertical motion or thermal uplift of air taking place in the atmosphere. The height of the cloud base depends upon the humidity of the rising air. The more humid the air, the lower the cloud base. The tops of these clouds can reach over 60,000 feet.

Strati-form—Stratus is Latin for "layer" or "blanket." These clouds consist of a featureless lower layer that can cover the entire sky like a blanket. The cloud bases are usually only a few hundred feet above the ground.

25. What are the three primary causes of turbulence?
(FAA-H-803-28)

a. Convective currents (called convective turbulence)
b. Obstructions in the wind flow (called mechanical turbulence)
c. Wind shear

26. What are the four intensity levels of turbulence? (FAA-H-8083-28)

Light—Causes slight, erratic changes in altitude and/or attitude (pitch, roll, or yaw).

Moderate—Changes in altitude and/or attitude occur, but the aircraft remains in positive control at all times. It usually causes variations in indicated airspeed.

Severe—Causes large, abrupt changes in altitude and/or attitude. It usually causes large variations in indicated airspeed. Aircraft may be momentarily out of control.

Extreme—The aircraft is violently tossed about and is practically impossible to control. It may cause structural damage.

27. Define the term *clear air turbulence* (CAT). (FAA-H-8083-28)

CAT is defined as sudden severe turbulence occurring in cloudless regions that causes violent buffeting of aircraft. CAT is a higher altitude turbulence (normally above 15,000 feet) particularly between the core of a jet stream and the surrounding air. CAT is especially troublesome because it is often encountered unexpectedly and frequently without visual clues to warn pilots of the hazard. The best available information on the location of CAT comes from pilots via PIREPs.

28. What are the factors necessary for a thunderstorm to form, and what are the three stages of thunderstorm development? (FAA-H-8083-28)

For a thunderstorm to form, the air must have sufficient water vapor, an unstable lapse rate, and an initial upward boost (lifting) to start the storm process in motion. During its life cycle, a thunderstorm cell progresses through three stages:

a. *Cumulus*—Characterized by a strong updraft.

b. *Mature*—Precipitation beginning to fall from the cloud base signals that a downdraft has developed and a cell has entered the mature stage.

c. *Dissipating*—Downdrafts characterize the dissipating stage and the storm dies rapidly.

29. What are the three principal types of thunderstorms? (FAA-H-8083-28)

Single cell—Also called ordinary cell thunderstorms, this type consists of only one cell; they are easily circumnavigated except at night or when embedded in other clouds. Single-cell thunderstorms are rare, as almost all thunderstorms are multi-celled.

Multicell (cluster and line)—Consists of a cluster of cells at different stages of their life cycles. As the first cell matures, it is carried downwind, and a new cell forms upwind to take its place. A multicell may have a lifetime of several hours (or more), which makes it tougher to circumnavigate than a single-cell thunderstorm. Supercells may be embedded within them.

Supercell—Consists primarily of a single, quasi-steady rotating updraft that persists for an extended period of time. Updraft speeds may reach 9,000 fpm (100 knots). They may persist for many hours (or longer), and their size and persistence make them tough to circumnavigate.

30. What are microbursts? (AIM 7-1-24)

Microbursts are small-scale, intense downdrafts which, on reaching the surface, spread outward in all directions from the downdraft center. This causes the presence of both vertical and horizontal wind shears that can be extremely hazardous to all types and categories of aircraft, especially at low altitudes. Due to their small size, short lifespan, and the fact that they can occur over areas without surface precipitation, microbursts are not easily detectable using conventional weather radar or wind shear alert systems.

31. Where are microbursts most likely to occur? (AIM 7-1-24)

Microbursts can be found almost anywhere there is convective activity. They may be embedded in heavy rain associated with a thunderstorm or in light rain in benign-appearing virga. When there is little or no precipitation at the surface accompanying the microburst, a ring of blowing dust may be the only visual clue of its existence.

32. What are the main types of icing an aircraft may encounter? (FAA-H-8083-28)

Structural, induction system, and instrument icing.

33. Name the three types of structural ice that may occur in flight. (FAA-H-8083-28)

Clear icing, or glaze ice, is a glossy, clear, or translucent ice formed by the relatively slow freezing of large, supercooled water droplets. Clear icing conditions exist more often in an environment with warmer temperatures, higher liquid water content, and larger droplets. It forms when only a small portion of the drop freezes immediately while the remaining unfrozen portion flows or smears over the aircraft surface and gradually freezes.

Rime icing is rough, milky, and opaque ice formed by the instantaneous freezing of small, supercooled water droplets after they strike the aircraft. It is the most frequently reported icing type. Rime icing formation favors colder temperatures, lower liquid water content, and small droplets.

Mixed icing is a mixture of clear ice and rime ice and forms as an airplane collects both rime and clear ice due to small-scale variations in liquid water content, temperature, and droplet sizes.

Note: In general, rime icing tends to occur at temperatures colder than −15°C, clear ice when the temperature is warmer than −10°C, and mixed ice at temperatures in between. This is only general guidance. The type of icing will vary depending on the liquid water content, droplet size, and aircraft-specific variables.

34. How does fog form? (FAA-H-8083-28)

Fog forms when the temperature and dew point of the air become identical (or nearly so). This may occur through cooling of the air to a little beyond its dew point (producing radiation fog, advection fog, or upslope fog), or by adding moisture and thereby elevating the dew point (producing frontal fog or steam fog).

35. Name several types of fog. (FAA-H-8083-28)

a. *Radiation fog*—Favorable conditions are clear skies, little or no wind, and small temperature-dew point spread (high relative humidity). This fog forms almost exclusively at night or near daybreak.

b. *Advection fog*—Forms when moist air moves over colder ground or water. It is most common along coastal areas but often develops deep in continental areas. It may occur with winds, cloudy skies, over a wide geographic area, and at any time of the day or night.

c. *Upslope fog*—Forms as a result of moist, stable air being cooled adiabatically as it moves up sloping terrain. Once the upslope wind ceases, the fog dissipates.

d. *Frontal fog or precipitation-induced fog*—When warm, moist air is lifted over a front, clouds and precipitation may form. If the cold air below is near its dew point, evaporation (or sublimation) from the precipitation may saturate the cold air and form fog.

e. *Steam fog*—When very cold air moves across relatively warm water, enough moisture may evaporate from the water surface to produce saturation. As the rising water vapor meets the cold air, it immediately re-condenses and rises with the air that is being warmed from below.

f. *Freezing fog*—Occurs when the temperature falls to 32°F (0°C) or below. Tiny, supercooled liquid water droplets in fog can freeze instantly on exposed surfaces when surface temperatures are at or below freezing.

36. What is frost and what conditions would be conducive to its formation? (FAA-H-8083-25)

Frost is ice crystal deposits formed by sublimation when the temperature and dew point are below freezing. Frost can form on an airplane sitting outside on a clear night when there is moisture present in the air and the airplane's skin temperature falls below freezing due to radiation cooling.

37. Describe several types of obstructions to visibility that may occur in the atmosphere. (FAA-H-8083-28)

Weather and obstructions to visibility include fog, mist, haze, smoke, precipitation, blowing snow, dust storms, sandstorms, and volcanic ash.

Preflight
Procedures

4

A. Preflight Assessment

1. Explain how a pilot can perform an effective self-assessment before flight. (FAA-H-8083-25)

Prior to each and every flight, all pilots must do a proper physical self-assessment to ensure safety. One of the best ways to accomplish this is to use the IMSAFE checklist to determine physical and mental readiness for flying:

Illness—Am I sick? Illness is an obvious pilot risk.

Medication—Am I taking any medicines that might affect my judgment or make me drowsy?

Stress—Am I under excessive stress or psychological pressure?

Alcohol—Have I been drinking within 8 hours? Within 24 hours?

Fatigue—Am I tired and not adequately rested?

Emotion—Am I emotionally upset?

2. What is the purpose of performing a preflight inspection on the airplane? (FAA-H-8083-3)

The purpose of the preflight inspection is to ensure that the airplane meets regulatory airworthiness standards and is in a safe mechanical condition prior to flight.

3. Who is responsible for ensuring that an aircraft is maintained in an airworthy condition? (14 CFR 91.403)

The owner or operator of an aircraft is primarily responsible for maintaining an aircraft in an airworthy condition.

4. Who is responsible for determining that an aircraft is airworthy and in a condition for safe flight? (14 CFR 91.7)

The pilot-in-command of a civil aircraft is responsible for determining whether that aircraft is in condition for safe flight. The pilot-in-command shall discontinue the flight when unairworthy mechanical, electrical, or structural conditions occur.

5. **For an aircraft to be considered airworthy, what two conditions must be met?** (FAA-H-8083-25)

   a. The aircraft must conform to its type design (type certificate). This is attained when the required and proper components are installed consistent with the drawings, specifications, and other data that are part of the type certificate. Conformity includes applicable supplemental type certificate(s) (STC) and field-approval alterations.

   b. The aircraft must be in a condition for safe operation, referring to the condition of the aircraft in relation to wear and deterioration.

6. **Explain how a pilot determines if an aircraft conforms to its approved type design and is in a condition for safe operation.** (14 CFR Parts 21, 43, and 91)

   a. To determine that the aircraft conforms to its type design, a pilot must determine that the maintenance, preventive maintenance, and alterations have been performed in accordance with Parts 21, 43, and 91 and that the aircraft is registered in the United States. The pilot does this by ensuring that all required inspections, maintenance, preventive maintenance, repairs, and alterations have been appropriately documented in the aircraft's maintenance records.

   b. To determine that the aircraft is in condition for safe operation, the pilot conducts a thorough preflight inspection of the aircraft for wear and deterioration, structural damage, fluid leaks, tire wear, inoperative instruments and equipment, etc. If an unsafe condition exists or inoperative instruments or equipment are found, the pilot uses the guidance in 14 CFR §91.213 for handling the inoperative equipment.

7. **Explain how a preflight inspection should be performed on an airplane.** (FAA-H-8083-3)

   Since each airplane has different features and equipment, the preflight inspection checklist provided in airplane's AFM/POH should be used to perform the preflight inspection. As a flight instructor, I will teach my learners the "what, why, and how" of preflight inspection. *What* they are looking at, *why* they are looking at it, and *how* they will determine if it is airworthy.

8. **Why is it important to inspect the airplane with reference to an appropriate checklist?** (FAA-H-8083-3)

   Checklists are guides for use in ensuring that all necessary items are not only checked, but checked in a logical sequence. The pilot should never assume that the checklist is merely a crutch for poor memory but instead should consider the checklist a necessary tool used to accomplish a complex task thoroughly and efficiently.

9. **Describe the additional inspections that may be required when conducting the preflight inspection of an airplane equipped with integrated flight deck (IFD) glass-panel avionics.** (FAA-H-8083-3)

   Ground-based inspections may include verification that the flight deck reference guide is in the aircraft and accessible; checking of system-driven removal of "Xs" over engine indicators; checking pitot/static and attitude displays; testing of low-level alarms and annunciator panels; setting of fuel levels; and verification that the avionics cooling fans, if equipped, are functional. The AFM/POH specifies how these preflight inspections are to take place.

10. **Explain the different types of airplane logbooks that should be available for inspection prior to flight.** (FAA-H-8083-3)

    Each airplane has a set of logbooks that include airframe and engine—and in some cases, propeller and appliance—logbooks, which are used to record maintenance, alterations, and inspections performed on a specific airframe, engine, propeller, or appliance.

11. **Where are the airplane logbooks located and when should they be inspected?** (FAA-H-8083-3)

    It is important that the logbooks be kept accurate, secure, and available for inspection. Airplane logbooks are not normally kept in the airplane. It should be a matter of procedure by the pilot to inspect the airplane logbooks or a summary of the airworthy status prior to flight to ensure that the airplane records of maintenance, alteration, and inspections are current and correct.

12. **How can the use of the "PAVE" checklist during preflight help a pilot to assess and mitigate risk?** (FAA-H-8083-9)

Use of the PAVE checklist provides pilots with a simple way to remember each category to examine for risk during flight planning. The pilot divides the risks of flight into four categories:

Pilot—illness, medication, stress, alcohol, fatigue, emotion (I'M SAFE), proficiency, currency.

Aircraft—airworthiness, aircraft equipped for flight, proficiency in aircraft, performance capability.

enVironment—weather hazards, type of terrain, airports/runways to be used, conditions.

External pressures—meetings, people waiting at destination, desire to impress, desire to get there, etc.

B. Flight Deck Management

1. **Do the regulations require pilots to provide a pre-takeoff safety briefing to their passengers?** (14 CFR 91.107)

Yes. No pilot may take off an aircraft unless the PIC of that aircraft ensures that each person on board is *briefed* on how to fasten and unfasten that person's safety belt and, if installed, shoulder harness. Also, no pilot may cause to be moved on the surface, take off, or land an aircraft unless the pilot-in-command of that aircraft ensures that each person on board has been *notified* to fasten his or her safety belt and, if installed, his or her shoulder harness.

2. **Explain the items that should be included in a passenger preflight briefing.** (FAA Safety)

Seat belts fastened for taxi, takeoff, landing. Shoulder harnesses fastened for takeoff, landing. Seat position adjusted and locked in place.

Air vents (location and operation). All environmental controls (discussed). Action in case of any passenger discomfort.

Fire extinguisher (location and operation).

Exit doors (how to secure; how to open). Emergency evacuation plan. Emergency/survival kit (location and contents).

(continued)

Traffic (scanning, spotting, notifying pilot). Talking (sterile cockpit expectations).

Your questions? (Speak up!)

3. Why is the use of sterile cockpit procedures important when conducting taxi operations? (AC 91-73)

Pilots must be able to focus on their duties without being distracted by non-flight-related matters unrelated to the safe and proper operation of the aircraft. Refraining from nonessential activities during ground operations is essential. Passengers should be briefed on the importance of minimizing conversations and questions during taxi as well as on arrival, from the time landing preparations begin until the aircraft is safely parked.

4. What are examples of hazards a pilot should consider when assessing flight deck management risk? (FAA-S-ACS-25)

a. Equipment, checklists, charts, etc., not readily available or not secured.

b. Not briefing crew and passengers.

c. Poor ADM, SRM, CRM.

d. Improper use of systems or equipment, to include automation and portable electronic devices.

e. Flying with unresolved discrepancies.

5. How can a pilot mitigate hazards and reduce the risk present when managing the flight deck? (FAA-S-ACS-25)

a. Secure all items in the aircraft.

b. Conduct an appropriate passenger briefing, including identifying the pilot-in-command (PIC); use of safety belts, shoulder harnesses, and doors; passenger conduct; sterile aircraft; propeller blade avoidance; and emergency procedures.

c. Properly program and manage the aircraft's automation, as applicable.

d. Appropriately manage risks by utilizing ADM, including SRM/CRM.

6. Are navigational databases required to be updated for VFR flight? What about for IFR flight? (FAA-H-8083-15, AIM 1-1-17, AC 90-100)

Databases are required per regulations to be updated for IFR operations and should but are not required to be updated for VFR operations. It is not recommended to use a moving map with an outdated database in and around critical airspace. Databases are updated every 28 days and are available from various commercial vendors. For IFR operations, all approach procedures to be flown must be retrievable from the current airborne navigation database.

7. Explain what the FAA policy is for carrying current charts. (FAA AIS FAQ)

The specific FAA regulation, 14 CFR §91.103, Preflight Action, states that each pilot-in-command shall, before beginning a flight, become familiar with all available information concerning that flight. Although the regulation does not specifically require it, you should always carry a current chart with you in flight. Expired charts may not show frequency changes or newly constructed obstructions, both of which, when unknown, could be a hazard.

C. Engine Starting

1. Explain why it is important to call "clear" prior to starting an aircraft engine. (FAA-H-8083-3)

The pilot needs to ensure that the ramp area surrounding the airplane is clear of persons, equipment, and other hazards that could come into contact with the airplane or the propeller. Just prior to starter engagement, the pilot should always call "CLEAR" out of the side window and wait for a response from anyone who may be nearby *before* engaging the starter.

2. Describe several other precautions that can be taken to reduce risk prior to engine start. (FAA-H-8083-3)

The pilot should always check the area behind the airplane prior to engine start as a standard practice. At all times before engine start, the anti-collision lights should be turned on. For night operations, the position (navigation) lights should also be on.

3. **Explain why an engine start procedure in the winter would be different from one in the summer.** (FAA-P-8740-24)

   a. Batteries can lose a high percentage of their effectiveness in cold weather.

   b. Oil can become partially congealed, and turning the engines is difficult for the starter or by hand.

   c. There is a tendency to overprime, which results in washed-down cylinder walls and possible scouring of the walls. This results in poor compression and, consequently, harder starting.

   d. Sometimes aircraft fires have been started by overprime, when the engine fires and the exhaust system contains raw fuel. Other fires are caused by backfires through the carburetor.

4. **When starting the engine, are there any limitations on the amount of time the starter can be operated?** (FAA-H-8083-3, POH/AFM)

   Starter motors are not designed for continuous duty. Their service life may be drastically shortened during a prolonged or difficult start, as an excess buildup of heat can damage internal starter components. Avoid continuous starter operation for periods longer than 30 seconds without a cool down period of at least 30 seconds to 1 minute (some POH/AFMs specify longer cool-down routines). Reference your POH/AFM.

5. **Explain how an airplane engine is started through use of external power.** (FAA-H-8083-3, POH/AFM)

   Some aircraft have receptacles to which an external ground power unit (GPU) may be connected to provide electrical energy for starting. These are very useful, especially during cold weather starting. Procedures for use of external power are not the same for all aircraft. Follow the manufacturer's recommendations in the POH/AFM.

6. **In warm weather, how long should it take for the oil pressure to rise and provide an indication on the oil pressure gauge?** (FAA-H-8083-3, POH/AFM)

   In most conditions, oil pressure should rise to at least the lower limit within 30 seconds. To prevent damage, the engine should be shut down immediately if the oil pressure does not rise to the POH/ AFM values within the required time.

7. Identify hazards that a pilot should consider prior to conducting an engine start procedure. (FAA-S-ACS-25)

   a. Propeller safety.
   b. Use of external power unit.
   c. Limitations during starting.
   d. Engine fire due to excessive priming.
   e. Foreign object debris (FOD) around airplane.

D. Taxiing, Airport Signs, and Lighting

1. Explain the recommended practices that can assist a pilot in maintaining situational awareness during taxi operations. (AC 91-73)

   a. A current airport diagram should be available for immediate reference during taxi.

   b. Monitor ATC instructions/clearances issued to other aircraft for the big picture.

   c. Focus attention outside the cockpit while taxiing.

   d. Use all available resources (airport diagrams, airport signs, markings, lighting, and ATC) to keep the aircraft on its assigned taxi route.

   e. Cross-reference heading indicator to ensure turns are being made in the correct direction and that you're on the assigned taxi route.

   f. Prior to crossing any hold short line, visually check for conflicting traffic; verbalize "clear left, clear right."

   g. Be alert for other aircraft with similar call signs on the frequency.

   h. Understand and follow all ATC instructions and if in doubt—ask!

2. Why is it important to perform a brake check immediately after the airplane begins moving? (FAA-H-8083-3)

If the brake check is unsatisfactory, the engine can be shut down immediately instead of delaying the check until later only to find out that the brakes will not stop the airplane from a collision with an obstacle or another airplane.

3. Explain the importance of using a safe taxi speed. (FAA-H-8083-3)

The primary requirements for safe taxiing are positive control, the ability to recognize any potential hazards in time to avoid them, and the ability to stop or turn where and when desired, without undue reliance on the brakes. Normally, the speed should be at the rate where movement of the airplane is dependent on the throttle. That is, slow enough so that when the throttle is closed, the airplane can be stopped promptly.

4. Preflight planning for taxi operations should be an integral part of the pilot's flight planning process. What information should this include? (AC 91-73)

a. Review and understand airport signage, markings and lighting.

b. Review the airport diagram and planned taxi route, and identify any hot spots.

c. Review the latest airfield NOTAMs and ATIS (if available) for taxiway/runway closures, construction activity, etc.

d. Conduct a pre-taxi/pre-landing briefing that includes the expected/assigned taxi route and any hold short lines and restrictions based on ATIS information or previous experience at the airport.

e. Plan for critical times and locations on the taxi route (complex intersections, crossing runways, etc.).

f. Plan to complete as many aircraft checklist items as possible prior to taxi.

5. Describe several sources of information that a pilot can reference for current airport data and conditions. (FAA-H-8083-25)

    a. Aeronautical charts

    b. *Chart Supplement U.S.*

    c. Notices to Air Missions (NOTAMs)

    d. Automated Terminal Information Service (ATIS)

6. Explain what NOTAMs are and why they should be reviewed prior to conducting taxi and flight operations. (FAA-H-8083-25)

Notices to Air Missions (NOTAMs) contain time-critical aeronautical information, which is of a temporary nature or not sufficiently known in advance to permit publication on aeronautical charts or in other operational publications; this information receives immediate dissemination by the NOTAM system. NOTAMs include information on taxiway and runway closures, construction, communications, changes in status of navigational aids, and other information essential to planned enroute, terminal, or landing operations.

7. When issued taxi instructions to an assigned takeoff runway, are you automatically authorized to cross any runway that intersects your taxi route? (AIM 4-3-18)

No; Aircraft must receive a runway crossing clearance for each runway that their taxi route crosses. When assigned a takeoff runway, ATC will first specify the runway, issue taxi instructions, and state any hold short instructions or runway crossing clearances if the taxi route will cross a runway. When issuing taxi instructions to any point other than an assigned takeoff runway, ATC will specify the point to which to taxi, issue taxi instructions, and state any hold short instructions or runway crossing clearances if the taxi route will cross a runway. ATC is required to obtain a read back from the pilot of all runway hold short instructions.

8. **When receiving taxi instructions from a controller, a pilot should always read back what information?** (AIM 4-3-18)

   a. The runway assignment.

   b. Any clearance to enter a specific runway.

   c. Any instruction to hold short of a specific runway or line up and wait.

9. **Explain the terms *confirmation bias* and *expectation bias*.** (FAA-H-8083-2)

   Confirmation bias—The human tendency to look for information to confirm a decision already made. This occurs when we only look for, listen to, or acknowledge information that confirms our own preconceptions. We tend not to seek out or pay attention to evidence that could disconfirm the belief.

   Expectation bias—When we have a strong belief or mindset towards something we expect to see or hear, and act according to those beliefs. This often occurs on the ground while taxiing where a pilot expects a particular taxi route and perceives the clearance as expected rather than as given by ATC.

   Note: The result of either, if uncorrected, may lead to an error. Either case results in the pilot continuing with a plan despite clues indicating the situation is not as perceived. Fatigue tends to stop pilots from taking extra steps to verify perceived reality and contributes to expectation and confirmation bias susceptibility.

10. **What can a pilot do to mitigate confirmation and expectation biases?** (FAA-H-8083-2)

    Understand that expectation bias often affects the verbal transmission of information. When issued instructions by ATC, focus on listening and repeat to yourself exactly what is said in your head, and then apply that information actively. Does the clearance make sense? If something doesn't make sense (incorrect call sign, runway assignment, altitude, etc.), then query the controller about it.

11. Describe the various types of taxiway markings.
(AIM 2-3-4)

Markings for taxiways are yellow and consist of the following types:

a. *Taxiway centerline*—Single continuous yellow line; aircraft should be kept centered over this line during taxi; however, being centered on the centerline does not guarantee wingtip clearance with other aircraft or objects.

b. *Taxiway edge*—Used to define the edge of taxiway; two types, continuous and dashed.

c. *Taxiway shoulder*—Usually defined by taxiway edge markings; denotes pavement unusable for aircraft.

d. *Surface painted taxiway direction*—Yellow background with black inscription; supplements direction signs or when not possible to provide taxiway sign.

e. *Surface painted location signs*—Black background with yellow inscription; supplements location signs.

f. *Geographic position markings*—Located at points along low-visibility taxi routes; used to identify the location of aircraft during low-visibility operations.

12. What are the three types of runway holding position markings? (AIM 2-3-5)

a. *Runway holding position markings on taxiways*—These markings identify the locations on taxiways where aircraft **must stop** when a clearance has not been issued to proceed on to the runway.

b. *Runway holding position markings on runways*—These markings identify the locations on runways where aircraft **must stop**. These markings are located on runways used by ATC for LAHSO and taxiing operations.

c. *Holding position markings on taxiways located in runway approach areas*—These markings are used at some airports where it is necessary to hold an aircraft on a taxiway located in the approach or departure area of a runway so that the aircraft does not interfere with the operations on that runway.

13. Describe the various types of runway markings (precision instrument runway). (AIM 2-3-3)

Markings for runways are white and consist of the following types:

a. *Runway designators*—Runway number is the whole number nearest one-tenth the magnetic azimuth of the centerline of the runway, measured clockwise from the magnetic north.

b. *Runway centerline marking*—Identifies the center of the runway and provides alignment guidance during takeoff and landings; consists of a line of uniformly spaced stripes and gaps.

c. *Runway aiming point marking*—Serves as a visual aiming point for a landing aircraft; two rectangular markings consist of a broad white stripe located on each side of the runway centerline and approximately 1,000 feet from the landing threshold.

d. *Runway touchdown zone markers*—Identifies the touchdown zone for landing operations and are coded to provide distance information in 500-feet increments; groups of one, two, and three rectangular bars symmetrically arranged in pairs about the runway centerline.

e. *Runway side stripe markings*—Delineate the edges of the runway and provide a visual contrast between runway and the abutting terrain or shoulders; continuous white stripes located on each side of the runway.

f. *Runway shoulder markings*—May be used to supplement runway side stripes to identify pavement areas contiguous to the runway sides that are not intended for use by aircraft; painted yellow.

g. *Runway threshold markings*—Used to help identify the beginning of the runway that is available for landing. Two configurations: either eight longitudinal stripes of uniform dimensions disposed symmetrically about the runway centerline, or the number of stripes is related to the runway width.

14. Describe the six types of signs installed at airports.
(AIM 2-3-7 through 2-3-13)

a. *Mandatory instruction sign*—Red background/white inscription; denotes an entrance to a runway, critical area, or prohibited area.

b. *Location sign*—Black background/yellow inscription/yellow border; do not have arrows; used to identify a taxiway or runway location, the boundary of the runway, or identify an ILS critical area.

c. *Direction sign*—Yellow background/black inscription; identifies the designation of the intersecting taxiway(s) leading out of an intersection that a pilot would expect to turn onto or hold short of.

d. *Destination sign*—Yellow background/black inscription, and contain arrows; provides information on locating runways, terminals, cargo areas, civil aviation areas, etc.

e. *Information sign*—Yellow background/black inscription; used to provide the pilot with information on areas that can't be seen from the control tower, applicable radio frequencies, noise abatement procedures, etc.

f. *Runway distance remaining sign*—Black background/white numeral inscription; indicates the distance of the remaining runway in thousands of feet.

15. Describe the following types of airport taxiway and runway lighting: runway edge lights; lights marking the ends of the runway; runway end identifier lights; taxiway edge lights; taxiway centerline lights. (AIM 2-1-4, 2-1-3, 2-1-10)

a. *Runway edge lights*—White. On instrument runways, yellow replaces white on the last 2,000 feet or half the runway length (whichever is less), to form a caution zone for landings.

b. *Lights marking the ends of the runway*—Emit red light toward the runway to indicate the end of the runway to a departing aircraft, and green light outward from the runway end to indicate the threshold to landing aircraft.

(continued)

    c. *Runway end identifier lights (REIL)*—Provide rapid and positive identification of the approach end of a particular runway. The system consists of a pair of synchronized flashing lights located laterally on each side of the runway threshold. REIL may be either omnidirectional or unidirectional facing the approach area.

    d. *Taxiway edge lights*—Emit blue light; used to outline the edges of taxiways during periods of darkness or restricted visibility conditions.

    e. *Taxiway centerline lights*—Steady-burning, green lights; used to facilitate ground traffic under low-visibility conditions.

16. Describe the different visual wind direction indicators at airports without operating control towers. (AIM 4-3-4)

    a. *Segmented circle*—Located in a position affording maximum visibility to pilots in the air and on the ground and providing a centralized location for other elements of the system.

    b. *Wind direction indicator*—A wind cone, wind sock, or wind tee installed near the operational runway to indicate wind direction.

    c. *Landing direction indicator*—A tetrahedron indicates the direction of landings and takeoffs. It may be located at the center of a segmented circle and may be lighted for night operations. The small end of the tetrahedron points in the direction of landing.

    d. *Landing strip indicators*—Installed in pairs within the airport segmented circle to show the alignment of landing strips.

    e. *Traffic pattern indicators*—Arranged in pairs in conjunction with landing strip indicators and used to indicate the direction of turns when there is a variation from the normal left traffic pattern.

17. Explain how a pilot can mitigate the risk of a runway incursion if it becomes necessary to taxi in low-visibility conditions. (AC 91-73)

During low-visibility conditions, all resources available should be used during taxi. Resources include the airport diagram, the heading indicators, and airport signs, markings, and lighting. These resources help keep the aircraft on its assigned taxi route and not crossing any runway hold lines without clearance.

18. When taxiing at a non-towered airport, what are several precautionary measures you should take prior to entering or crossing a runway? (AC 91-73)

Listen on the appropriate frequency (CTAF) for inbound aircraft information, and always scan the full length of the runway, including the final approach and departure paths, before entering or crossing the runway. Self-announce your position and intentions and remember that not all aircraft are radio-equipped.

19. How can a pilot use aircraft exterior lighting to enhance situational awareness and safety during airport surface operations? (AC 91-73)

To the extent possible and consistent with aircraft equipment, operating limitations, and pilot procedures, pilots should illuminate exterior lights as follows:

a. *Engines running*—Turn on the rotating beacon whenever an engine is running.

b. *Taxiing*—Prior to commencing taxi, turn on navigation/position lights; when aircraft is moving, turn on taxi light; strobe lights should be off if they adversely affect vision of other pilots or ground personnel.

c. *Crossing a runway*—All exterior lights should be illuminated.

d. *Entering the departure runway for takeoff*—All exterior lights (except landing lights) should be on to make your aircraft more conspicuous to aircraft on final and ATC.

e. *Cleared for takeoff*—All exterior lights including takeoff/landing lights should be on.

Note: If you see an aircraft in takeoff position on a runway with landing lights ON, that aircraft has most likely received its takeoff clearance and will be departing immediately.

20. **Explain how the flight control surfaces should be positioned when taxiing in a quartering headwind and in a quartering tailwind.** (FAA-H-8083-3)

Quartering headwind—The wing on the upwind side (the side that the wind is coming from) tends to be lifted by the wind unless the aileron control is held in that direction (upwind aileron up). Moving the aileron into the up position reduces the effect of the wind striking that wing, thus reducing the lifting action. This control movement also causes the downwind aileron to be placed in the down position, thus a small amount of lift and drag on the downwind wing, further reducing the tendency of the upwind wing to rise.

Quartering tailwind—The elevator should be held in the down position, and the upwind aileron down. Since the wind is striking the airplane from behind, these control positions reduce the tendency of the wind to get under the tail and the wing and to nose the airplane over. The application of these crosswind taxi corrections helps to minimize the weathervaning tendency and ultimately results in easier steering.

21. **Identify hazards that should be considered when conducting taxi operations at a controlled airport.** (FAA-S-ACS-25)

    a. Activities and distractions.
    b. Confirmation or expectation bias as related to taxi instructions.
    c. A taxi route or departure runway change.
    d. Runway incursion.

22. **During preflight planning, describe the types of information a learner can review that will mitigate risk and enhance safety when conducting taxi operations.** (FAA-H-8083-3)

    a. Review and understand airfield signage and markings.

    b. Review the appropriate airport diagrams. Review any hot spots identified on the diagram. Print a copy for use in the cockpit.

    c. Review airfield NOTAMs and current ATIS for any taxiway closures, runway closures, construction activity, or other airfield-specific risks.

23. **Describe the common errors that can occur when taxiing an airplane.** (FAA-H-8083-3)

   a. Improper use of brakes.

   b. Improper positioning of the flight controls for various wind conditions.

   c. Taxiing too fast.

   d. Failure to comply with markings, signals, or clearances.

   e. Failure to use or the improper use of the checklist.

   f. Improper positioning of the airplane.

   g. Acceptance of marginal engine performance.

   h. An improper check of flight controls.

   i. Failure to review takeoff and emergency procedures.

   j. Failure to check for hazards and other traffic.

E. Before Takeoff Check

1. **Explain the purpose of performing a before takeoff checklist.** (FAA-H-8083-3)

   The before-takeoff check is the systematic AFM/POH procedure for checking the engine, controls, systems, instruments, and avionics prior to flight. Its purpose is to verify that the airplane is ready and safe for flight.

2. **Why do aircraft checklists call for the engine run-up/ magneto checks to be performed just before takeoff instead of prior to taxi?** (FAA-H-8083-3)

   a. Taxiing to the run-up position usually allows sufficient time for the engine to warm up to at least minimum operating temperature. Most engines require that oil temperature reach a minimum value before takeoff power is applied.

   b. Taxiing to a run-up position near the takeoff end of a runway provides a suitable location that is free of debris. Otherwise, the propeller may pick up pebbles, dirt, mud, sand, or other loose objects that could damage the propeller and also damage the tail of the airplane.

3. **When checking the carburetor heat (if equipped) during the before-takeoff check, explain why a drop in RPM occurs.** (FAA-H-8083-25)

   The use of carburetor heat causes a decrease in engine power, sometimes up to 15 percent, because the heated air is less dense than the outside air that had been entering the engine. This enriches the mixture. A mixture that is too rich or too lean will result in the engine losing power, which is indicated by a loss of RPM (on fixed-pitch propellers).

4. **Explain how the learner should properly position the airplane in the run-up area prior to performing the before takeoff check.** (FAA-H-8083-3)

   a. To minimize overheating, the airplane should be headed as nearly as possible into the wind.

   b. The airplane should be positioned clear of other aircraft and the taxiway.

   c. There should not be anything behind the airplane that might be damaged by the propeller airflow blasting rearward.

   d. The airplane should be allowed to roll forward slightly to ensure that the nose wheel or tail wheel is in alignment with the longitudinal axis of the airplane.

5. **Identify the hazards that can exist while performing a before-takeoff checklist.** (FAA-S-ACS-25)

   a. Not dividing attention while conducting the before-takeoff checks.

   b. Unexpected runway changes by air traffic control (ATC).

   c. Wake turbulence.

   d. If a problem is not detected, the potential for powerplant failure and other malfunctions during takeoff.

6. **Explain what a pilot can do to minimize the possibility of overheating the engine during the engine run-up prior to takeoff.** (FAA-H-8083-3)

   To minimize overheating during engine run-up, it is recommended that the airplane be headed as nearly as possible into the wind and, if equipped, engine instruments that indicate cylinder head temperatures should be monitored. Cowl flaps, if available, should be set according to the POH/AFM.

Airport
Operations

5

A. Communications, Light Signals, and Runway Lighting Systems

1. Explain where a pilot would look for radio communication frequencies and other airport data. (FAA-H-8083-25)

Communication frequencies and airport data may be found in:

a. Aeronautical charts (on the chart tab).

b. The *Chart Supplement U.S.*

c. Notices to Air Missions (NOTAMs).

d. Automated Terminal Information Service (ATIS) broadcasts.

e. GPS navigation databases and charting apps.

2. Explain how you would teach a learner when to communicate and how to obtain appropriate radio frequencies.

With a VFR sectional chart and a *Chart Supplement* available, I would locate examples of each of the following frequencies and explain when they would use them: ATIS, clearance delivery, ground control, tower, departure control, approach control, Air Route Traffic Control Center (ARTCC) frequencies, FSS frequencies on navigation and communication boxes, remote communications outlet (RCO), ground communication outlet (GCO), CTAF, UNICOM, ASOS/AWOS, VOR with voice, VOR without voice, and Special Use Airspace frequencies.

3. Where can a learner find information on recommended radio communication procedures and air traffic control (ATC) phraseology? (FAA-H-8083-25, AIM 4-2-1)

A review of the Pilot/Controller Glossary contained in the *AIM* assists a pilot in the use and understanding of standard terminology. *AIM* Chapter 4, Section 2, also contains many examples of radio communications phraseology and techniques.

4. Explain the phraseology a learner should use on initial contact with an ATC facility. (AIM 4-2-3)

Use the following format:

a. Name of the facility being called.

b   Your full aircraft identification.

c. If on the ground, your position; if in the air, your location.

d. Your request if it is short.

Example: "Columbia Ground, Cessna Three One Six Zero Foxtrot, south ramp, ready to taxi, with information Bravo."

5. What would be an indication that a microphone/PTT switch is stuck in the transmit position in your airplane? What would you do? (AIM 4-2-2)

One indication would be a lack of sounds from the receiver. Some aircraft transmitters will indicate that they're transmitting by displaying a "T" on the display. Check your volume, recheck your frequency, and make sure that your microphone/push-to-talk (PTT) button is not stuck in the transmit position. Depending on the airplane, other possible actions would be unplugging the microphone/PTT, unplugging a headset, etc.

6. If operating into an airport *without* an operating control tower that is located within the Class D airspace of an airport with an operating control tower, is it always necessary to communicate with the tower? (14 CFR 91.129)

Yes; operations to or from an airport in Class D airspace (airport traffic area) require communication with the tower even when operating to/from a satellite airport.

7. When conducting flight operations into an airport with an operating control tower, when should initial contact be established? (AIM 4-3-2)

Initial call-up should be made about 15 miles from the airport.

8. When departing a Class D surface area, what communications procedures are recommended? (AIM 4-3-2)

Unless there is good reason to leave the tower frequency before exiting the Class B, Class C, and Class D surface areas, it is good operating practice to remain on the tower frequency for the purpose of receiving traffic information. In the interest of reducing tower frequency congestion, pilots are reminded that it is not necessary to request permission to leave the tower frequency once outside of Class B, Class C, and Class D surface areas.

9. **In the event of radio failure while operating an aircraft to, from, through or on an airport having an operational tower, what are the different types and meanings of light gun signals you might receive from an ATC tower?** (14 CFR 91.125)

Light	On Ground	In Air
Steady green	Cleared for takeoff	Cleared to land
Flashing green	Cleared to taxi	Return for landing
Steady red	Stop	Yield, continue circling
Flashing red	Taxi clear of runway	Unsafe, do not land
Flashing white	Return to start	Not used
Alternate red/green	Exercise extreme caution	Exercise extreme caution

10. **Explain when transponder and ADS-B Out equipment should be operated while on the ground.** (AIM 4-1-20)

Civil and military aircraft should operate with the transponder in the altitude reporting mode and ADS-B Out transmissions enabled at all airports, any time the aircraft is positioned on any portion of the airport movement area. This includes all defined taxiways and runways. Pilots must pay particular attention to ATIS and airport diagram notations, general notes (included on airport charts), and comply with directions pertaining to transponder and ADS-B usage.

11. **What procedures should be used when attempting communications with a tower when the aircraft transmitter or receiver or both are inoperative?** (AIM 4-2-13, 6-4-2)

Arriving aircraft receiver inoperative:

a. Remain outside or above Class D surface area.

b. Determine direction and flow of traffic.

c. Advise tower of aircraft type, position, altitude, and intention to land. Request to be controlled by light signals.

d. At 3 to 5 miles, advise tower of position and join traffic pattern.

e. Watch tower for light gun signals.

Arriving aircraft transmitter inoperative:

a. Remain outside or above Class D surface area.

b. Determine direction and flow of traffic.

c. Monitor frequency for landing or traffic information.

d. Join the traffic pattern and watch for light gun signals.

e. During daytime, acknowledge by rocking wings. At night, acknowledge by flashing landing light or navigation lights.

Arriving aircraft transmitter and receiver inoperative:

a. Remain outside or above Class D surface area.

b. Determine direction and flow of traffic.

c. Join the traffic pattern and watch for light gun signals.

d. Acknowledge light signals as noted above.

Note: When an aircraft with a coded radar beacon transponder experiences a loss of two-way radio capability, the pilot should adjust the transponder to reply on Mode A/3, Code 7600. The pilot should understand that the aircraft may not be in an area of radar coverage.

12. Describe the type of information provided when receiving VFR radar assistance from ATC. (FAA-H-8083-25, AIM 4-1-17)

Radar-equipped ATC facilities provide radar assistance to aircraft on instrument flight plans and VFR aircraft provided the aircraft can communicate with the facility and are within radar coverage. This basic service includes safety alerts, traffic advisories, limited vectoring when requested, and sequencing at locations where this procedure has been established. ATC issues traffic advisories based on observed radar targets. This service is not intended to relieve the pilot of the responsibility to see and avoid other aircraft.

13. Describe the various types of terminal radar services available for VFR aircraft. (AIM 4-1-18)

Basic radar service—Safety alerts, traffic advisories, limited radar vectoring (on a workload-permitting basis), and sequencing at locations where procedures have been established for this purpose and/or when covered by a letter of agreement.

(continued)

TRSA service—Radar sequencing and separation service for participating VFR aircraft in a TRSA.

Class C service—This service provides, in addition to basic radar service, approved separation between IFR and VFR aircraft, and sequencing of VFR arrivals to the primary airport.

Class B service—This service provides, in addition to basic radar service, approved separation of aircraft based on IFR, VFR, and/or weight, and sequencing of VFR arrivals to the primary airport(s).

14. When is immediate notification to the National Transportation Safety Board (NTSB) required? (49 CFR 830.5)

The operator of an aircraft shall immediately, and by the most expeditious means available, notify the nearest NTSB office when an aircraft accident or any of the following listed serious incidents occur:

a. Flight control system malfunction.

b. Crewmember unable to perform normal duties.

c. Inflight fire.

d. Aircraft collision in flight.

e. Property damage, other than aircraft, estimated to exceed $25,000.

f. Overdue aircraft (believed to be in accident).

g. Release of all or a portion of a propeller blade from an aircraft.

h. Complete loss of information (excluding flickering) from more than 50 percent of an aircraft's EFIS cockpit displays.

15. Explain the difference between an aircraft incident and an aircraft accident. (49 CFR 830.2)

Aircraft incident means an occurrence other than an accident associated with the operation of an aircraft, which affects or could affect the safety of operations.

Aircraft accident means an occurrence associated with the operation of an aircraft which takes place between the time any person boards the aircraft with the intention of flight and all such persons have disembarked, and in which any person suffers death or serious injury, or in which the aircraft receives substantial damage.

16. **Define the term *serious injury*.** (49 CFR 830.2)

    Serious injury means any injury that:

    a. Requires hospitalization for more than 48 hours, commencing within 7 days from the date the injury was received;

    b. Results in a fracture of any bone (except simple fractures of fingers, toes, or nose);

    c. Causes severe hemorrhages, nerve, muscle, or tendon damage;

    d. Involves any internal organ; or

    e. Involves second- or third-degree burns affecting more than 5 percent of the body surface.

17. **Define the term *substantial damage*.** (49 CFR 830.2)

    Substantial damage means damage or failure that adversely affects the structural strength, performance, or flight characteristics of the aircraft and that would normally require major repair or replacement of the affected component. Engine failure or damage limited to an engine if only one engine fails or is damaged; bent fairings or cowling; dented skin; small punctured holes in the skin or fabric; ground damage to rotor or propeller blades; and damage to landing gear, wheels, tires, flaps, engine accessories, brakes, or wing tips are not considered substantial damage for the purpose of this 49 CFR Part 830.

18. **Will notification to the NTSB always be necessary in any aircraft accident even if there were no injuries?** (49 CFR Part 830)

    Refer to the definition of accident. An aircraft accident can involve substantial damage and/or injuries, and the NTSB always requires a report if this is the case.

19. **Where are accident or incident reports filed?** (49 CFR Part 830)

    The operator of an aircraft shall file any report with the NTSB field office nearest the accident or incident.

20. **After an accident or incident has occurred, how soon must a report be filed with the NTSB?** (49 CFR Part 830)

The operator shall file a report on NTSB Form 6120.1/2, available from NTSB field offices, the NTSB in Washington, DC, or the FAA Flight Standards District Office:

a. Within 10 days after an accident.

b. When, after 7 days, an overdue aircraft is still missing.

Note: A report on an incident for which notification is required as described shall be filed only as requested by an authorized representative of the NTSB.

21. **An airport diagram indicates the letters "RWSL." Explain what these letters indicate.** (AIM 2-1-6, P/CG)

Runway Status Lights system—The RWSL is a system of runway and taxiway lighting to provide pilots increased situational awareness by illuminating runway entry lights (REL) when the runway is unsafe for entry or crossing, and takeoff hold lights (THL) when the runway is unsafe for departure. The lights automatically turn red when other traffic makes it dangerous to enter, cross, or begin takeoff.

22. **Describe the common errors related to radio communications and ATC light signal interpretation.**

a. Use of improper frequencies.

b. Improper procedure and phraseology when using radio communications.

c. Failure to acknowledge or properly comply with ATC clearances and instructions.

d. Failure to understand or to properly comply with ATC light signals.

e. Confirmation or expectation bias.

B. Traffic Patterns

1. What are the two main categories of airports?
(FAA-H-8083-25)

Towered airport—Pilots are required to maintain two-way radio communication with ATC and to acknowledge and comply with their instructions.

Non-towered airport—Two-way radio communications are not required, although it is a good operating practice for pilots to transmit their intentions on the specified frequency for the benefit of other traffic in the area.

Note: These two types of airports can be further subdivided into civil airports, military/federal government airports, and private airports.

2. Explain the purpose of an airport traffic pattern.
(FAA-H-8083-3)

An airport traffic pattern is the traffic flow or "pattern" that is prescribed for aircraft landing at, taxiing on, or taking off from the airport. To ensure that air traffic flows into and out of an airport in an orderly manner, a traffic pattern is established based on the local conditions, to include the direction and altitude of the pattern and the procedures for entering and leaving the pattern.

3. What are the basic components of an airport traffic pattern? (FAA-H-8083-3)

a. *Upwind leg*—A flight path parallel to the landing runway in the direction of landing.

b. *Crosswind leg*—A flight path at right angles to the landing runway off its upwind end.

c. *Downwind leg*—A flight path parallel to the landing runway in the direction opposite to landing. The downwind leg normally extends between the crosswind leg and the base leg.

d. *Base leg*—A flight path at right angles to the landing runway off its approach end. The base leg normally extends from the downwind leg to the intersection of the extended runway centerline.

(continued)

e. *Final approach*—A flight path in the direction of landing along the extended runway centerline. The final approach normally extends from the base leg to the runway. An aircraft making a straight-in approach VFR is also considered to be on final approach.

4. When approaching an airport with an operating control tower, when should initial contact be made with the ATC tower? (AIM 4-3-2)

Initial call-up should be made about 15 miles from the airport unless otherwise advised.

5. Explain the general rules that apply when conducting traffic pattern operations at a non-towered airport within Class E or G airspace. (14 CFR 91.126, 91.127)

Each person operating an aircraft to or from an airport without an operating control tower shall:

a. in the case of an airplane approaching to land, make all turns of that airplane to the left unless the airport displays approved light signals or visual markings indicating that turns should be made to the right, in which case the pilot shall make all turns to the right.

b. in the case of an aircraft departing an airport, comply with any traffic patterns established for that airport in 14 CFR Part 93.

6. Explain the recommended traffic pattern entry procedure at a non-towered airport. (AC 90-66, AIM 4-3-3)

Arriving aircraft should be at traffic pattern altitude and allow for sufficient time to view the entire traffic pattern before entering. Entries into traffic patterns while descending may create collision hazards and should be avoided. Entry to the downwind leg should be at a 45-degree angle abeam the midpoint of the runway to be used for landing. The pilot may use discretion to choose an alternate type of entry, especially when intending to cross over midfield, based upon the traffic and communication at the time of arrival.

7. **Explain the recommended traffic pattern departure procedure at a non-towered airport.** (AC 90-66, AIM 4-3-3)

   When departing the traffic pattern, airplanes should continue straight out or exit with a 45-degree left turn (right turn for right traffic pattern) beyond the departure end of the runway after reaching pattern altitude. Pilots need to be aware of any traffic entering the traffic pattern prior to commencing a turn.

8. **What is considered standard for a traffic pattern altitude?** (AIM 4-3-3)

   Unless otherwise required by the applicable distance from cloud criteria (14 CFR §91.155):

   a. Propeller-driven aircraft enter the traffic pattern at 1,000 feet AGL.

   b. Large and turbine-powered aircraft enter the traffic pattern at an altitude of not less than 1,500 feet AGL or 500 feet above the established pattern altitude.

   c. Helicopters operating in the traffic pattern may fly a pattern similar to the fixed-wing aircraft pattern, but at a lower altitude (500 AGL) and closer to the runway. This pattern may be on the opposite side of the runway from fixed-wing traffic when airspeed requires or for practice power-off landings (autorotation) and if local policy permits. Landings not to the runway must avoid the flow of fixed-wing traffic.

9. **Explain the different methods a pilot may use to determine the proper runway and traffic pattern in use at an airport without an operating control tower.** (AIM 4-1-9, 4-3-4)

   a. At an airport with a full or part-time UNICOM station in operation, an advisory may be obtained that will usually include wind direction and velocity, favored or designated runway, right or left traffic, altimeter setting, known traffic, NOTAMs, etc.

   b. Many airports are now providing completely automated weather, radio check capability, and airport advisory information on an automated UNICOM system. Availability of the automated UNICOM will be published in the *Chart Supplement U.S.* and approach charts.

(continued)

   c. At those airports where these services are not available, a segmented circle visual indicator system, if installed, is designated to provide traffic pattern information. The segmented circle system consists of the following components:

- The segmented circle
- The wind direction indicator (wind sock, cone, or tee)
- The landing direction indicator (a tetrahedron)
- Landing strip indicators
- Traffic pattern indicators

10. Explain the right-of-way rules that apply when two or more aircraft are approaching an airport for the purpose of landing. (14 CFR 91.113)

Aircraft on final approach to land or while landing have the right-of-way over aircraft in flight or operating on the surface, except that they shall not take advantage of this rule to force an aircraft off the runway surface which has already landed and is attempting to make way for an aircraft on final approach. When two or more aircraft are approaching an airport for the purpose of landing, the aircraft at the lower altitude has the right-of-way, but it shall not take advantage of this rule to cut in front of another which is on final approach to land or to overtake that aircraft.

11. Identify several hazards that a pilot should consider when operating in an airport traffic pattern. (FAA-S-ACS-25)

   a. Collision hazards.

   b. Distractions, task prioritization, loss of situational awareness, or disorientation.

   c. Wind shear and wake turbulence.

12. Explain how a pilot can mitigate the risk of an in-flight collision when operating in the traffic pattern at a non-towered airport. (FAA Safety)

   a. Be conspicuous—use landing lights and strobes.

   b. Announce your positions and intentions on the CTAF.

   c. Be aware of possible no-radio aircraft.

   d. Don't assert right-of-way if it will result in a collision hazard.

e. If there is an unresolved conflict, break off the approach and go around to the non-pattern side of the runway.

13. Define the term *wake turbulence*. (P/CG)

A phenomenon resulting from the passage of an aircraft through the atmosphere. The term includes vortices, thrust stream turbulence, jet blast, jet wash, propeller wash, and rotor wash, both on the ground and in the air.

14. Explain how wake vortices are created. (FAA-H-8083-25)

Lift is generated by the creation of a pressure differential over the wing surface. The lowest pressure occurs over the upper wing surface and the highest pressure under the wing. This pressure differential triggers the rollup of the airflow aft of the wing, resulting in swirling air masses trailing downstream of the wingtips. After the rollup is completed, the wake consists of two counter rotating cylindrical vortices.

15. Where are wake turbulence and wingtip vortices likely to occur? (AIM 7-4-1, 7-4-3)

All aircraft generate turbulence and associated wingtip vortices. In general, avoid the area behind and below the generating aircraft, especially at low altitudes. Also of concern is the weight, speed, and shape of the wing of the generating aircraft. The greatest vortex strength occurs when the generating aircraft is *heavy*, *clean*, and *slow*.

16. Explain the operational procedures that should be followed when wake vortices are suspected to exist? (AIM 7-4-6)

a. *Landing behind a larger aircraft on the same runway*—Stay at or above the larger aircraft's final approach flight path. Note its touchdown point and land beyond it.

b. *Landing behind a larger aircraft, when parallel runway is closer than 2,500 feet*—Consider possible drift to your runway. Stay at or above the larger aircraft's final approach flight path, and note its touchdown point.

c. *Landing behind a larger aircraft, crossing runway*—Cross above the larger aircraft's flight path.

(continued)

d. *Landing behind a departing larger aircraft on the same runway*—Note the larger aircraft's rotation point, and land well prior to that rotation point.

e. *Landing behind a departing larger aircraft, crossing runway*—Note the larger aircraft's rotation point. If past the intersection, continue the approach and land prior to the intersection. If larger aircraft rotates prior to the intersection, avoid flight below the larger aircraft's flight path. Abandon the approach unless a landing is ensured well before reaching the intersection.

f. *Departing behind a large aircraft*—Note the larger aircraft's rotation point and rotate prior to the that rotation point. Continue climbing above the larger aircraft's climb path until turning clear of the larger aircraft's wake. Avoid subsequent headings that will cross below and behind a larger aircraft.

g. *Intersection takeoffs, same runway*—Be alert to adjacent larger aircraft operations, particularly upwind of your runway. If intersection takeoff clearance is received, avoid subsequent heading which will cross below a larger aircraft's path.

h. *Departing or landing after a larger aircraft executing a low approach, missed approach, or touch-and-go landing*—Vortices settle and move laterally near the ground. Because of this, the vortex hazard may exist along the runway and in your flight path after a larger aircraft has executed a low approach, missed approach, or touch-and-go landing, particularly in light quartering wind conditions. You should ensure that an interval of at least 2 minutes has elapsed before your takeoff or landing.

i. *En route VFR (thousand-foot altitude plus 500 feet)*—Avoid flight below and behind a large aircraft's path. If a larger aircraft is observed above or on the same track (meeting or overtaking), adjust your position laterally, preferably upwind.

Remember: Acceptance of instructions from ATC is an acknowledgment that the pilot will ensure safe takeoff and landing intervals and accept the responsibility for providing wake turbulence separation.

17. What type of automated weather is provided at most controlled airports? (AIM 4-1-13)

The Automated Terminal Information Service (ATIS) is a recording of the local weather conditions and other pertinent non-control information broadcast on a local frequency in a looped format. It is normally updated once per hour but is updated more often when changing local conditions warrant. Important information is broadcast on ATIS, including weather, runways in use, specific ATC procedures, and any airport construction activity that could affect taxi planning.

18. What type of automated weather is available at uncontrolled airports? (AIM 4-3-26)

Many airports throughout the National Airspace System are equipped with either Automated Surface Observing System (ASOS) or Automated Weather Observing System (AWOS). At uncontrolled airports that are equipped with ASOS/AWOS with ground-to-air broadcast capability, the one-minute updated airport weather should be available to you within approximately 25 NM of the airport below 10,000 feet. The frequency for the weather broadcast will be published on sectional charts and in the *Chart Supplement U.S.*

19. Describe the common errors that can occur when operating in the traffic pattern.

a. Failure to comply with traffic pattern instructions, procedures, and rules.

b. Improper correction for wind drift.

c. Inadequate spacing from other traffic.

d. Poor altitude or airspeed control.

e. Distractions

f. Loss of situational awareness.

Takeoffs, Landings, and Go-Arounds

6

A. Normal Takeoff and Climb

1. Describe a normal takeoff and climb procedure.
(FAA-H-8083-3)

A normal takeoff and climb is one in which the airplane is headed directly into the wind or the wind is very light, and the takeoff surface is firm with no obstructions along the takeoff path and is of sufficient length to permit the airplane to gradually accelerate to normal climbing speed.

2. Discuss the importance of a thorough knowledge of normal takeoff and climb procedures. (FAA-H-8083-3)

A thorough knowledge of takeoff and climb principles, both in theory and practice, will prove to be of great value throughout the pilot's career. It often may prevent an attempt to take off under critical conditions that would require performance beyond the capability of the airplane or skill of the pilot. The takeoff itself, though relatively simple, often presents the most hazards of any part of a flight.

3. What are the steps involved in performing a normal takeoff and climb procedure? (FAA-H-8083-3)

Although the takeoff and climb process is one continuous maneuver, it can be divided into three main steps in order to explain the process:

a. The takeoff roll:
- Align the airplane with the runway centerline.
- Apply throttle smoothly and continuously to maximum allowable power.
- Maintain directional control with rudder; slight rudder pressure will be required to compensate for torque.
- Glance at the engine instruments for any sign of malfunction.

b. The liftoff:
- As soon as all flight controls become effective during the takeoff roll, gradually apply back pressure to lift the nose wheel off of the runway (rotation).
- Adjust and maintain liftoff attitude for V_X or V_Y.
- Keep the wings level and establish an initial heading.

c. The initial climb after becoming airborne:
- Establish pitch attitude for V_X or V_Y as necessary.
- Retrim aircraft for appropriate speed.
- Maintain takeoff power until 500 feet AGL above surrounding terrain.
- Adjust heading to maintain track of extended runway centerline.

4. Identify the hazards that a learner should consider when performing a normal takeoff and climb procedure. (FAA-S-ACS-25)

a. Runway selection based on pilot capability, airplane performance and limitations, available distance, and wind.

b. Effects of crosswind.

c. Effects of wind shear.

d. Effects of tailwind.

e. Effects of wake turbulence.

f. Effects of takeoff surface/condition.

g. Abnormal operations, including planning for:
- Rejected takeoff.
- Potential engine failure in takeoff and climb phase of flight.

h. Collision hazards.

i. Low-altitude maneuvering, including stall, spin, or controlled flight into terrain (CFIT).

j. Distractions, task prioritization, loss of situational awareness, or disorientation.

k. Runway incursion.

5. What skill standards are expected when demonstrating a normal takeoff and climb procedure? (FAA-S-ACS-25)

The applicant demonstrates and simultaneously explains how to:

a. Complete the appropriate checklist(s).

b. Make radio calls as appropriate.

c. Verify assigned/correct runway or takeoff path.

(continued)

d. Determine wind direction with or without visible wind direction indicators.

e. Position the flight controls for the existing wind, if applicable.

f. Clear the area, taxi into takeoff position, and align the airplane on the runway centerline.

g. Advance the throttle smoothly to takeoff power and confirm proper engine and flight instrument indications prior to rotation.

h. Rotate and lift off at the recommended airspeed and accelerate to V_Y.

i. Establish a pitch attitude to maintain the manufacturer's recommended speed or V_Y, ±5 knots.

j. Configure the airplane in accordance with manufacturer's guidance.

k. Maintain V_Y ±5 knots to a safe maneuvering altitude.

l. Maintain directional control and proper wind-drift correction throughout takeoff and climb.

m. Comply with noise abatement procedures, as applicable.

n. Analyze and correct common errors related to this task.

6. **What common errors may occur when performing a normal takeoff and departure climb?** (FAA-H-8083-3)

a. Failure to review AFM/POH and performance charts prior to takeoff.

b. Failure to adequately clear the area prior to taxiing into position on the active runway.

c. Abrupt use of the throttle.

d. Failure to check engine instruments for signs of malfunction after applying takeoff power.

e. Failure to anticipate the airplane's left-turning tendency on initial acceleration.

f. Overcorrecting for left-turning tendency.

g. Relying solely on the airspeed indicator rather than developing an understanding of visual references and tracking clues of airplane airspeed and controllability during acceleration and liftoff.

h. Failure to attain proper liftoff attitude.

i. Inadequate compensation for torque/P-factor during initial climb, resulting in a sideslip.

j. Over-control of elevators during initial climb-out and lack of elevator trimming.

k. Limiting scan to areas directly ahead of the airplane (pitch attitude and direction), causing a wing (usually the left) to drop immediately after liftoff.

l. Failure to attain/maintain best rate-of-climb airspeed (V_Y) or desired climb airspeed.

m. Failure to employ the principles of attitude flying during climb-out, resulting in "chasing" the airspeed indicator.

B. Normal Approach and Landing

1. Describe a normal approach and landing. (FAA-H-8083-3)

These are techniques for what is considered a normal situation—that is, when engine power is available; the wind is light and the final approach is made directly into the wind; the final approach path has no obstacles; and the landing surface is firm and of ample length to gradually bring the airplane to a stop. The selected landing point is normally beyond the runway approach threshold but within the first one-third of the runway

2. What is the learning objective of a normal approach and landing? (FAA-H-8083-3)

The objective of a good, stabilized approach and landing is to establish an angle of descent and airspeed that will permit the airplane to reach the desired touchdown point at an airspeed which will result in a minimum floating just before touchdown.

3. Explain the procedure for performing a normal approach and landing. (FAA-H-8083-3)

a. Establish a normal traffic pattern.

b. At midfield, on downwind, complete a pre-landing checklist.

c. Abeam the touchdown point on downwind, reduce power.

d. Maintain altitude and level pitch attitude momentarily to dissipate airspeed.

(continued)

e. Retrim aircraft to establish airspeed within flap operating range (white arc).

f. Lower flaps to 10°.

g. Establish initial approach airspeed ($1.4 \times V_{S0}$); retrim if necessary.

h. At an approximate 45° point from the landing threshold, clear for traffic and turn base.

i. Extend flaps and retrim if necessary to maintain approach airspeed; apply wind-drift correction.

j. Lead turn to final to roll out on runway extended centerline.

k. Once the field is assured, extend final flaps.

l. Simultaneously adjust power and pitch attitude as necessary to control the airspeed and the descent angle, or to attain the desired altitudes along the approach path.

m. As the airplane approaches to within what appears to be 10 to 20 feet above the ground, the round out or flare should be started and the power reduced.

n. Continue applying back pressure as the airplane decelerates.

o. Land on the main wheels first.

p. Brake as necessary.

4. **Identify the hazards that a learner should consider when performing a normal approach and landing procedure.**
(FAA-S-ACS-25)

a. Selection of runway/landing surface, approach path, and touchdown area based on pilot capability, aircraft performance and limitations, available distance, and wind.

b. Effects of crosswind.

c. Effects of wind shear.

d. Effects of tailwind.

e. Effects of wake turbulence.

f. Effects of landing surface/condition.

g. Rejected landing and go-around.

h. Land and hold short operations (LAHSO).

i. Collision hazards.

j. Low-altitude maneuvering, including stall, spin, or controlled flight into terrain (CFIT).

k. Distractions, task prioritization, loss of situational awareness, or disorientation.

5. What skill standards are expected when demonstrating a normal approach and landing procedure?
(FAA-H-8083-25)

The applicant demonstrates and simultaneously explains how to:

a. Complete the appropriate checklist(s).

b. Make radio calls as appropriate.

c. Ensure the airplane is aligned with the correct/assigned runway or landing surface.

d. Scan the runway or landing surface and adjoining area for traffic and obstructions.

e. Select and aim for a suitable touchdown point considering the wind conditions, landing surface, and obstructions.

f. Establish the recommended approach and landing configuration, airspeed, and trim, and adjust pitch attitude and power as required to maintain a stabilized approach.

g. Maintain manufacturer's published approach airspeed or in its absence not more than 1.3 times the stalling speed or the minimum steady flight speed in the landing configuration (V_{S0}), ±5 knots with gust factor applied.

h. Maintain directional control and appropriate crosswind correction throughout the approach and landing.

i. Make smooth, timely, and correct control application during round out and touchdown.

j. Touch down at a proper pitch attitude, within 200 feet beyond or on the specified point, with no side drift, and with the airplane's longitudinal axis aligned with and over the runway center/landing path.

k. Execute a timely go-around if the approach cannot be made within the tolerances specified above or for any other condition that may result in an unsafe approach or landing.

l. Analyze and correct common errors related to this task.

6. **What common errors can occur when performing a normal approach and landing?** (FAA-H-8083-3)

   a. Failure to complete the landing checklist in a timely manner.

   b. Inadequate wind-drift correction on the base leg.

   c. An overshooting, undershooting, too steep, or too shallow turn onto final approach.

   d. A skidding turn from base leg to final approach as a result of overshooting/inadequate wind-drift correction.

   e. Poor coordination during turn from base to final approach.

   f. Unstable approach.

   g. Failure to adequately compensate for flap extension.

   h. Poor trim technique on final approach.

   i. Attempting to maintain altitude or reach the runway using elevator alone.

   j. Focusing too close to the airplane, resulting in a too high round out.

   k. Focusing too far from the airplane, resulting in a too low round out.

   l. Touching down prior to attaining proper landing attitude.

   m. Failure to hold sufficient back-elevator pressure after touchdown.

   n. Excessive braking after touchdown.

   o. Loss of aircraft control during touchdown and rollout.

C. Soft-Field Takeoff and Climb

1. **What is the purpose of the soft-field takeoff and climb procedure?** (FAA-H-8083-3)

   It is used when operating an airplane off of an unimproved surface such as grass, soft sand, mud, snow, rough terrain, etc.

2. **Why is it important that a learner be familiar with the soft-field takeoff and climb procedure?** (FAA-H-8083-3)

   This procedure requires the use of operational techniques for getting the airplane airborne as quickly as possible. Soft surfaces such as tall grass, soft sand, mud, snow, etc., usually retard the airplane's acceleration during the takeoff roll so much that adequate takeoff speed might not be attained with normal techniques. It is also useful when operating an airplane from a rough field where it is advisable to get the airplane off the ground as soon as possible to avoid damaging the landing gear.

3. **Explain the steps for performing a soft-field takeoff and climb procedure.** (FAA-H-8083-3)

   a. Wing flaps should be lowered prior to starting the takeoff roll (if recommended by the manufacturer).

   b. Taxi the airplane at as fast a speed as possible, consistent with safety and surface conditions. Avoid making sharp turns, using brakes, and any other action that might bog the airplane down.

   c. Keep the airplane in continuous motion with sufficient power while lining up for the takeoff roll.

   d. As the airplane is aligned, apply power smoothly to maximum allowable power.

   e. As the airplane accelerates, apply enough elevator back pressure to reduce the weight supported by the nose wheel.

   f. Maintain a nose-high attitude throughout the takeoff run sufficient to relieve the main gear of progressively more and more weight. This will minimize drag caused by surface irregularities or adhesion.

   g. As the airplane becomes airborne, lower pitch attitude slightly to gain additional airspeed while in ground effect.

   h. Accelerate to V_X with obstacle or V_Y without obstacle before leaving ground effect.

   i. Continue climb at V_X or V_Y as appropriate.

   j. Retract the wing flaps and/or landing gear when clear of obstacles.

4. Identify the hazards that a learner should consider when performing a soft-field takeoff and climb procedure. (FAA-S-ACS-25)

a. Selection of runway based on pilot capability, airplane performance and limitations, available distance, and wind.

b. Effects of crosswind.

c. Effects of wind shear.

d. Effects of tailwind.

e. Effects of wake turbulence.

f. Effects of takeoff surface/condition.

g. Abnormal operations, including planning for:
   • Rejected takeoff.
   • Potential engine failure in takeoff/climb phase of flight.

h. Collision hazards.

i. Low-altitude maneuvering, including stall, spin, or controlled flight into terrain (CFIT).

j. Distractions, task prioritization, loss of situational awareness, or disorientation.

5. What skill standards are expected when demonstrating a soft-field takeoff and climb procedure? (FAA-H-8083-25)

The applicant demonstrates and simultaneously explains how to:

a. Complete the appropriate checklist(s).

b. Make radio calls as appropriate.

c. Verify assigned/correct runway.

d. Determine wind direction with or without visible wind direction indicators.

e. Position the flight controls for the existing wind, if applicable.

f. Clear the area, maintain necessary flight control inputs, and taxi into takeoff position and align the airplane on the runway centerline without stopping, while advancing the throttle smoothly to takeoff power.

g. Confirm takeoff power and proper engine and flight instrument indications.

h. Establish and maintain a pitch attitude that transfers the weight of the airplane from the wheels to the wings as rapidly as possible.

i. Lift off at the lowest possible airspeed and remain in ground effect while accelerating to V_X or V_Y, as appropriate.

j. Establish a pitch attitude for V_X or V_Y, as appropriate, and maintain selected airspeed ±5 knots during the climb.

k. Configure the airplane after a positive rate of climb has been verified or in accordance with airplane manufacturer's instructions.

l. Maintain V_X or V_Y, as appropriate, ±5 knots to a safe maneuvering altitude.

m. Maintain directional control and proper wind-drift correction throughout takeoff and climb.

n. Comply with noise abatement procedures, as applicable.

o. Analyze and correct common errors related to this task.

6. What common errors can occur when performing a soft-field takeoff and climb procedure? (FAA-H-8083-3)

a. Failure to review AFM/POH and performance charts prior to takeoff.

b. Failure to adequately clear the area.

c. Insufficient back-elevator pressure during initial takeoff roll, resulting in inadequate AOA.

d. Failure to cross-check engine instruments for indications of proper operation after applying power.

e. Poor directional control.

f. Climbing too high after liftoff and not leveling off low enough to maintain ground effect attitude.

g. Abrupt and/or excessive elevator control while attempting to level off and accelerate after liftoff.

h. Allowing the airplane to mush or settle, resulting in an inadvertent touchdown after liftoff.

i. Attempting to climb out of ground effect area before attaining sufficient climb speed.

j. Failure to anticipate an increase in pitch attitude as the airplane climbs our of ground effect.

D. Soft-Field Approach and Landing

1. What is a soft-field approach and landing procedure? (FAA-H-8083-3)

When landing on rough fields or those with soft surfaces such as snow, sand, mud, or tall grass, the pilot must control the airplane so that the wings support the weight of the airplane as long as is practical in order to minimize drag and stresses imposed on the landing gear by the surface. The approach for the soft-field landing is similar to the normal approach used for operating into long, firm landing areas, the major difference being that during the soft-field landing, the airplane is held 1 to 2 feet off the surface as long as possible to dissipate the forward speed enough so the wheels touch down gently at minimum speed.

2. What is the objective for practicing soft-field approaches and landings? (FAA-H-8083-3)

Operations into and out of airports with paved runways will not always be possible. Soft-field approach and landing techniques are used when normal approach and landing procedures will not be effective or particularly safe.

3. How is a soft-field approach and landing performed? (FAA-H-8083-3)

a. Establish a normal traffic pattern.

b. At midfield, on downwind, complete a pre-landing checklist.

c. Abeam the touchdown point on downwind, reduce power.

d. Maintain altitude and level pitch attitude momentarily to dissipate airspeed.

e. Retrim aircraft to establish airspeed within flap operating range (white arc).

f. Lower flaps to 10°.

g. Establish initial approach airspeed ($1.4 \times V_{S0}$); retrim if necessary.

h. At an approximate 45° point from the landing threshold (30° point for a short field with obstacle), clear for traffic and turn base.

i. Extend flaps and retrim if necessary to maintain approach airspeed; apply wind-drift correction.

j. Lead turn to final to roll out on runway extended centerline.

k. Extend full flaps on final.

l. Simultaneously adjust power and pitch attitude as necessary to control rate of descent and obtain an airspeed of $1.3 \times V_{S0}$.

m. Touch down at the lowest possible airspeed with the airplane in a nose-high pitch attitude.

n. After the main wheels touch the surface, hold sufficient back elevator pressure to keep the nose wheel off the ground until it can no longer aerodynamically be held off the field surface.

o. Gently lower the nose wheel to the surface.

p. A slight addition of power during and immediately after the touchdown will aid in easing the nose wheel down.

q. Avoid the use of brakes.

r. Increase power, as necessary, to keep the airplane moving and prevent it from becoming stuck in the surface.

4. Identify the hazards that a learner should consider when performing a soft-field approach and landing procedure. (FAA-S-ACS-25)

a. Selection of runway based on pilot capability, airplane performance and limitations, available distance, and wind.

b. Effects of crosswind.

c. Effects of wind shear.

d. Effects of tailwind.

e. Effects of wake turbulence.

f. Effects of landing surface/condition.

g. Rejected landing and go-around.

h. Land and hold short operations (LAHSO).

i. Collision hazards.

j. Low-altitude maneuvering, including stall, spin, or controlled flight into terrain (CFIT).

k. Distractions, task prioritization, loss of situational awareness, or disorientation.

5. What skill standards are expected when demonstrating a soft-field approach and landing? (FAA-S-ACS-25)

The applicant demonstrates and simultaneously explains how to:

a. Complete the appropriate checklist(s).

b. Make radio calls as appropriate.

c. Ensure the airplane is aligned with the correct/assigned runway.

d. Scan the landing runway and adjoining area for traffic and obstructions.

e. Select and aim for a suitable touchdown point considering the wind conditions, landing surface, and obstructions.

f. Establish the recommended approach and landing configuration, airspeed, and trim, and adjust pitch attitude and power as required to maintain a stabilized approach.

g. Maintain manufacturer's published approach airspeed or in its absence not more than 1.3 times the stalling speed or the minimum steady flight speed in the landing configuration (V_{S0}), ±5 knots with gust factor applied.

h. Maintain directional control and appropriate crosswind correction throughout the approach and landing.

i. Make smooth, timely, and correct control inputs during the round out and touchdown, and, for tricycle gear airplanes, keep the nose wheel off the surface until loss of elevator effectiveness.

j. Touch down at a proper pitch attitude with minimum sink rate, no side drift, and with the airplane's longitudinal axis aligned with the center of the runway.

k. Maintain elevator as recommended by manufacturer during rollout and exit the "soft" area at a speed that would preclude sinking into the surface.

l. Execute a timely go-around if the approach cannot be made within the tolerances specified above or for any other condition that may result in an unsafe approach or landing.

m. Maintain proper position of the flight controls and sufficient speed to taxi while on the soft surface.

n. Analyze and correct common errors related to this task.

6. **What common errors can occur when performing a soft-field approach and landing?** (FAA-H-8083-3)

    a. Excessive descent rate on final approach.

    b. Excessive airspeed on final approach.

    c. Unstable approach.

    d. Round out too high above the runway surface.

    e. Poor power management during round out and touchdown.

    f. Hard touchdown.

    g. Inadequate control of the airplane weight transfer from wings to wheels after touchdown.

    h. Allowing the nose wheel to "fall" to the runway after touchdown rather than controlling its descent.

E. Short-Field Takeoff and Maximum Performance Climb

1. **What is the purpose of a short-field takeoff and maximum performance climb procedure?** (FAA-H-8083-3)

    As the name implies, short-field takeoff procedures are used when an airplane must be operated out of an area with either a short runway or the available takeoff area is restricted by obstructions.

2. **Why is it important that a learner be familiar with this procedure?** (FAA-H-8083-3)

    A takeoff and climb from a field where the takeoff area is short or the available takeoff area is restricted by obstructions requires that the pilot operate the airplane at the limit of its takeoff performance capabilities. The pilot must exercise positive and precise control of the airplane attitude and airspeed so that takeoff and climb performance results in the shortest ground roll and the steepest angle of climb. To takeoff and depart safely, the pilot must be well indoctrinated in the use and effectiveness of best-angle-of-climb speed and best-rate-of-climb speed for the specific airplane flown.

3. **Describe the short-field takeoff and maximum performance climb procedure.** (FAA-H-8083-3)

   a. Set flaps as recommended by manufacturer.

   b. Taxi onto runway using all available runway length.

   c. Momentarily apply brakes (if recommended) while applying maximum allowable power.

   d. Check all engine instruments are in the green and release brakes.

   e. Adjust airplane pitch attitude/angle of attack for minimum drag and maximum acceleration.

   f. Accelerate to recommended liftoff airspeed.

   g. On liftoff, adjust pitch attitude for V_X (best angle) until obstacles cleared or if no obstacles until an altitude of at least 50 feet AGL is obtained.

   h. Retract flaps and gear (if retractable) when well clear of obstacles and best rate-of-climb has been established.

   Note: The pilot should consult and follow the performance section of the AFM/POH to obtain the power setting, flap setting, airspeed, and procedures prescribed by the airplane's manufacturer.

4. **Identify the hazards that a learner should consider when performing a short-field takeoff and maximum performance climb procedure.** (FAA-S-ACS-25)

   a. Selection of runway based on pilot capability, airplane performance and limitations, available distance, and wind.

   b. Effects of crosswind.

   c. Effects of wind shear.

   d. Effects of tailwind.

   e. Effects of wake turbulence.

   f. Effects of takeoff surface/condition.

   g. Abnormal operations, including planning for:
      • Rejected takeoff
      • Potential engine failure in takeoff/climb phase of flight

   h. Collision hazards.

i.   Low-altitude maneuvering, including stall, spin, or controlled flight into terrain (CFIT).

j.   Distractions, task prioritization, loss of situational awareness, or disorientation.

5. What skill standards are expected when demonstrating a short-field takeoff and maximum performance climb? (FAA-S-ACS-25)

The applicant demonstrates and simultaneously explains how to:

a.   Complete the appropriate checklist(s).

b.   Make radio calls as appropriate.

c.   Verify assigned/correct runway.

d.   Determine wind direction with or without visible wind direction indicators.

e.   Position the flight controls for the existing wind, if applicable.

f.   Clear the area, taxi into takeoff position, and align the airplane on the runway centerline utilizing maximum available takeoff area.

g.   Apply brakes while setting engine power to achieve maximum performance.

h.   Confirm takeoff power prior to brake release and verify proper engine and flight instrument indications prior to rotation.

i.   Rotate and lift off at the recommended airspeed and accelerate to the recommended obstacle clearance airspeed or V_X, ±5 knots.

j.   Establish a pitch attitude to maintain the recommended obstacle clearance airspeed or V_X, ±5 knots, until the obstacle is cleared or until the airplane is 50 feet above the surface

k.   Establish a pitch attitude for V_Y and accelerate to V_Y ±5 knots after clearing the obstacle or at 50 feet above ground level (AGL) if simulating an obstacle.

l.   Configure the airplane in accordance with the manufacturer's guidance after a positive rate of climb has been verified.

m.   Maintain V_Y ±5 knots to a safe maneuvering altitude.

(continued)

n. Maintain directional control and proper wind-drift correction throughout takeoff and climb.

o. Comply with noise abatement procedures, as applicable.

p. Analyze and correct common errors related to this task.

6. **What common errors can occur when performing a short-field takeoff and maximum performance climb?** (FAA-H-8083-3)

a. Failure to review AFM/POH and performance charts prior to takeoff.

b. Failure to adequately clear the area.

c. Failure to utilize all available runway/takeoff area.

d. Failure to have the airplane properly trimmed prior to takeoff.

e. Premature liftoff resulting in high drag.

f. Holding the airplane on the ground unnecessarily with excessive forward-elevator pressure.

g. Inadequate rotation resulting in excessive speed after liftoff.

h. Inability to attain/maintain V_X.

i. Fixation on the airspeed indicator during initial climb.

j. Premature retraction of landing gear and/or wing flaps.

F. Short-Field Approach and Landing

1. **Describe a short-field approach and landing procedure.** (FAA-H-8083-3)

The short-field approach and landing is a maximum performance operation that requires the use of procedures and techniques for the approach and landing at fields that have a relatively short landing area or where an approach must be made over obstacles that limit the available landing area. It is one of the most critical of the maximum performance operations, since it requires that the pilot fly the airplane at one of its crucial performance capabilities while close to the ground in order to safely land within confined areas.

2. Why is it important to practice short-field approaches and landings? (FAA-H-8083-3)

To land within a short field or confined area, the pilot must have precise, positive control of the rate of descent and airspeed to produce an approach that will clear any obstacles, result in little or no floating during the roundout, and permit the airplane to be stopped in the shortest possible distance.

3. How is a short-field approach and landing procedure performed? (FAA-H-8083-3)

a. Establish a wider-than-normal pattern so that the airplane can be properly configured and trimmed.

b. At midfield, on downwind, complete a pre-landing checklist.

c. Abeam the touchdown point on downwind, reduce power.

d. Maintain altitude and level pitch attitude momentarily to dissipate airspeed.

e. Retrim aircraft to establish airspeed within flap operating range (white arc).

f. Lower flaps to $10°$.

g. Establish initial approach airspeed ($1.4 \times V_{S0}$); retrim if necessary.

h. At an approximate $45°$ point from the landing threshold ($30°$ point for a short field with obstacle), clear for traffic and turn base.

i. Extend flaps and retrim if necessary to maintain approach airspeed; apply wind-drift correction.

j. Lead turn to final to roll out on runway extended centerline.

k. Extend full flaps on final.

l. Simultaneously adjust power and pitch attitude as necessary to control rate of descent and obtain an airspeed of $1.3 \times V_{S0}$.

m. If landing over a 50-foot obstacle, when clear, adjust pitch attitude slightly to establish rate of descent. Do not reduce power until in ground effect.

n. If landing with no obstacle, adjust descent angle to land just inside of the desired touchdown point.

(continued)

o. After landing, identify and retract flaps, and apply maximum braking and full elevator back pressure.

Note: The procedures for landing on a short field or for landing approaches over obstacles as recommended in the AFM/POH should be used.

4. **Identify the hazards that a learner should consider when performing a short-field approach and landing procedure.** (FAA-S-ACS-25)

a. Selection of runway based on pilot capability, airplane performance and limitations, available distance, and wind.

b. Effects of crosswind.

c. Effects of wind shear.

d. Effects of tailwind.

e. Effects wake turbulence.

f. Effects of landing surface/condition.

g. Rejected landing and go-around.

h. Land and hold short operations (LAHSO).

i. Collision hazards.

j. Low-altitude maneuvering, including stall, spin, or controlled flight into terrain (CFIT).

k. Distractions, task prioritization, loss of situational awareness, or disorientation.

5. **What skill standards are expected when demonstrating a short-field approach and landing procedure?** (FAA-S-ACS-25)

The applicant demonstrates and simultaneously explains how to:

a. Complete the appropriate checklist(s).

b. Make radio calls as appropriate.

c. Ensure the airplane is aligned with the correct/assigned runway.

d. Scan the landing runway and adjoining area for traffic and obstructions.

e. Select and aim for a suitable touchdown point considering the wind conditions, landing surface, and obstructions.

f. Establish the recommended approach and landing configuration, airspeed, and trim, and adjust pitch attitude and power as required to maintain a stabilized approach.

g. Maintain manufacturer's published approach airspeed or in its absence not more than 1.3 times the stalling speed or the minimum steady flight speed in the landing configuration (V_{S0}), ±5 knots with gust factor applied.

h. Maintain directional control and appropriate crosswind correction throughout the approach and landing.

i. Make smooth, timely, and correct control application before, during, and after touchdown.

j. Touch down at a proper pitch attitude within 100 feet beyond or on the specified point, threshold markings, or runway numbers, with no side drift, minimum float, and with the airplane's longitudinal axis aligned with and over the runway centerline.

k. Use manufacturer's recommended procedures for airplane configuration and braking.

l. Execute a timely go-around if the approach cannot be made within the tolerances specified above or for any other condition that may result in an unsafe approach or landing.

m. Analyze and correct common errors related to this task.

6. **What common errors can occur when a learner is performing a short-field approach and landing?** (FAA-H-8083-3)

a. A final approach that necessitates an overly steep approach and high sink rate.

b. Unstable approach.

c. Undue delay in initiating glidepath corrections.

d. Too low an airspeed on final, resulting in inability to flare properly and landing hard.

e. Too high an airspeed, resulting in floating on round out.

f. Prematurely reducing power to idle on round out, resulting in hard landing.

g. Touch down with excessive airspeed.

(continued)

h. Excessive and/or unnecessary braking after touchdown.

i. Failure to maintain directional control.

j. Failure to recognize and abort a poor approach that cannot be completed safely.

G. Slip to a Landing

1. What is a forward slip? (FAA-H-8083-3)

A forward slip is one in which the airplane's direction of motion continues the same as before the slip was begun. The wing on the side toward which the slip is to be made is lowered and, simultaneously, the airplane's nose is yawed in the opposite direction by applying opposite rudder so that the airplane's longitudinal axis is at an angle to its original flight path.

2. What is the purpose of a forward slip to a landing? (FAA-H-8083-3)

The primary purpose of forward slips is to dissipate altitude and increase decent rate without increasing the airplane's speed, particularly in airplanes not equipped with flaps. There are many circumstances requiring the use of forward slips, such as in a landing approach over obstacles and in making forced landings, when it is always wise to allow an extra margin of altitude for safety in the original estimate of the approach.

3. How is a forward slip to a landing performed? (FAA-H-8083-3)

a. Reduce power to idle.

b. The wing on the side toward which the slip is to be made should be lowered by use of ailerons.

c. Simultaneously, the airplane's nose must be yawed in the opposite direction by applying opposite rudder so that the airplane's longitudinal axis is at an angle to its original flight path.

d. The degree to which the nose is yawed in the opposite direction from the bank should be such that the original ground track is maintained.

e. The pitch should be adjusted as necessary to maintain the appropriate airspeed.

f. Discontinuing the slip is accomplished by leveling the wings and simultaneously releasing rudder pressure while readjusting pitch attitude to the normal glide attitude.

4. What should a learner be aware of regarding instrument error in a forward slip? (FAA-H-8083-3)

Because of the location of the pitot tube and static vents, airspeed indicators in some airplanes may have considerable error when the airplane is in a slip. The pilot must be aware of this possibility and recognize a properly performed slip by the attitude of the airplane, the sound of the airflow, and the feel of the flight controls. Forward slips with the wing flaps extended should not be done in airplanes wherein the manufacturer's operating instructions prohibit such operation.

5. What is a sideslip? (FAA-H-8083-3)

A sideslip is a slip in which the airplane's longitudinal axis remains parallel to the original flight path. It is entered by lowering a wing and applying just enough opposite rudder to prevent a turn. The horizontal component of wing lift forces the airplane to move somewhat sideways toward the low wing. The amount of slip, and therefore the rate of sideward movement, is determined by the bank angle.

6. What is the objective of learning sideslips? (FAA-H-8083-3)

Learning and becoming proficient in sideslips provides a pilot with an effective procedure for counteracting wind drift during a crosswind landing. If done correctly, it prevents an airplane from touching down in a sideward motion, imposing damaging side loads to the landing gear and possible loss of directional control.

7. How is a sideslip to a landing performed? (FAA-H-8083-3)

a. Align the airplane's heading with the centerline of the runway.

b. Note the rate and direction of drift and promptly apply wind-drift correction by lowering the upwind wing into the wind; the amount the wing must be lowered depends on the rate of drift.

(continued)

   c. As the wing is lowered, simultaneously apply sufficient opposite rudder to prevent a turn and keep the airplane's longitudinal axis aligned with the runway.

   d. Drift is controlled with aileron and heading with rudder.

   e. As crosswind diminishes or increases, the amount of aileron and rudder must be adjusted accordingly.

   f. As airspeed decreases for round-out and landing, gradually increase deflection of rudder and ailerons to maintain correct amount of wind-drift correction.

   g. During landing round-out, keep the upwind wing down sufficient to control drift and rudder sufficient to align the longitudinal axis with the runway.

   h. Touchdown should be made on the upwind main wheel.

   i. As forward speed decreases, the weight of the airplane will cause the downwind main wheel to settle to the runway.

   j. As the airplane comes to a stop, maintain full aileron control into the wind.

8. Identify the hazards that a learner should consider when performing a slip to a landing. (FAA-S-ACS-25)

   a. Selection of runway/landing surface, approach path, and touchdown area based on pilot capability, aircraft performance and limitations, available distance, and wind.

   b. Effects of crosswind.

   c. Effects of wind shear.

   d. Effects of tailwind.

   e. Effects of wake turbulence.

   f. Effects of landing surface/condition.

   g. Rejected landing and go-around.

   h. Land and hold short operations (LAHSO).

   i. Collision hazards.

   j. Low-altitude maneuvering, including stall, spin, or controlled flight into terrain (CFIT).

   k. Distractions, task prioritization, loss of situational awareness, or disorientation.

l. Forward slip operations, including fuel flowage, tail stalls with flaps, and airspeed control.

m. Surface contact with the airplane's longitudinal axis misaligned.

n. Unstable approach.

9. **What skill standards are expected when demonstrating a slip to a landing?** (FAA-S-ACS-25)

The applicant demonstrates and simultaneously explains how to:

a. Complete the appropriate checklist(s).

b. Make radio calls as appropriate.

c. Plan and follow a flight path to the selected landing area considering altitude, wind, terrain, and obstructions.

d. Select the most suitable touchdown point based on wind, landing surface, obstructions, and airplane limitations.

e. Position airplane on downwind leg, parallel to landing runway or selected landing surface.

f. Configure the airplane correctly.

g. As necessary, correlate crosswind with direction of slip and transition to sideslip as appropriate before touchdown.

h. Touch down at a proper pitch attitude, within 400 feet beyond or on the specified point, with no side drift, and with the airplane's longitudinal axis aligned with and over the runway center/landing path.

i. Maintain a ground track aligned with the runway center/landing path.

j. Analyze and correct common errors related to this task.

10. **What common errors can occur when a learner is performing a slip to a landing?** (FAA-H-8083-3)

a. Incorrect pitch adjustments that result in poor airspeed control.

b. Reacting to erroneous airspeed indications.

c. Using excess power while trying to lose altitude.

d. A slip in the same direction as any crosswind.

e. Poor glidepath control.

(continued)

f. Late transition to a sideslip during landing with crosswinds.

g. Landing without the longitudinal axis parallel to the runway.

h. Landing off the centerline.

Exam Tip: Be capable of explaining the difference between a sideslip and a forward slip. What are the aerodynamics of each? Provide examples of when you would use a sideslip or a forward slip.

H. Go-Around/Rejected Landing

1. Describe a go-around/rejected landing procedure. (FAA-H-8083-3)

A go-around is a procedure used when it may be advisable for safety reasons to discontinue the landing approach and make another approach under more favorable conditions. A go-around involves procedures including establishing full power, drag reduction, and traffic pattern procedures.

2. Explain why a learner should not wait to make the decision to reject a landing and go around. (FAA-H-8083-3)

The earlier a dangerous situation is recognized and the sooner the landing is rejected and the go-around started, the safer the procedure will be. Extremely low base to final turns, overshot or low final approaches, the unexpected appearance of hazards on the runway, wake turbulence from a preceding airplane, or overtaking another airplane on the approach are hazardous conditions that would demand a go-around.

3. How is the go-around executed? (FAA-H-8083-3)

a. Make the decision to go-around as early as possible.

b. Simultaneously increase pitch attitude to stop the descent and apply takeoff power.

c. If the aircraft has been trimmed for the approach, expect to hold considerable forward elevator pressure to maintain a safe climb attitude.

d. After the descent has been stopped, the landing flaps may be partially retracted or placed in the takeoff position, as recommended by the manufacturer.

e. Roughly retrim the aircraft to relieve control pressure.

f. Establish a best angle (V_X) or best rate (V_Y) of climb as appropriate.

g. Retract the landing gear when a positive rate of climb has been established.

h. Retract remaining flaps.

i. Retrim aircraft.

4. Identify the hazards that a learner should consider when performing a go-around procedure. (FAA-S-ACS-25)

a. Delayed recognition of the need for a go-around/rejected landing.

b. Delayed performance of a go-around at low altitude.

c. Power application.

d. Configuring the airplane.

e. Collision hazards.

f. Low-altitude maneuvering, including stall, spin, or controlled flight into terrain (CFIT).

g. Distractions, task prioritization, loss of situational awareness, or disorientation.

h. Managing a go-around/rejected landing after accepting a LAHSO clearance.

i. Runway incursion.

5. What skill standards are expected when demonstrating a go-around procedure? (FAA-S-ACS-25)

The applicant demonstrates and simultaneously explains how to:

a. Complete the appropriate checklist(s).

b. Make radio calls as appropriate.

c. Make a timely decision to discontinue the approach to landing.

d. Apply takeoff power immediately and transition to climb pitch attitude for V_X or V_Y as appropriate ±5 knots.

e. Configure the airplane after a positive rate of climb has been verified or in accordance with airplane manufacturer's instructions.

(continued)

   f. Maneuver to the side of the runway/landing area when necessary to clear and avoid conflicting traffic.

   g. Maintain V_Y ±5 knots to a safe maneuvering altitude.

   h. Maintain directional control and proper wind-drift correction throughout the climb.

   i. Analyze and correct common errors related to this task.

6. What common errors can occur when a learner is performing a go-around? (FAA-H-8083-3)

   a. Failure to recognize a condition that warrants a rejected landing.

   b. Indecision.

   c. Delay in initiating a go-around.

   d. Failure to apply maximum allowable power in a timely manner.

   e. Abrupt power application.

   f. Improper pitch attitude.

   g. Failure to configure the airplane appropriately.

   h. Attempting to climb out of ground effect prematurely.

   i. Failure to adequately compensate for torque/P-factor.

   j. Loss of aircraft control.

I. Power-Off 180° Accuracy Approach and Landing

1. What is a power-off 180° accuracy approach and landing? (FAA-H-8083-3)

Power-off accuracy approaches and landings involve gliding to a touchdown at a given point (or within a specified distance beyond that point) while using a specific pattern and with the engine idling.

2. What is the objective of learning a power-off 180° accuracy approach and landing? (FAA-H-8083-3)

The objective is to instill in the pilot the judgment and procedures necessary for accurately flying the airplane, without power, to a safe landing.

3. **Explain how to perform a power-off 180° accuracy approach and landing.** (FAA-H-8083-3)

   a. Fly the airplane on a downwind heading parallel to the landing runway.

   b. When opposite the desired landing spot, close the throttle.

   c. Maintain altitude while decelerating to manufacturer's recommended glide speed or 1.4 V_{S0}. The point where throttle is closed is the downwind key position.

   d. Turn from downwind leg to base leg with medium or slightly steeper bank. The degree of bank and amount of this initial turn depends on the glide angle of the airplane and the velocity/direction of the wind.

   e. Position base leg as needed for the altitude or wind condition. Position base leg to conserve or dissipate altitude so as to reach the desired landing spot.

   f. After turn to base leg is complete, airspeed is allowed to decrease to the normal base-leg speed.

   g. On the base leg, airspeed, wind-drift correction, and altitude are maintained while proceeding to 45° key position.

   h. At 45° key position, intended landing spot appears to be at a 45° angle from the airplane's nose.

   i. The strength and direction of the wind determines the amount of crab necessary to hold the desired ground track on base leg.

   j. At the 45° key position, advance propeller control (if equipped) to the full increase RPM position, and maintain altitude until the airspeed decreases to recommended glide speed. In the absence of a recommended speed, use 1.4 V_{S0}.

   k. When airspeed is attained, the nose should be lowered to maintain the glide speed, and the controls retrimmed.

   l. The base-to-final turn should be planned so that rolling out of the turn will result in the airplane aligned with the runway centerline.

   m. On final, lower wing flaps and adjust pitch attitude as necessary to establish the proper descent angle and airspeed (1.3 V_{S0}), then retrim the controls.

   n. Slight adjustments in pitch attitude or flaps setting may be necessary to control glide angle and airspeed.

o. A crab or sideslip can be used to maintain desired flight path. A forward slip may be used momentarily to steepen descent without changing airspeed.

p. Full flaps should be delayed until it is clear that adding them will not cause the landing to be short of the point.

q. After the final-approach glide has been established, full attention is then given to making a good, safe landing rather than concentrating on the selected landing spot.

Note: The base-leg position and the flap setting already determined the probability of landing on the spot. In any event, it is better to execute a good landing 200 feet from the spot than to make a poor landing precisely on the spot.

4. Identify the hazards that a learner should consider when performing a power-off 180° accuracy approach and landing? (FAA-S-ACS-25)

a. Selection of runway/landing surface, approach path, and touchdown area based on pilot capability, aircraft performance and limitations, available distance, and wind.

b. Effects of crosswind.

c. Effects of wind shear.

d. Effects of tailwind.

e. Effects of wake turbulence.

f. Effects of landing surface/condition.

g. Rejected landing and go-around.

h. Land and hold short operations (LAHSO).

i. Collision hazards.

j. Low-altitude maneuvering, including stall, spin, or controlled flight into terrain (CFIT).

k. Distractions, task prioritization, loss of situational awareness, or disorientation.

l. Forward slip operations, including fuel flowage, tail stalls with flaps, and airspeed control.

5. **What skill standards are expected when demonstrating a power-off 180° approach and landing?** (FAA-S-ACS-25)

The applicant demonstrates and simultaneously explains how to:

a. Complete the appropriate checklist(s).

b. Make radio calls as appropriate.

c. Plan and follow a flight path to the selected landing area considering altitude, wind, terrain, and obstructions.

d. Select the most suitable touchdown point based on wind, landing surface, obstructions, and aircraft limitations.

e. Position airplane on downwind leg, parallel to landing runway.

f. Correctly configure the airplane.

g. As necessary, correlate crosswind with direction of forward slip and transition to sideslip before touchdown.

h. Touch down at a proper pitch attitude, within 200 feet beyond or on the specified point with no side drift and with the airplane's longitudinal axis aligned with and over the runway centerline or landing path, as applicable.

i. Analyze and correct common errors related to this task.

6. **What common errors can occur to a learner performing a power-off 180° accuracy approach and landing?** (FAA-H-8083-3)

a. Downwind leg is too far from the runway/landing area.

b. Overextension of downwind leg resulting from a tailwind.

c. Inadequate compensation for wind drift on base leg.

d. Skidding turns in an effort to increase gliding distance.

e. Failure to lower landing gear in retractable gear airplanes.

f. Attempting to "stretch" the glide during an undershoot.

g. Premature flap extension/landing gear extension.

h. Use of throttle to increase the glide instead of merely clearing the engine.

i. Forcing the airplane onto the runway in order to avoid overshooting the designated landing spot.

Fundamentals
of Flight

7

A. Straight-and-Level Flight

1. What is straight-and-level flight? (FAA-H-8083-3)

Flight in which a constant heading and altitude are maintained. It is accomplished by making immediate corrections for deviations in direction and altitude from unintentional slight turns, descents, and climbs.

2. What is the objective in learning straight-and-level flight maneuvers? (FAA-H-8083-3)

To learn the proper use of the controls for maneuvering the airplane, to attain the proper attitude in relation to the horizon by use of inside and outside references (the integrated flight instruction method), and to emphasize the importance of dividing attention and constantly checking all reference points.

3. How is straight-and-level flight achieved? (FAA-H-8083-3)

The pitch attitude for level flight (constant altitude) is usually obtained by selecting some portion of the airplane's nose as a reference point, and then keeping that point in a fixed position relative to the horizon. That position should be cross-checked occasionally against the altimeter and attitude indicator to determine whether or not the pitch attitude is correct.

To achieve straight flight (laterally level flight) the pilot should select two or more outside visual reference points directly ahead of the airplane (such as fields, towns, lakes) to form points along an imaginary line and keep the airplane's nose headed along that line. While using these references, an occasional check of the heading indicator and attitude indicator should be made to determine that the airplane is actually maintaining flight in a constant direction.

4. Identify the hazards that a learner should consider when performing straight-and-level flight. (FAA-S-ACS-25)

a. Distractions, task prioritization, loss of situational awareness, or disorientation.

b. Collision hazards.

5. What are the skill standards when demonstrating straight-and-level flight? (FAA-S-ACS-25)

The applicant demonstrates and simultaneously explains how to:

a. Establish and maintain straight-and-level flight.

b. Analyze and correct common errors related to this task.

6. What common errors can occur when a learner performs straight-and-level flight? (FAA-H-8083-3)

a. Attempting to use improper pitch and bank references during flight.

b. Forgetting the location of preselected reference points on subsequent flights.

c. Attempting to establish or correct airplane attitude using flight instruments rather than the natural horizon.

d. "Chasing" the flight instruments rather than adhering to the principles of attitude flying.

e. Mechanically pushing or pulling on the flight controls rather than exerting accurate and smooth pressure.

f. Not scanning outside the aircraft for other traffic and weather and terrain influences.

g. Using a tight palm grip on the flight controls, resulting in a desensitized feeling of the hand and fingers.

h. Over-controlling the airplane.

i. Habitually flying with one wing low or maintaining directional control using only the rudder control.

j. Failure to make timely and measured control inputs after a deviation from straight-and-level.

k. Inadequate attention to sensory inputs in developing feel for reference points on the airplane to establish attitude.

B. Level Turns

1. Describe a level turn. (FAA-H-8083-3)

A turn is a basic flight maneuver used to change or return to a desired heading. It involves close coordination of all three flight controls—aileron, rudder, and elevator.

2. Discuss the importance of the level turn as a basic maneuver. (FAA-H-8083-3)

Since turns are a part of almost every other flight maneuver, it is important that the pilot thoroughly understand the factors involved and learn to perform them well.

3. What are the steps involved in performing a level turn? (FAA-H-8083-3)

a. Perform the appropriate clearing procedure before beginning the turn.

b. Roll into the banked attitude by coordinated use of aileron and rudder in the direction of turn.

c. When the desired angle of bank is obtained, neutralize the ailerons and rudder to maintain bank.

d. Apply back pressure in the turn to compensate for the loss of vertical lift and to maintain altitude.

e. Roll out of the turn by applying coordinated aileron and rudder pressure in the opposite direction of the turn until level attitude is reached. As the angle of bank is decreased, the elevator should be released smoothly as necessary to maintain altitude.

4. Identify the hazards that a pilot should consider when performing a level turn. (FAA-S-ACS-25)

a. Distractions, task prioritization, loss of situational awareness, or disorientation.

b. Collision hazards.

5. What are the skill standards when demonstrating a level turn? (FAA-S-ACS-25)

The applicant demonstrates and simultaneously explains how to:

a. Establish, maintain, and roll out of a level turn.

b. Analyze and correct common errors related to this task.

6. What common errors can occur when a learner is performing level turns? (FAA-H-8083-3)

a. Failure to adequately clear in the direction of turn for aircraft traffic.

b. Gaining or losing altitude during the turn.

c. Not holding the desired bank angle constant.

d. Attempting to execute the turn solely by instrument reference.

e. Leaning away from the direction of the turn while seated.

f. Insufficient feel for the airplane as evidenced by the inability to detect slips or skids without flight instruments.

g. Attempting to maintain a constant bank angle by referencing only the airplane's nose.

h. Making skidding, flat turns to avoid banking the airplane.

i. Holding excessive rudder in the direction of the turn.

j. Gaining proficiency in turns in only one direction.

k. Failure to coordinate the controls.

C. Straight Climbs and Climbing Turns

1. What are straight climbs and climbing turns? (FAA-H-8083-3)

A straight climb is one in which the airplane gains altitude while traveling straight ahead. It is a basic flight maneuver in which an increase in both the pitch attitude and power result in a gain in altitude. Climbing turns are those in which the airplane gains altitude while turning.

2. What is the objective in learning straight climbs and climbing turns? (FAA-H-8083-3)

The objective of this maneuver, as with the other basic flight maneuvers, is to learn the proper use of the controls for maneuvering the airplane, to attain the proper attitude in relation to the horizon by use of inside and outside references, and to emphasize the importance of dividing attention and constantly checking all reference points.

3. Describe how to achieve the straight climb/climbing turn maneuver. (FAA-H-8083-3)

a. Perform the appropriate clearing turn before beginning a climbing turn.

b. Establish a climb by applying back pressure on the elevator to increase pitch attitude. Simultaneously establish the desired bank angle if performing a climbing turn.

c. Apply full power and establish a pitch attitude for the climbing airspeed (V_Y).

d. Cross-check the airspeed indicator with the position of the airplane's nose in relation to the horizon as well as the attitude indicator.

e. Trim the aircraft for this attitude/airspeed.

f. Use right rudder to correct for torque effect.

g. Maintain a constant heading by cross-checking visual references as well as instrument references. Maintain wings level while cross-checking heading indicator, attitude indicator, and turn coordinator. If performing a climbing turn, maintain the desired bank angle by cross-checking visual references as well as instrument references.

4. Identify the hazards that a learner should consider when performing a straight climb or climbing turn. (FAA-S-ACS-25)

a. Distractions, task prioritization, loss of situational awareness, or disorientation.

b. Collision hazards.

5. What are the skill standards when demonstrating straight climbs and climbing turns? (FAA-S-ACS-25)

The applicant demonstrates and simultaneously explains how to:

a. Establish, maintain, and level off from climbs and climbing turns.

b. Analyze and correct common errors related to this task.

6. What are examples of common errors that can occur when a learner performs straight climbs/climbing turns? (FAA-H-8083-3)

a. Attempting to establish climb pitch attitude by primarily referencing the airspeed indicator and chasing the airspeed.

b. Applying elevator pressure too aggressively, resulting in an excessive climb angle.

c. Inadequate or inappropriate rudder pressure during climbing turns.

d. Allowing the airplane to yaw during climbs usually due to inadequate right rudder pressure.

e. Fixation on the airplane's nose during straight climbs, resulting in climbing with one wing low.

f. Initiating a climbing turn without coordinated use of flight controls, resulting in no turn and a climb with one wing low.

g. Improper coordination resulting in a slip that counteracts the rate of climb, resulting in little or no altitude gain.

h. Inability to keep pitch and bank attitude constant during climbing turns.

i. Attempting to exceed the airplane's climb capability.

j. Using excessive forward elevator pressure during level-off, resulting in a loss of altitude or excessive low G-force.

D. Straight Descents and Descending Turns

1. Describe the straight descent and descending turn maneuvers. (FAA-H-8083-3)

A straight descent or descending turn is a basic maneuver in which the airplane changes its flight path from level to an inclined plane in a controlled descent with or without engine power. The three types of descents are partial power descents, descents at minimum airspeed, and glides without power.

2. Explain the objective in learning straight descents/descending turns and why these maneuvers are especially important. (FAA-H-8083-3)

Learning and becoming proficient in descents and descending turns is important because these maneuvers have a specific operational purpose, including enroute descents, descents for a normal landing, forced landing procedures, and descents used for clearing obstacles on approach to a runway. It is necessary that they be performed more subconsciously than other maneuvers because, most of the time during their execution, the pilot will be giving full attention to details other than the mechanics of performing the maneuver. Since a majority of descents and descending turns are performed relatively close to the ground, accuracy of their execution and the formation of proper procedures and habits are of special importance.

3. How is a straight descent or descending turn maneuver performed? (FAA-H-8083-3)

a. Perform the appropriate clearing turn before beginning a descending turn.

b. Apply carburetor heat (if applicable) and reduce power to the appropriate setting.

c. Maintain a level pitch attitude momentarily to reduce airspeed to the desired airspeed for descent.

d. Establish the desired bank angle if performing a descending turn.

e. Allow the pitch attitude to decrease as necessary to maintain desired descent airspeed.

f. When airspeed is stabilized, the aircraft should be re-trimmed.

Chapter 7 **Fundamentals of Flight**

4. **Identify the hazards that a learner should consider when performing straight descents and descending turns.** (FAA-S-ACS-25)

   a. Distractions, task prioritization, loss of situational awareness, or disorientation.

   b. Collision hazards.

5. **What are the skill standards when demonstrating straight descents and descending turns?** (FAA-S-ACS-25)

   The applicant demonstrates and simultaneously explains how to:

   a. Establish, maintain, and level off from straight descents and descending turns.

   b. Analyze and correct common errors related to this task.

6. **What common errors can occur when a learner performs straight descents and descending turns?** (FAA-H-8083-3)

   a. Failure to adequately clear for aircraft traffic in the turn direction or descent.

   b. Inadequate elevator back pressure during glide entry, resulting in an overly steep glide.

   c. Failure to slow the airplane to approximate glide speed prior to lowering pitch attitude.

   d. Attempting to establish/maintain a normal glide solely by reference to flight instruments.

   e. Inability to sense changes in airspeed through sound and feel.

   f. Inability to stabilize the glide (chasing the airspeed indicator).

   g. Attempting to stretch the glide by applying back-elevator pressure.

   h. Skidding or slipping during gliding turns and not recognizing the difference in rudder forces with and without power.

   i. Failure to lower pitch attitude during gliding turn entry, resulting in a decrease in airspeed.

   j. Excessive rudder pressure during recovery from gliding turns.

   k. Inadequate pitch control during recovery from a straight glide.

   l. Cross-controlling during gliding turns near the ground.

   m. Failure to maintain constant bank angle during gliding turns.

Performance and Ground Reference Maneuvers

8

A. Steep Turns

1. Describe a steep turn. (FAA-H-8083-3)

Steep turns consist of single to multiple 360° to 720° turns, in either or both directions, using a bank angle between 45° and 60°. When performing steep turns, pilots will be exposed to higher load factors, the airplane's inherent overbanking tendency, the loss of vertical component of lift when the wings are steeply banked, the need for substantial pitch control pressures, and the need for additional power to maintain altitude and airspeed during the turn.

2. What is the objective of practicing a steep turn? (FAA-H-8083-3)

The objective of the steep turn is to develop a pilot's skill in flight control smoothness and coordination, an awareness of the airplane's orientation to outside references, division of attention between flight control application, and the constant need to scan for hazards.

3. Explain how to perform a steep turn maneuver. (FAA-H-8083-3)

a. Establish a specific heading (and an outside reference) and altitude.

b. Perform clearing turns.

c. Establish manufacturer's recommended entry speed or the design maneuvering speed.

d. Roll into a 45° to 60° bank while maintaining altitude with necessary back pressure.

e. Complete a left and right 360° heading change. (It may be necessary to add additional power to maintain airspeed above a stall.)

f. Lead rollout to heading by one half the bank angle.

g. Use horizon and glare shield/cowling to maintain pitch attitude.

h. If loss of altitude occurs, decrease bank, add back pressure to regain altitude, and establish higher pitch attitude.

i. If gain of altitude occurs, increase bank (maximum 55°) and decrease pitch attitude and/or power.

4. **Identify the hazards that a learner should consider when performing steep turns.** (FAA-S-ACS-25)

   a. Division of attention between aircraft control and orientation.

   b. Collision hazards.

   c. Low-altitude maneuvering, including stall, spin, or controlled flight into terrain (CFIT).

   d. Distractions, task prioritization, loss of situational awareness, or disorientation.

   e. Uncoordinated flight.

5. **What are the skill standards expected when demonstrating steep turns?** (FAA-S-ACS-25)

   The applicant demonstrates and simultaneously explains how to:

   a. Clear the area.

   b. Establish the manufacturer's recommended airspeed; or if one is not available, an airspeed not to exceed maneuvering speed (V_A).

   c. Roll into a coordinated 360° steep turn with approximately a 50° bank.

   d. Perform the task in the opposite direction.

   e. Maintain the entry altitude ±100 feet, airspeed ±10 knots, bank ±5°, and roll out on the entry heading ±10°.

   f. Analyze and correct common errors related to this task.

6. **Describe the common errors made by learners when performing steep turns?** (FAA-H-8083-3)

   a. Not clearing the area.

   b. Inadequate pitch control on entry or rollout.

   c. Gaining or losing altitude.

   d. Failure to maintain constant bank angle.

   e. Poor flight control coordination.

   f. Ineffective use of trim.

   g. Ineffective use of power.

   h. Inadequate airspeed control.

(continued)

    i. Becoming disoriented.

    j. Performing by reference to the flight instruments rather than visual references.

    k. Failure to scan for other traffic during the maneuver.

    l. Attempting to start recovery prematurely.

    m. Failure to stop the turn on the designated heading.

7. Explain the relationship of bank angle, load factor, and stalling speed when performing a steep turn. (FAA-H-8083-3)

Stall speed increases with the square root of the load factor. A steeper bank angle will result in a higher load factor and a higher stall speed.

8. Explain the overbanking tendency encountered when performing a steep turn. (FAA-H-8083-3)

During a steep turn, the wing on the outside of the turn travels a longer path than the inside wing, yet both complete their respective paths in the same unit of time. Therefore, the outside wing travels at a faster airspeed than the inside wing and, as a result, it develops more lift. This creates an overbanking tendency that must be controlled by the use of opposite aileron when the desired bank angle is reached. Because the outboard wing is developing more lift, it also produces more drag. The drag causes a slight slip during steep turns that must be corrected by use of the rudder.

9. Explain how torque effect is a factor in right and left steep turns. (FAA-H-8083-3)

Torque effect (left-turning tendency) requires more rudder when rolling into a right turn.

10. Explain the relationship between airspeed, bank, and rate and radius of turn. (FAA-H-8083-3)

The rate of turn at any given true airspeed depends on the horizontal lift component. The horizontal lift component varies in proportion to the amount of bank. Therefore, the rate of turn at a given airspeed increases as the angle of bank is increased. On the other hand, when a turn is made at a higher airspeed at a given bank angle, the inertia is greater and the horizontal lift component required for the turn is greater, causing the turning rate to become slower. Therefore, at a given angle of bank, a higher airspeed makes the radius of turn larger because the airplane turns at a slower rate.

B. Steep Spiral

1. What is a steep spiral? (FAA-H-8083-3)

A steep spiral is a gliding turn wherein the pilot maintains a constant radius around a surface-based reference point—similar to the turns around a point maneuver, but in this case the airplane is rapidly descending. The maneuver consists of the completion of at least three 360° turns, and it should begin at sufficient altitude such that the maneuver concludes no lower than 1,500 feet AGL.

2. What is the objective of a steep spiral? (FAA-H-8083-3)

The objective of the steep spiral is to provide a flight maneuver for rapidly dissipating substantial amounts of altitude while remaining over a selected spot. Its most practical application is for dissipating altitude while remaining over a selected spot in preparation for landing, especially for emergency forced landings.

3. Explain how to perform a steep spiral. (FAA-H-8083-3)

a. Select an altitude that will allow completion of at least three 360° turns and concludes at no lower than 1,500 feet AGL.

b. Choose a reference point and perform clearing turns.

c. Close throttle, apply carb heat if equipped, and establish gliding speed.

d. Once gliding speed is established, pitch should be lowered and the airplane rolled to the desired bank angle as the reference point is reached.

e. The pilot should consider the distance from the reference point, since that establishes the turning radius.

f. The steepest bank should not exceed 60°.

g. The gliding spiral should be a turn of constant radius while maintaining the airplane's position relative to the reference.

(continued)

h. Correct for wind drift by steepening the bank on downwind headings and shallowing the bank on upwind headings.

i. During descent, continually correct for any changes in wind direction and velocity to maintain a constant radius around reference point

j. Maintain airspeed, ±10 knots, roll out toward an object or specified heading, ±10°, and complete the maneuver no lower than 1,500 feet AGL.

4. **Identify the hazards that a learner should consider when performing a steep spiral.** (FAA-S-ACS-25)

a. Division of attention between aircraft control and orientation.

b. Collision hazards.

c. Low-altitude maneuvering, including stall, spin, or controlled flight into terrain (CFIT).

d. Distractions, task prioritization, loss of situational awareness, or disorientation.

e. Uncoordinated flight.

f. Effects of wind.

g. Airframe or airspeed limitations.

5. **What are the skill standards expected when demonstrating a steep spiral?** (FAA-S-ACS-25)

The applicant demonstrates and simultaneously explains how to:

a. Clear the area.

b. Select an altitude sufficient to continue through a series of at least three, 360° turns.

c. Establish and maintain a steep spiral, not to exceed 60° angle of bank, to maintain a constant radius about a suitable ground reference point.

d. Apply wind-drift correction to track a constant-radius circle around selected reference point with bank not to exceed 60° at steepest point in turn.

e. Divide attention between airplane control, traffic avoidance, and the ground track while maintaining coordinated flight.

   f. Maintain the specified airspeed, ±10 knots, roll out toward an object or specified heading, ±10°, and complete the maneuver no lower than 1,500 feet above ground level (AGL).

   g. Analyze and correct common errors related to this task.

6. What common errors can occur when a learner is performing a steep spiral? (FAA-H-8083-3)

   a. Not clearing the area.

   b. Inadequate pitch control on entry or rollout.

   c. Not correcting the bank angle to compensate for wind.

   d. Poor flight control coordination.

   e. Ineffective use of trim.

   f. Inadequate airspeed control.

   g. Becoming disoriented.

   h. Performing by reference to the flight instruments rather than visual references.

   i. Not scanning for other traffic during the maneuver.

   j. Not completing the turn on the designated heading or reference.

C. Chandelles

1. What is a chandelle? (FAA-H-8083-3)

A chandelle is a maximum performance climbing turn that begins from approximately straight-and-level flight and ends at the completion of 180° of turn in a wings-level, nose-high attitude at the minimum controllable airspeed.

2. What is the objective of the chandelle maneuver? (FAA-H-8083-3)

To develop the pilot's coordination, orientation, planning, feel for maximum-performance flight, and positive control techniques at varying airspeeds and attitudes. Maximum flight performance of the airplane is obtained. The airplane should gain the most amount of altitude possible for a given degree of bank and power setting without stalling.

3. Explain how to perform a chandelle. (FAA-H-8083-3)

a. Establish a specific heading and altitude (no lower than 1,500 feet AGL).

b. Perform clearing turns.

c. Pick a prominent reference point and plan to perform the maneuver into the wind to prevent drift from the training area.

d. Establish a coordinated 30°-bank turn and plan on maintaining this bank angle for the first 90° of turn.

e. Apply takeoff or climb power and begin a climbing turn by smoothly applying back pressure to increase pitch attitude at a constant rate and to attain the highest pitch attitude as 90° of turn is completed.

f. When the turn has progressed 90° from the original heading, begin rolling out of the bank at a constant rate while maintaining a constant pitch attitude.

g. As the wings are being leveled at the completion of 180° of turn, the pitch attitude should be held momentarily while the airplane is at minimum controllable speed.

Note: First 90°—constant bank, changing pitch
Second 90°—constant pitch, changing bank

4. Identify the hazards that a learner should consider when performing a chandelle. (FAA-S-ACS-25)

a. Division of attention between aircraft control and orientation.

b. Collision hazards.

c. Low-altitude maneuvering, including stall, spin, or controlled flight into terrain (CFIT).

d. Distractions, task prioritization, loss of situational awareness, or disorientation.

e. Uncoordinated flight.

f. Energy management.

g. Rate and radius of turn with confined-area operations.

5. **What are the skill standards expected when demonstrating a chandelle?** (FAA-S-ACS-25)

The applicant demonstrates and simultaneously explains how to:

a. Clear the area.

b. Select an altitude that allows the maneuver to be performed no lower than 1,500 feet above ground level (AGL).

c. Establish the appropriate entry configuration, power, and airspeed.

d. Establish the angle of bank at approximately 30°.

e. Simultaneously apply power and pitch to maintain a smooth, coordinated, climbing turn, in either direction, to the 90° point, with a constant bank and continuously decreasing airspeed.

f. Begin a coordinated constant-rate rollout from the 90° point to the 180° point, maintaining power and a constant pitch attitude.

g. Complete rollout at the 180° point, ±10°, just above a stall airspeed, and maintaining that airspeed momentarily avoiding a stall.

h. Resume a straight-and-level flight with minimum loss of altitude.

i. Analyze and correct common errors related to this task.

6. **What common errors can a learner make when performing chandelles?** (FAA-H-8083-3)

a. Not clearing the area.

b. Initial bank is too shallow, resulting in a stall.

c. Initial bank is too steep, resulting in failure to gain maximum performance.

d. Allowing the bank angle to increase after initial establishment.

e. Not starting the recovery at the 90° point in the turn.

f. Allowing the pitch attitude to increase as the bank is rolled out during the second 90° of turn.

g. Leveling the wings prior to the 180° point being reached.

h. Pitch attitude is low on recovery, resulting in airspeed well above stall speed.

(continued)

    i. Application of flight control pressures is not smooth.

    j. Poor flight control coordination.

    k. Stalling at any point during the maneuver.

    l. Execution of a steep turn instead of a climbing maneuver.

    m. Not scanning for other traffic during the maneuver.

    n. Performing by reference to the instruments rather than visual references.

D. Lazy Eights

1. What is a lazy eight? (FAA-H-8083-3)

A lazy eight consists of two 180° turns in opposite directions, while making a climb and a descent in a symmetrical pattern during each of the turns.

2. Explain the objective for learning and practicing lazy eights. (FAA-H-8083-3)

The objective of the lazy eight is to develop the pilot's feel for varying control forces and the ability to plan and remain oriented while maneuvering the airplane with positive, accurate control. Constantly changing control pressures are needed due to changing combinations of climbing and descending turns at varying airspeeds. It is often used to develop and demonstrate a pilot's mastery of the airplane in maximum performance flight situations.

3. Describe the steps involved in performing a lazy eight maneuver. (FAA-H-8083-3)

    a. Establish a specific heading and altitude (no lower than 1,500 feet AGL).

    b. Perform clearing turns.

    c. Select prominent reference points (45°, 90°, and 135°) on the horizon.

    d. Establish maneuvering speed or manufacturer's recommended speed.

    e. Start the maneuver from level flight with a gradual climbing turn toward reference points.

    f. At the 45° point—maximum pitch-up attitude; bank 15° (approximately).

g. At the 90° point—bank approximately 30°; minimum airspeed; maximum altitude; level pitch attitude.

h. At the 135° point—maximum pitch down; bank 15° (approximately).

i. At the 180° point—level flight; entry airspeed; altitude same as entry altitude.

4. Identify the hazards that a learner should consider when performing lazy eights. (FAA-S-ACS-25)

a. Division of attention between aircraft control and orientation.

b. Collision hazards.

c. Low-altitude maneuvering, including stall, spin, or controlled flight into terrain (CFIT).

d. Distractions, task prioritization, loss of situational awareness, or disorientation.

e. Uncoordinated flight.

f. Energy management.

g. Accelerated stalls.

5. What are the skill standards expected when demonstrating lazy eights? (FAA-S-ACS-25)

The applicant demonstrates and simultaneously explains how to:

a. Clear the area.

b. Select an altitude that allows the maneuver to be performed no lower than 1,500 feet above ground level (AGL).

c. Establish the recommended entry configuration, power, and airspeed.

d. Maintain coordinated flight throughout the maneuver.

e. Complete the maneuver in accordance with the following:

- Approximately 30° bank at the steepest point.
- Constant change of pitch and roll rate and airspeed.
- Altitude at the 180° point ±100 feet from entry altitude.
- Airspeed at the 180° point ±10 knots from entry airspeed.
- Heading at the 180° point, ±10°.

(continued)

    f. Continue the maneuver through the number of symmetrical loops specified, then resume straight-and level flight.

    g. Analyze and correct common errors related to this task.

6. What common errors can occur when a learner performs lazy eights? (FAA-H-8083-3)

    a. Not clearing the area.

    b. Maneuver is not symmetrical across each 180°.

    c. Inadequate or improper selection or use of 45°, 90°, and 135° references.

    d. Ineffective planning.

    e. Gain or loss of altitude at each 180° point.

    f. Poor control at the top of each climb segment, resulting in the pitch rapidly falling through the horizon.

    g. Airspeed or bank angle standards not met.

    h. Control roughness.

    i. Poor flight control coordination.

    j. Stalling at any point during the maneuver.

    k. Execution of a steep turn instead of a climbing maneuver.

    l. Not scanning for other traffic during the maneuver.

    m. Performing by reference to the flight instruments rather than visual references.

E. Ground Reference Maneuvers

Rectangular Course

1. Describe a rectangular course maneuver. (FAA-H-8083-3)

This a practice maneuver in which the ground track of the airplane is equidistant from all sides of a selected rectangular area on the ground. While performing the rectangular course maneuver, the pilot should maintain a constant altitude, airspeed, and distance from the ground references.

2. What are the objectives of practicing a rectangular course? (FAA-H-8083-3)

The maneuver assists the pilot with developing and maintaining proficiency in the following:

a. Maintaining a specific relationship between the airplane and the ground.

b. Dividing attention between the flight path, ground-based references, manipulating the flight controls, and scanning for outside hazards and instrument indications.

c. Adjusting the bank angle during turns to correct for ground speed changes in order to maintain constant-radius turns.

d. Rolling out from a turn with the required wind correction angle to compensate for any drift cause by the wind.

e. Establishing and correcting the wind correction angle in order to maintain the track over the ground.

f. Preparing the pilot for the airport traffic pattern and subsequent landing pattern practice.

3. Describe the procedure for performing a rectangular course. (FAA-H-8083-3)

a. Establish an altitude 600 to 1,000 feet AGL (500 feet above obstructions).

b. Perform clearing turns.

c. Select a square or rectangular field, the sides of which are approximately 1 mile in length.

d. Enter a left or right pattern, 45° to the downwind leg, at an appropriate distance (one-half to three-fourths of a mile) from field boundaries. Maneuver as necessary to maintain a uniform distance from field boundaries.

e. The bank in each of the turns should be adjusted to compensate for wind drift.

Note:

- Upwind to crosswind: Shallow bank, increasing to medium, and less than 90° of turn.
- Crosswind to downwind: Increasing to steepest bank necessary and more than 90° of turn.

(continued)

- Downwind to crosswind: Steepest bank necessary, decreasing to medium, and more than 90° of turn.
- Crosswind to upwind: Medium bank, decreasing to shallow, and less than a 90° turn.

4. Identify the hazards that a learner should consider when performing a rectangular course. (FAA-S-ACS-25)

a. Division of attention between aircraft control and orientation.

b. Collision hazards.

c. Low-altitude maneuvering, including stall, spin, or controlled flight into terrain (CFIT).

d. Distractions, task prioritization, loss of situational awareness, or disorientation.

e. Uncoordinated flight.

5. What are the skill standards expected when demonstrating a rectangular course? (FAA-S-ACS-25)

The applicant demonstrates and simultaneously explains how to:

a. Clear the area.

b. Select a suitable ground reference area.

c. Plan the maneuver: Enter a left or right pattern, 600 to 1,000 feet above ground level (AGL) at an appropriate distance from the selected reference area, 45° to the downwind leg.

d. Apply adequate wind-drift correction during straight and turning flight to maintain a constant ground track around a rectangular reference area.

e. Divide attention between airplane control, traffic avoidance, and the ground track while maintaining coordinated flight.

f. Maintain altitude ±100 feet; maintain airspeed ±10 knots.

g. Analyze and correct common errors related to this task.

6. What common errors can occur when a learner is performing a rectangular course? (FAA-H-8083-3)

a. Failure to adequately clear the surrounding area for safety hazards, initially and throughout the maneuver.

b. Failure to establish a constant, level altitude prior to entering the maneuver.

c. Failure to maintain altitude during the maneuver.

d. Failure to properly assess wind direction.

e. Failure to establish the appropriate wind correction angle.

f. Failure to apply coordinated aileron and rudder pressure, resulting in slips and skids.

g. Failure to manipulate the flight controls in a smooth and continuous manner.

h. Failure to properly divide attention between airplane control and orientation with ground references.

i. Failure to execute turns with accurate timing.

S-Turns

1. Describe an S-turn ground reference maneuver. (FAA-H-8083-3)

An S-turn is a ground reference maneuver in which the airplane's ground track resembles two opposite but equal half-circles on each side of a selected ground-based straight-line reference. This ground reference maneuver presents a practical application for the correction of wind during a turn.

2. What are the objectives of practicing S-turns across a road? (FAA-H-8083-3)

a. Maintaining a specific relationship between the airplane and the ground.

b. Dividing attention between the flight path, ground-based references, manipulating the flight controls, and scanning for outside hazards and instrument indications.

c. Adjusting the bank angle during turns to correct for ground speed changes in order to maintain a constant-radius turn—steeper bank angles for higher ground speeds, shallow bank angles for slower ground speeds.

d. Rolling out from a turn with the required wind correction angle to compensate for any drift cause by the wind.

e. Establishing and correcting the wind correction angle in order to maintain the track over the ground.

(continued)

    f. Developing the ability to compensate for drift in quickly changing orientations.

    g. Arriving at specific points on required headings.

3. Describe how S-turns across a road are performed. (FAA-H-8083-3)

    a. Establish an altitude 600 to 1,000 feet AGL (500 feet above obstructions).

    b. Perform clearing turns.

    c. Select a straight ground reference line or road that lies 90° to the direction of the wind.

    d. Approach the road from the upwind side on a downwind heading and when directly over the road, roll into the first turn, which should be the steepest.

    e. As the airplane gradually turns back into the wind, begin to shallow the bank angle so as to arrive over the road as the wings roll level.

    f. When directly over the road, roll into the next turn, using a shallow bank initially (upwind), then gradually increasing bank to the steepest (downwind).

4. Identify the hazards that a learner should consider when performing S-turns across a road. (FAA-S-ACS-25)

    a. Division of attention between aircraft control and orientation.

    b. Collision hazards.

    c. Low-altitude maneuvering, including stall, spin, or controlled flight into terrain (CFIT).

    d. Distractions, task prioritization, loss of situational awareness, or disorientation.

    e. Uncoordinated flight.

5. What are the skill standards expected when demonstrating S-turns? (FAA-S-ACS-25)

The applicant demonstrates and simultaneously explains how to:

    a. Clear the area.

    b. Select a suitable straight-line ground reference.

   c. Plan the maneuver: Enter perpendicular to the selected reference line, 600 to 1,000 feet AGL at an appropriate distance from the selected reference area.

   d. Apply adequate wind-drift correction to maintain a constant-radius turn on each side of the selected reference line.

   e. Reverse the turn directly over the selected reference line.

   f. Divide attention between airplane control, traffic avoidance, and the ground track while maintaining coordinated flight.

   g. Maintain altitude ±100 feet; maintain airspeed ±10 knots.

   h. Analyze and correct common errors related to this task.

6. What common errors can occur when a learner is performing S-turns? (FAA-H-8083-3)

   a. Failure to adequately clear surrounding area for safety hazards, initially and throughout the maneuver.

   b. Failure to establish a constant, level altitude prior to entering the maneuver.

   c. Failure to maintain altitude during the maneuver.

   d. Failure to properly assess wind direction.

   e. Failure to properly execute constant-radius turns.

   f. Failure to manipulate the flight controls in a smooth and continuous manner when transitioning into turns.

   g. Failure to establish the appropriate wind correction angle.

   h. Failure to apply coordinated aileron and rudder pressure, resulting in slips or skids.

Turns Around a Point

1. Describe the turns around a point maneuver.
(FAA-H-8083-3)

The maneuver is a 360° constant-radius turn around a single ground-based reference point. Turns around a point are a logical extension of both the rectangular course and S-turns across a road. The principles are the same in any turning ground reference maneuver—higher ground speeds require steeper banks and slower ground speeds require shallower banks.

2. What are the objectives when practicing turns around a point? (FAA-H-8083-3)

a. Maintaining a specific relationship between the airplane and the ground.

b. Dividing attention between the flight path, ground-based references, manipulating of the flight controls, and scanning for outside hazards and instrument indications.

c. Adjusting the bank angle during turns to correct for ground speed changes in order to maintain a constant-radius turn; steeper bank angles for higher ground speeds, shallow bank angles for slower ground speeds.

d. Improving competency in managing the quickly changing bank angles.

e. Establishing and adjusting the wind correction angle in order to maintain the track over the ground.

f. Developing the ability to compensate for drift in quickly changing orientations.

g. Developing further awareness that the radius of a turn is correlated to the bank angle.

3. How are turns around a point performed? (FAA-H-8083-3)

a. Establish an altitude 600 to 1,000 feet AGL (500 feet above obstructions).

b. Perform clearing turns.

c. Select a prominent reference point.

d. Enter the maneuver downwind at a distance equal to the desired radius of turn.

e. Roll into a bank when abeam reference. If any significant wind is present, this will be the steepest bank in the maneuver (highest ground speed).

f. Decrease the bank angle as the aircraft turns into the wind (low ground speed).

Note:

• Downwind turn: Steepest bank.

• Downwind to crosswind: Gradually decrease to medium bank.

- Crosswind to upwind: Gradually decrease from medium to shallow bank.
- Upwind to crosswind: Gradually increase from shallow to medium bank.
- Crosswind to downwind: Increase from medium to steep bank.

4. Identify the hazards that a learner should consider when performing turns around a point. (FAA-S-ACS-25)

a. Division of attention between aircraft control and orientation.

b. Collision hazards.

c. Low-altitude maneuvering, including stall, spin, or controlled flight into terrain (CFIT).

d. Distractions, task prioritization, loss of situational awareness, or disorientation.

e. Uncoordinated flight.

5. What are the skill standards expected when demonstrating turns around a point? (FAA-S-ACS-25)

The applicant demonstrates and simultaneously explains how to:

a. Clear the area.

b. Select a suitable ground reference point.

c. Plan the maneuver: Enter at an appropriate distance from the reference point, 600 to 1,000 feet AGL at an appropriate distance from the selected reference area.

d. Apply adequate wind-drift correction during straight and turning flight to maintain a constant-radius turn on each side of the selected point.

e. Complete turns in either direction, as specified by the evaluator.

f. Divide attention between airplane control, traffic avoidance, and the ground track while maintaining coordinated flight.

g. Maintain altitude ±100 feet; maintain airspeed ±10 knots.

h. Analyze and correct common errors related to this task.

6. **What common errors can occur when a learner is performing turns around a point?** (FAA-H-8083-3)

   a. Failure to adequately clear the surrounding area for safety hazards, initially and throughout the maneuver.

   b. Failure to establish a constant, level altitude prior to entering the maneuver.

   c. Failure to maintain altitude during the maneuver.

   d. Failure to properly assess wind direction.

   e. Failure to properly execute constant-radius turns.

   f. Failure to manipulate the flight controls in a smooth and continuous manner.

   g. Failure to establish the appropriate wind correction angle.

   h. Failure to apply coordinated aileron and rudder pressure, resulting in slips or skids.

F. Eights on Pylons

1. **Describe eights-on-pylons.** (FAA-H-8083-3)

   Eights-on-pylons is an advanced ground reference maneuver in which you fly the airplane in circular paths, alternately left and right, in the form of a figure 8 around two selected points or pylons on the ground. No attempt is made to maintain a uniform distance from the pylon. Instead, the airplane is flown at such an altitude and airspeed that a line parallel to the airplane's lateral axis, and extending from the pilot's eye, appears to pivot on each of the pylons.

2. **What is the objective of the eights-on-pylons maneuver?** (FAA-H-8083-3)

   To develop the ability to maneuver the airplane accurately while dividing attention between the flight path and maintaining a pivotal position on selected pylons on the ground.

3. Describe the procedure for performing eights-on-pylons.
(FAA-H-8083-3)

a. Establish an approximate pivotal altitude.

b. Perform clearing turns.

c. Select two points on the ground along a line that lies 90° to the wind. The points should be prominent and adequately spaced to provide planning for the turns (approximately 3 to 5 seconds straight-and-level flight).

d. Begin the maneuver by flying diagonally crosswind between the pylons to a point downwind from the first pylon so that the first turn can be made into the wind.

e. As the airplane approaches the pylon, a turn should be started by lowering the wing to place the pilot's line of sight reference on the pylon.

f. As the airplane heads into the wind, the ground speed decreases, and consequently, the pivotal altitude is lower and the airplane must descend to hold the reference line on the pylon.

g. As the turn progresses on the upwind side of the pylon, the wind becomes more of a crosswind and drifts the airplane closer to the pylon. Since a constant distance is not required, no correction should be applied.

h. With the airplane drifting closer to the pylon, the angle of bank must be increased to hold the reference line on the pylon.

i. If the reference line appears to move ahead of the pylon, the pilot should increase altitude.

j. As the airplane turns toward a downwind heading, the rollout from the turn should be started to allow the airplane to proceed diagonally to a point on the downwind side of the second pylon.

k. The rollout must be completed in the proper crab angle to correct for wind drift so that the airplane will arrive at a point downwind from the second pylon the same distance it was from the first pylon.

l. Upon reaching the second pylon, a turn is started in the opposite direction by lowering the upwind wing to again place the pilot's line of sight reference on the pylon.

4. **Identify the hazards that a pilot should consider when performing eights-on-pylons.** (FAA-S-ACS-25)

   a. Division of attention between aircraft control and orientation.

   b. Collision hazards.

   c. Low-altitude maneuvering, including stall, spin, or controlled flight into terrain (CFIT).

   d. Distractions, task prioritization, loss of situational awareness, or disorientation.

   e. Uncoordinated flight.

   f. Energy management.

   g. Emergency landing considerations.

5. **What are the skill standards expected when demonstrating eights-on-pylons?** (FAA-S-ACS-25)

   The applicant demonstrates and simultaneously explains how to:

   a. Clear the area.

   b. Determine the approximate pivotal altitude.

   c. Select suitable pylons that permit straight-and-level flight between the pylons.

   d. Enter the maneuver in the correct direction and position using an appropriate altitude and airspeed.

   e. Establish the correct bank angle for the conditions, not to exceed 40°.

   f. Apply smooth and continuous corrections so that the line-of-sight reference line remains on the pylon.

   g. Divide attention between accurate, coordinated airplane control and outside visual references.

   h. Maintain pylon position using appropriate pivotal altitude, avoiding slips and skids.

   i. Analyze and correct common errors related to this task.

6. **What common errors can occur when a learner is performing eights-on-pylons?** (FAA-H-8083-3)

   a. Failure to adequately clear the surrounding area for safety hazards, initially and throughout the maneuver.

   b. Skidding or slipping in turns (whether trying to hold the pylon with rudder or not).

   c. Excessive gain or loss of altitude.

   d. Poor choice of pylons.

   e. Not entering the pylon turns into the wind.

   f. Failure to assume a heading when flying between pylons that will compensate sufficiently for drift.

   g. Failure to time the bank so that the turn entry is completed with the pylon in position.

   h. Abrupt control usage.

   i. Inability to select pivotal altitude.

Slow Flight, Stalls, and Spins

9

A. Maneuvering During Slow Flight

1. Describe the maneuvering during slow flight procedure. (FAA-H-8083-3)

Slow flight is flight at an airspeed where any further increase in angle of attack, increase in load factor, or reduction in power will result in a stall warning (e.g., aircraft buffet, stall horn, etc.). Slow flight includes two main elements:

- Slowing to, maneuvering at, and recovering from an airspeed at which the airplane is still capable of maintaining controlled flight without activating the stall warning—5 to 10 knots above the 1G stall speed is a good target.

- Performing slow flight in configurations appropriate to takeoffs, climbs, descents, approaches to landing, and go-arounds.

2. What is the objective in learning how to maneuver an airplane during slow flight? (FAA-H-8083-3)

The objective of maneuvering in slow flight is to develop the pilot's ability to fly at low speeds and high angles of attack (AOAs). Through practice, the pilot becomes familiar with the feel, sound, and visual cues of flight in this regime, where there is a degraded response to control inputs and where it is more difficult to maintain a selected altitude. It is essential that pilots:

a. Understand the aerodynamics associated with slow flight in various aircraft configurations and attitudes;

b. Recognize airplane cues in these flight conditions;

c. Smoothly manage coordinated flight control inputs while maneuvering without a stall warning; and

d. Make prompt appropriate correction should a stall warning occur.

3. Explain the procedure for maneuvering during slow flight. (FAA-H-8083-3)

a. Establish a specific heading and altitude (recovery by 1,500 feet AGL).

b. Perform clearing turns.

c. Perform a pre-maneuver checklist (GUMPS).

d. Apply carburetor heat (if applicable) and reduce power from cruise to slow the airplane to gear and/or flap operating range.

e. Extend gear (if retractable); extend flaps and adjust pitch attitude to maintain altitude. Retrim aircraft.

f. As the airspeed approaches target slow flight speed, which is an airspeed just above the stall warning in the desired configuration (i.e., approximately 5–10 knots above the stall speed for that flight condition), additional power will be needed to maintain altitude.

g. During these changing flight conditions, trim the airplane to compensate for changes in control pressures.

h. Continually cross-check the heading indicator, altimeter, airspeed indicator, and vertical speed indicator, as well as outside references, to ensure accurate control is maintained.

i. Right rudder should be applied to correct for left-turning tendencies.

j. For maneuvering in slow flight, establish straight-ahead climbs and medium-banked (approximately 20-degree) climbing turns, and straight-ahead power-off gliding descents and descending turns.

Recovery:

a. Add power.

b. As airspeed and lift increase, apply forward control pressure to reduce the AOA and maintain altitude.

c. Maintain coordinated flight, level the wings as necessary, and return to the desired flight path.

d. As airspeed increases, clean up the airplane by retracting flaps and landing gear, if they were extended, and adjust trim as needed.

e. Anticipate the changes to the AOA as the landing gear and flaps are retracted to avoid a stall.

4. Identify the hazards that a learner should consider when performing maneuvering during slow flight. (FAA-S-ACS-25)

a. Inadvertent slow flight and flight with a stall warning, which could lead to loss of control.

b. Range and limitations of stall warning indicators (e.g., aircraft buffet, stall horn, etc.).

c. Uncoordinated flight.

d. Effect of environmental elements on airplane performance (e.g., turbulence, microbursts, and high density altitude).

e. Collision hazards.

f. Distractions, task prioritization, loss of situational awareness, or disorientation.

5. What are the skill standards expected when demonstrating maneuvering during slow flight? (FAA-S-ACS-25)

The applicant demonstrates and simultaneously explains how to:

a. Clear the area.

b. Select an entry altitude that allows the task to be completed no lower than 1,500 feet AGL.

c. Establish and maintain an airspeed at which any further increase in angle of attack, increase in load factor, or reduction in power would result in a stall warning (e.g., aircraft buffet, stall horn, etc.).

d. Accomplish coordinated straight-and-level flight, turns, climbs, and descents with the aircraft configured as specified by the evaluator without a stall warning (e.g., aircraft buffet, stall horn, etc.).

e. Maintain the specified altitude, ±50 feet; specified heading, ±10°; airspeed, +5/−0 knots; and specified angle of bank, ±5°.

f. Analyze and correct common errors related to this task.

Note: Evaluation criteria for this task should recognize that environmental factors (e.g., turbulence) may result in a momentary activation of stall warning indicators such as the stall horn. If the applicant recognizes the stall warning indication and promptly makes an appropriate correction, a momentary activation does not constitute unsatisfactory performance on this task. As with other tasks, unsatisfactory performance would arise from an applicant's continual deviation from the standard, lack of correction, and/or lack of recognition.

6. **What common errors can occur when a learner is performing the maneuvering during slow flight task?** (FAA-H-8083-3)

   a. Failure to adequately clear the area.

   b. Inadequate back-elevator pressure as power is reduced, resulting in altitude loss.

   c. Excessive back-elevator pressure as power is reduced, resulting in a climb followed by rapid reduction in airspeed.

   d. Insufficient right rudder to compensate for left yaw.

   e. Fixation on the flight instruments.

   f. Failure to anticipate changes in AOA as flaps are extended or retracted.

   g. Inadequate power management.

   h. Inability to adequately divide attention between airplane control and orientation.

   i. Failure to properly trim the airplane.

   j. Failure to respond to a stall warning.

B. Demonstration of Flight Characteristics at Various Configurations and Airspeeds

1. **Describe the demonstration of flight characteristics at various configurations and airspeeds task.** (FAA-H-8083-3)

   This task demonstrates the flight characteristics, controllability, and power required of an airplane operated in various configurations and at different airspeeds. It develops the pilot's sense of feel and ability to determine characteristic control responses of an airplane when operated at airspeeds between cruise airspeed and critically slow airspeeds near the critical angle of attack. The pilot learns to slow the airplane smoothly and promptly from maneuvering speed to approach speed to minimum controllable airspeed (MCA), noting power settings required, in both the clean and the landing configurations of the airplane.

2. **What is the objective of the demonstration of flight characteristics at various configurations and airspeeds task?** (FAA-S-ACS-25)

    To determine the applicant understands flight characteristics and power required at different airspeeds and configurations appropriate to the make and model of airplane flown, can apply that knowledge, manage associated risks, demonstrate appropriate skills, and provide effective instruction.

3. **Explain how to demonstrate the flight characteristics at various configurations and airspeeds task.**
    (FAA-S-ACS-25)

    a. Conduct and explain the procedure, manage the associated risk, and fly the airplane, while maintaining altitude ±100 feet, airspeed +5/−0 knots, heading ±10°, and specified bank angle ±5°, as appropriate.

    b. Select an entry altitude that allows the task to be completed no lower than 1,500 feet AGL.

    c. Clear the area.

    Clean configuration demonstration:

    a. Establish and maintain design/operating maneuvering speed appropriate to the airplane's weight while describing pitch, power, and trim inputs to maintain altitude and airspeed, then;

    b. With gear and flaps retracted (as applicable), slow the airplane to, and maintain, best glide speed (or as specified by evaluator), noting the power setting required, then;

    c. Continue to slow the airplane to, and maintain, an airspeed at which any further increase in angle of attack, increase in load factor, or reduction in power would result in an immediate stall, and maintain that airspeed in level flight, noting the airspeed and power setting required, while;

    d. Verbally acknowledging stall warning indications, then;

e. Without changing the power setting, lower the pitch attitude and accelerate to a faster airspeed until reestablishing the airplane in level flight, noting the new airspeed and amount of altitude lost, then;

f. Return to normal cruise flight at the altitude and heading specified by the evaluator.

Landing configuration demonstration:

a. Establish and maintain design/operating maneuvering speed appropriate to the airplane's weight while describing pitch, power, and trim inputs to maintain altitude and airspeed, then;

b. Slow the airplane to, and maintain, the appropriate limiting airspeeds and fully extend the landing gear and flaps (as appropriate), then;

c. With gear and flaps fully extended (as applicable), slow the airplane to, and maintain, reference landing speed (or as specified by the evaluator), noting the power setting required, then;

d. With gear and flaps fully extended, continue to slow the airplane to, and maintain, an airspeed at which any further increase in angle of attack, increase in load factor, or reduction in power would result in an immediate stall, and maintain that airspeed in level flight, noting the airspeed and power setting required, while;

e. Verbally acknowledging stall warning indications, then;

f. Without changing the power setting, lower the pitch attitude and accelerate to a faster airspeed until re-establishing the airplane in level flight, noting the new airspeed and amount of altitude lost, then;

g. Return to normal cruise flight at the altitude and heading specified by the evaluator, and;

h. Analyze and correct common errors related to this task.

4. **Identify the hazards that should be considered when performing the demonstration of flight characteristics at various configurations and airspeeds task.** (FAA-S-ACS-25)

   a. Lack of familiarity with airplane airspeed limitations and interpretation of the airspeed indicator.

   b. Exceeding airspeed limitations.

   c. Flight characteristics in the region of reversed command and the potential for loss of control.

   d. Inadvertent exceedance of the critical angle of attack.

   e. Range, limitations, and operational characteristics of airspeed indicators and stall warning indicators (e.g., airplane buffet, stall horn, etc.).

   f. Unacknowledged stall warning indications.

   g. Effects of environmental elements on airplane performance and controllability (e.g., turbulence, microbursts, and high density altitude).

   h. Collision hazards.

   i. Maneuvering at critically slow airspeeds.

5. **What common errors can occur when demonstrating flight characteristics at various configurations and airspeeds?** (FAA-H-8083-3)

   a. Failure to adequately clear the area.

   b. Inadequate back-elevator pressure as power is reduced, resulting in altitude loss.

   c. Excessive back-elevator pressure as power is reduced, resulting in a climb followed by rapid reduction in airspeed.

   d. Insufficient right rudder to compensate for left yaw.

   e. Fixation on the flight instruments.

   f. Failure to anticipate changes in AOA as flaps are extended or retracted.

   g. Inadequate power management.

   h. Inability to adequately divide attention between airplane control and orientation.

i. Failure to properly trim the airplane.

j. Failure to respond to a stall warning.

6. Explain the power required at various airspeeds between cruise airspeed and critically slow airspeeds near the critical angle of attack. (FAA-H-8083-25)

When flying above the minimum drag speed (L/D$_{MAX}$), more power is required to fly even faster. When flying at speeds below L/D$_{MAX}$, more power is required to fly even slower. Since slow flight will be performed well below L/D$_{MAX}$, the pilot should be aware that large power inputs or a reduction in AOA will be required to prevent the aircraft from decelerating.

7. When flying in the region of reversed command, with speed decreasing and the AOA increasing towards the critical AOA, how will small changes in pitch control affect drag and airspeed? (FAA-H-8083-25)

As the AOA increases toward the critical AOA and the airplane's speed continues to decrease, small changes in the pitch control result in disproportionally large changes in induced drag and therefore changes in airspeed. As a result, pitch becomes a more effective control of airspeed when flying below L/D$_{MAX}$, and power is an effective control of the altitude profile (i.e., climbs, descents, or level flight).

8. Explain the basic difference between flight in the region of normal command and flight in the region of reversed command. (FAA-H-8083-25, FAA-H-8083-15)

Flight in the region of normal command means that a higher airspeed requires a higher power setting and a lower airspeed requires a lower power setting to hold a constant altitude. This region exists at speeds higher than the minimum drag point primarily as a result of parasite drag.

Flight in the region of reversed command means that a higher airspeed requires a lower power setting and a lower airspeed requires a higher power setting in order to maintain altitude. This region exists at speeds slower than the minimum drag point (L/D$_{MAX}$ on the thrust-required curve) and is primarily due to induced drag.

9. **Explain the minimum power required speed and its role in differentiating the region of normal command and the region of reversed command on the power-required curve.** (FAA-H-8083-25)

The lowest point on the power-required curve represents the speed at which the lowest brake horsepower sustains level flight. This is termed the *maximum endurance airspeed* (minimum power required speed). Flight speeds below the speed for maximum endurance (lowest point on the power curve) require higher power settings with a decrease in airspeed. Since the need to increase the required power setting with decreased speed is contrary to the normal command of flight, the regime of flight speeds between the speed for minimum required power setting and the stall speed (or minimum control speed) is termed the *region of reversed command*. In the region of reversed command, a decrease in airspeed must be accompanied by an increased power setting in order to maintain steady flight.

10. **Explain the airspeeds specific to the airplane for various operations, how to identify them on the airspeed indicator (if applicable), and their significance on an airplane's performance.** (FAA-H-8083-25)

V_{S0}—The calibrated power-off stalling speed or the minimum steady flight speed at which the aircraft is controllable in the landing configuration. Identified on the airspeed indicator by the lower limit of the white arc.

V_{S1}—The calibrated power-off stalling speed or the minimum steady flight speed at which the aircraft is controllable in a specified configuration. Identified on the airspeed indicator by the lower limit of the green arc.

V_{LE}—The maximum speed at which the aircraft can be safely flown with the landing gear extended. This is a problem involving stability and controllability.

V_{LO}—The maximum speed at which the landing gear can be safely extended or retracted. This is a problem involving the air loads imposed on the operating mechanism during extension or retraction of the gear.

V_{FE}—The highest speed permissible with the wing flaps in a prescribed extended position. This is because of the air loads imposed on the structure of the flaps. Identified on the airspeed indicator by the upper limit of the white arc.

V_A—The calibrated design maneuvering airspeed. This is the maximum speed at which the limit load can be imposed (either by gusts or full deflection of the control surfaces) without causing structural damage. Operating at or below maneuvering speed does not provide structural protection against multiple full control inputs in one axis or full control inputs in more than one axis at the same time.

V_{REF}— Reference landing speed is the airspeed used for final approach, which adjust the normal approach speed for winds and gusty conditions. V_{REF} is 1.3 times the stall speed in the landing configuration.

11. Explain the difference between the best glide speed and minimum sink speed. (FAA-H-8083-3)

Best glide speed—The speed and configuration that provides the greatest forward distance for a given loss of altitude. In most airplanes, best glide airspeed will be roughly halfway between V_X (best angle of climb speed) and V_Y (best rate of climb speed).

Minimum sink speed—Used to maximize the time that the airplane remains in flight. Use of the minimum sink speed will result in the airplane losing altitude at the lowest rate. It is important that pilots realize that flight at the minimum sink airspeed results in less distance traveled and is useful in flight situations where time in flight is more important than distance flown (i.e., more time to fix problem, ditching at sea, etc.). Minimum sink speed is not an often-published airspeed but is generally a few knots less than best glide speed.

C. Power-Off Stalls

1. What is a power-off stall? (FAA-H-8083-3)

A power-off stall is a maneuver designed to simulate an accidental stall occurring during a segment of a landing approach. Airplanes equipped with flaps and/or retractable gear will be in the landing configuration. Power-off stalls are practiced from straight-ahead flight as well as from moderately banked turns to simulate an accidental stall during a turn from base leg to final.

2. Explain the benefits of practicing power-off stalls. (FAA-H-8083-3)

Power-off stalls are practiced to show what could happen if the controls are improperly used during a turn from the base leg to the final approach. The power-off straight-ahead stall simulates the attitude and flight characteristics of a particular airplane during the final approach and landing. During the practice of intentional stalls, the real objective is not to learn how to stall the airplane but to learn how to recognize an incipient stall and take prompt corrective action. Practice of stalls is important because it simulates stall conditions that could occur during normal flight maneuvers.

3. Explain the procedure for performing a fully developed power-off stall. (FAA-H-8083-3)

a. Establish a specific heading and altitude (recovery by 1,500 feet AGL).

b. Perform clearing turns.

c. Extend landing gear (if applicable).

d. Carburetor heat ON.

e. Reduce power and maintain back pressure to slow aircraft to flap operating speed.

f. Extend approach flaps.

g. Reduce power to idle and establish approach airspeed.

h. Bring the nose smoothly upward until the full stall occurs.

i. Immediately reduce angle of attack to regain flying speed.

j. Simultaneously apply full power (carburetor heat off).

k. Retract flaps incrementally.

l. Control any yawing tendency with rudder.

m. Use ailerons to level wings as soon as possible.

n. As airspeed approaches V_X or V_Y, establish a climb attitude to maintain V_X or V_Y. After establishing V_X or V_Y positive rate of climb, retract final flaps.

o. Return to cruise flight.

4. Identify the hazards that a learner should consider when performing a power-off stall. (FAA-S-ACS-25)

a. Factors and situations that could lead to an inadvertent power-off stall, spin, and loss of control.

b. Range and limitations of stall warning indicators (e.g., aircraft buffet, stall horn, etc.).

c. Stall warning(s) during normal operations.

d. Stall recovery procedure.

e. Secondary stalls, accelerated stalls, and cross-control stalls.

f. Effect of environmental elements on airplane performance related to power-off stalls (e.g., turbulence, microbursts, and high density altitude).

g. Collision hazards.

h. Distractions, task prioritization, loss of situational awareness, or disorientation.

5. What are the skill standards expected when demonstrating a power-off stall? (FAA-S-ACS-25)

The applicant demonstrates and simultaneously explains how to:

a. Clear the area.

b. Select an entry altitude that allows the task to be completed no lower than 1,500 feet AGL.

c. Configure the airplane in the approach or landing configuration, as specified by the evaluator, and maintain coordinated flight throughout the maneuver.

d. Establish a stabilized descent.

e. Transition smoothly from the approach or landing attitude to a pitch attitude that induces a stall.

(continued)

f. Maintain a specified heading, ±10°, if in straight flight; maintain a specified angle of bank not to exceed 20°, ±5°, if in turning flight, until an impending or full stall occurs, as specified by the evaluator.

g. Acknowledge the cues at the first indication of a stall (e.g., aircraft buffet, stall horn, etc.).

h. Recover at the first indication of a stall or after a full stall has occurred, as specified by the evaluator.

i. Configure the airplane as recommended by the manufacturer, and accelerate to best angle of climb speed (V_X) or best rate of climb speed (V_Y).

j. Return to the altitude, heading, and airspeed specified by the evaluator.

k. Analyze and correct common errors related to this task.

Note: Evaluation criteria for a recovery from an approach to stall should not mandate a predetermined value for altitude loss and should not mandate maintaining altitude during recovery. Proper evaluation criteria should consider the multitude of external and internal variables that affect the recovery altitude.

6. What common errors can occur when a learner is performing a power-off stall? (FAA-H-8083-3)

a. Failure to adequately clear the area.

b. Over-reliance on the airspeed indicator and slip-skid indicator while excluding other cues after recovery.

c. Inadvertent accelerated stall by pulling too fast on the controls during a power-off stall entry.

d. Inability to recognize an impending stall condition.

e. Failure to take timely action to prevent a full stall during the conduct of impending stalls.

f. Failure to maintain a constant bank angle during turning stalls.

g. Failure to maintain proper coordination with the rudder throughout the stall and recovery.

h. Recovering before reaching the critical AOA when practicing the full stall maneuver.

i. Not disconnecting the wing leveler or autopilot, if equipped, prior to reducing AOA.

j. Attempting recovery without recognizing the importance of pitch control and AOA.

k. Not maintaining a nose down control input until the stall warning is eliminated.

l. Attempting to level the wings before reducing AOA.

m. Attempting to recover with power before reducing AOA.

n. Failure to roll wings level after AOA reduction and stall warning is eliminated.

o. Inadvertent secondary stall during recovery.

p. Excessive forward-elevator pressure during recovery, resulting in low or negative G load.

q. Excessive airspeed buildup during recovery.

r. Losing situational awareness and failing to return to desired flight path or follow ATC instructions.

D. Power-On Stalls

1. What is a power-on stall? (FAA-H-8083-3)

Power-on stalls are, as the name implies, stalls in which full power is being developed as the aircraft stalls. They are intended to simulate the characteristics of an airplane that has stalled in a takeoff and departure configuration.

2. Explain the objective in practicing power-on stalls. (FAA-H-8083-3)

The objectives in performing stalls are to familiarize the pilot with the conditions that produce stalls, to assist in recognizing a takeoff and departure stall, and to develop the habit of taking prompt preventive or corrective action.

3. **Explain the procedure for performing a fully developed power-on stall.** (FAA-H-8083-3)

   a. Establish a specific heading and altitude (recovery by 1,500 feet AGL).

   b. Perform clearing turns.

   c. Establish the takeoff and departure configuration.

   d. Slow the airplane to normal liftoff airspeed.

   e. Apply takeoff power for a takeoff stall, or the recommended climb power for a departure stall.

   f. Establish a climb attitude.

   g. After the climb attitude is established, the nose should be brought smoothly upward to an attitude obviously impossible for the airplane to maintain and held at that attitude until a full stall occurs.

   h. Recovery should be accomplished by immediately reducing the pitch attitude/angle of attack, applying maximum power (or confirm at maximum power), and maintaining directional control through coordinated use of controls.

   i. Control any yawing tendency with rudder.

   j. Use ailerons to level wings as soon as possible.

   k. Retract flaps to the recommended setting and retract landing gear (if retractable), after a positive rate of climb is established.

   l. Accelerate to V_X or V_Y speed before the final flap retraction, and return to initial altitude, heading, and airspeed.

4. **Identify the hazards that a learner should consider when performing a power-on stall.** (FAA-S-ACS-25)

   a. Factors and situations that could lead to an inadvertent power-on stall, spin, and loss of control.

   b. Range and limitations of stall warning indicators (e.g., aircraft buffet, stall horn, etc.).

   c. Stall warning(s) during normal operations.

   d. Stall recovery procedure.

   e. Secondary stall, accelerated stall, elevator stall, and cross-controlled stalls.

f. Effect of environmental elements on airplane performance related to power-on stalls (e.g., turbulence, microbursts, and high density altitude).

g. Collision hazards.

h. Distractions, task prioritization, loss of situational awareness, or disorientation.

5. What are the skill standards expected when demonstrating a power-on stall? (FAA-S-ACS-25)

The applicant demonstrates and simultaneously explains how to:

a. Clear the area.

b. Select an entry altitude that allows the task to be completed no lower than 1,500 feet AGL.

c. Establish the takeoff, departure, or cruise configuration, as specified by the evaluator, and maintain coordinated flight throughout the maneuver.

d. Set power to no less than 65 percent power.

e. Transition smoothly from the takeoff or departure attitude to the pitch attitude that induces a stall.

f. Maintain a specified heading, ±10°, if in straight flight; maintain a specified angle of bank not to exceed 20°, ±10°, if in turning flight, until an impending or full stall is reached, as specified by the evaluator.

g. Acknowledge the cues at the first indication of a stall (e.g., aircraft buffet, stall horn, etc.).

h. Recover at the first indication of a stall or after a full stall has occurred, as specified by the evaluator.

i. Configure the airplane as recommended by the manufacturer, and accelerate to best angle of climb speed (V_X) or best rate of climb speed (V_Y).

j. Return to the altitude, heading, and airspeed specified by the evaluator.

k. Analyze and correct common errors related to this task.

(continued)

Note: In some high-performance airplanes, the power setting may have to be reduced below the ACS guidelines power setting to prevent pitch attitudes greater than 30° nose up. Evaluation criteria for a recovery from an approach to stall does not mandate a predetermined value for altitude loss and does not mandate maintaining altitude during recovery. Proper evaluation criteria considers the multitude of external and internal variables that affect the recovery altitude.

6. **What common errors can occur when a learner performs a power-on stall?** (FAA-H-8083-3)

   a. Failure to adequately clear the area.

   b. Over-reliance on the airspeed indicator and slip-skid indicator while excluding other cues after recovery.

   c. Inadvertent accelerated stall by pulling too fast on the controls during a power-on stall entry.

   d. Inability to recognize an impending stall condition.

   e. Failure to take timely action to prevent a full stall during the conduct of impending stalls.

   f. Failure to maintain a constant bank angle during turning stalls.

   g. Failure to maintain proper coordination with the rudder throughout the stall and recovery.

   h. Recovering before reaching the critical AOA when practicing the full stall maneuver.

   i. Not disconnecting the wing leveler or autopilot, if equipped, prior to reducing AOA.

   j. Attempting recovery without recognizing the importance of pitch control and AOA.

   k. Not maintaining a nose down control input until the stall warning is eliminated.

   l. Attempting to level the wings before reducing AOA.

   m. Attempting to recover with power before reducing AOA.

   n. Failure to roll wings level after AOA reduction and stall warning is eliminated.

   o. Inadvertent secondary stall during recovery.

p. Excessive forward-elevator pressure during recovery, resulting in low or negative G load.

q. Excessive airspeed buildup during recovery.

r. Losing situational awareness and failing to return to desired flight path or follow ATC instructions.

E. Accelerated Stalls

1. Explain how an accelerated stall occurs. (FAA-H-8083-3)

At the same gross weight, airplane configuration, and power setting, a given airplane will consistently stall at the same indicated airspeed if no acceleration is involved. The airplane will, however, stall at a higher indicated airspeed when excessive maneuvering loads are imposed by steep turns, pull-ups, or other abrupt changes in its flight path. Stalls entered from these flight situations are called accelerated maneuver stalls. These stalls would most frequently occur inadvertently during improperly executed turns, stall and spin recoveries, pullouts from steep dives, or when overshooting a base to final turn.

2. What are the objectives when demonstrating an accelerated stall? (FAA-H-8083-3)

The objectives of demonstrating an accelerated stall are to determine the stall characteristics of the airplane, experience stalls at speeds greater than the +1G stall speed, and develop the ability to instinctively recover at the onset of such stalls. This is a maneuver only commercial pilot and flight instructor applicants may be required to perform or demonstrate on a practical test. However, all pilots should be familiar with the situations that can cause an accelerated stall, how to recognize this type of stall, and how to execute the appropriate recovery should one occur.

3. **Describe the procedure for demonstrating an accelerated stall.** (FAA-H-8083-3)

   a. Establish a specific heading and altitude (recovery by 3,000 feet AGL).

   b. Perform clearing turns.

   c. From straight-and-level flight at maneuvering speed or less, roll the airplane into a steep, level flight turn and gradually apply back-elevator pressure.

   d. After the turn and bank are established, smoothly and steadily increase back-elevator pressure. The resulting apparent centrifugal force will push the pilot's body down in the seat, increase the wing loading, and decrease the airspeed.

   e. After the airspeed reaches the design maneuvering speed or within 20 knots above the unaccelerated stall speed, firmly increase back-elevator pressure until a definite stall occurs. These speed restrictions must be observed to prevent exceeding the load limit of the airplane.

   f. At the first indication of a stall, recovery should be made promptly by releasing sufficient back-elevator pressure and increasing power to reduce the angle of attack.

   g. If an uncoordinated turn is made, one wing may tend to drop suddenly, causing the airplane to roll in that direction. If this occurs, release the excessive back-elevator pressure, add power, and return the airplane to straight-and-level flight with coordinated control pressure.

   h. The pilot should recognize when the stall is imminent and take prompt action to prevent a completely stalled condition. It is imperative to avoid a prolonged stall, excessive airspeed, excessive loss of altitude, or spin.

4. **Identify the hazards a learner should consider when performing accelerated stalls.** (FAA-S-ACS-25)

   a. Factors and situations that could lead to an inadvertent accelerated stall, spin, and loss of control.

   b. Range and limitations of stall warning indicators (e.g., aircraft buffet, stall horn, etc.).

   c. Stall warning(s) during normal operations.

   d. Stall recovery procedure.

e. Secondary stalls, cross-control stalls, and spins.

f. Effect of environmental elements on airplane performance related to accelerated stalls (e.g., turbulence, microbursts, and high density altitude).

g. Collision hazards.

h. Distractions, task prioritization, loss of situational awareness, or disorientation.

5. **What are the skill standards expected when demonstrating an accelerated stall?** (FAA-S-ACS-25)

The applicant demonstrates and simultaneously explains how to:

a. Clear the area.

b. Select an entry altitude that allows the task to be completed no lower than 3,000 feet AGL.

c. Establish the configuration as specified by the evaluator.

d. Set power appropriate for the configuration, such that the airspeed does not exceed the maneuvering speed (V_A) or any other applicable POH/AFM limitation.

e. Establish and maintain a coordinated turn in a 45° bank, increasing elevator back pressure smoothly and firmly until an impending stall is reached.

f. Acknowledge the cues at the first indication of a stall (e.g., aircraft buffet, stall horn, etc.).

g. Execute a stall recovery in accordance with procedures set forth in the POH/AFM.

h. Configure the airplane as recommended by the manufacturer, and accelerate to best angle of climb speed (V_X) or best rate of climb speed (V_Y).

i. Return to the altitude, heading, and airspeed specified by the evaluator.

j. Analyze and correct common errors related to this task.

Note: Evaluation criteria for a recovery from an approach to stall should not mandate a predetermined value for altitude loss and should not mandate maintaining altitude during recovery. Proper evaluation criteria should consider the multitude of external and internal variables that affect the recovery altitude.

6. **What common errors can occur when demonstrating and explaining an accelerated stall?** (FAA-H-8083-3)

   a. Failure to adequately clear the area before beginning the maneuver.

   b. Failure to establish proper configuration prior to entry.

   c. Improper or inadequate demonstration of the recognition of and recovery from an accelerated maneuver stall.

   d. Failure to present simulated learner instruction that adequately emphasizes the hazards of poor procedures in recovering from an accelerated stall.

F. Cross-Controlled Stall Demonstration

1. **Explain how cross-controlled stalls occur.** (FAA-H-8083-3)

   A cross-controlled stall occurs when the pilot allows the aircraft to be flown in uncoordinated flight with the flight controls crossed—that is, aileron pressure applied in one direction and rudder pressure in the opposite direction. If excessive back pressure is applied, a cross-controlled stall may result. A skidding cross-controlled stall is most likely to occur in the traffic pattern during a poorly planned and executed base-to-final approach turn.

2. **What is the objective of a cross-controlled stall demonstration?** (FAA-H-8083-3)

   The objective of the cross-controlled stall demonstration is to show the effects of uncoordinated flight on stall behavior and to emphasize the importance of maintaining coordinated flight while making turns. This is a demonstration-only maneuver; only flight instructor applicants may be required to perform it on a practical test. However, all pilots should be familiar with the situations that can lead to a cross-controlled stall, how to recognize and avoid this stall, and how to recover should one occur.

3. **How is the cross-controlled stall demonstrated?** (FAA-H-8083-3)

   a. Establish a specific heading and safe altitude (recovery by 3,000 feet AGL).

   b. Perform clearing turns.

c. Reduce power.

d. Extend landing gear (if applicable).

e. Maintain altitude until airspeed approaches normal glide speed.

f. Retrim aircraft.

g. Roll into a medium-banked turn.

h. During the turn, excessive rudder pressure should be applied in direction of turn but the bank held constant by applying opposite aileron pressure.

i. Increase back-elevator pressure to keep the nose from lowering.

j. Increase control pressures until airplane stalls.

k. When stall occurs, recover by releasing control pressures and increasing power as necessary.

l. Control any yawing tendency with rudder.

m. Use ailerons to level wings as soon as possible.

n. As airspeed approaches V_X, establish climb attitude to maintain V_X, and to establish a positive rate of climb.

o. Return to cruise flight.

Note: The flight instructor normally demonstrates this task to learners for the purposes of familiarization and stall/spin awareness. Private and commercial pilot certification does not include this task.

4. Identify the hazards that a learner should consider when performing a cross-controlled stall. (FAA-S-ACS-25)

a. Stall recovery procedure.

b. Effect of environmental elements on airplane performance related to cross-controlled stalls (e.g., turbulence, microbursts, and high density altitude).

c. Collision hazards.

d. Aircraft limitations.

e. Distractions, task prioritization, loss of situational awareness, or disorientation.

5. **What are the skill standards when demonstrating and explaining a cross-controlled stall?** (FAA-S-ACS-25)

The applicant exhibits the skill to:

a. Clear the area.

b. Select an entry altitude that allows the task to be completed no lower than 3,000 feet AGL.

c. Configure the airplane (with gear down) and close the throttle.

d. Establish a normal glide airspeed and trim the airplane.

e. Roll into a medium-banked turn, apply excess rudder in the turn while holding bank constant with opposite aileron input, and add elevator pressure to keep the nose from lowering.

f. Acknowledge the cues at the first indication of a stall (e.g., aircraft buffet, stall horn, etc.).

g. Recover at the first indication of a stall or after a full stall has occurred, as specified by the evaluator.

h. Describe and demonstrate conditions that lead to a cross-controlled stall for future avoidance.

i. Analyze and correct common errors related to this task.

6. **What common errors can occur when demonstrating and explaining cross-controlled stalls?** (FAA-H-8083-3)

a. Failure to adequately clear the area before beginning the maneuver.

b. Failure to establish selected configuration prior to entry.

c. Failure to establish a cross-controlled turn and stall condition that will adequately demonstrate the hazards of a cross-controlled stall.

   • Not reducing power initially to slow the airplane to a typical approach speed.

   • Not increasing cross-controlled pressures enough to induce a stall.

   • Not increasing back-elevator pressure enough to induce a stall.

d. Improper or inadequate demonstration of the recognition of and recovery from a cross-controlled stall.

e. Failure to present simulated learner instruction that adequately emphasizes the hazards of a cross-controlled condition in a gliding or reduced airspeed condition.

f. Not adequately explaining the "what, why, and how" of cross-controlled stalls.

G. Elevator Trim Stall Demonstration

1. Explain how and where elevator trim stalls occur. (FAA-H-8083-3)

Elevator trim stalls occur when full power is applied to an airplane configured with excessive nose-up trim. Positive control of the airplane is not maintained, resulting in a stall. This type of stall usually occurs during a go-around procedure from a normal landing approach or a simulated forced landing approach, or immediately after takeoff, with the trim set for a normal landing approach glide at idle power.

2. What is the objective when demonstrating an elevator trim stall? (FAA-H-8083-3)

The objective is to show the importance of making smooth power applications, overcoming strong trim forces, and maintaining positive control of the airplane to hold safe flight attitudes, and using proper and timely trim techniques. It also develops the pilot's ability to avoid actions that could result in this stall, to recognize when an elevator trim stall is approaching, and to take prompt and correct action to prevent a full stall condition. It is imperative to avoid the occurrence of an elevator trim stall during an actual go-around from an approach to landing.

3. How is an elevator trim stall demonstrated? (FAA-H-8083-3)

a. Establish a specific heading and altitude (recovery by 3,000 feet AGL).

b. Perform clearing turns.

c. Slowly retard the throttle and extend landing gear (if retractable).

d. Extend one-half to full flaps.

(continued)

   e. Close throttle.

   f. Maintain altitude until airspeed approaches normal glide speed.

   g. When normal glide is established, retrim the airplane just as would be done during a normal landing approach.

   h. Advance throttle to maximum power as in a go-around procedure. The combined forces of thrust, torque, and back-elevator trim will tend to make the nose rise sharply and turn to the left. To demonstrate what could occur if positive control of the airplane were not maintained, no immediate attempt should be made to correct these forces.

   i. When a stall is imminent, apply forward pressure to return the airplane to normal climbing attitude.

   j. Adjust trim to relieve the heavy control pressures, and complete the normal go-around and level-off procedures.

Note: The flight instructor normally demonstrates this task to learners for the purposes of familiarization and stall/spin awareness. Private and commercial pilot certification does not include this task.

4. Identify the hazards that a learner should consider when performing an elevator trim stall. (FAA-S-ACS-25)

   a. Stall recovery procedure.

   b. Effect of environmental elements on airplane performance related to cross-controlled stalls (e.g., turbulence, microbursts, and high density altitude).

   c. Collision hazards.

   d. Aircraft limitations.

   e. Distractions, task prioritization, loss of situational awareness, or disorientation.

5. What are the skill standards expected when demonstrating an elevator trim stall? (FAA-S-ACS-25)

The applicant exhibits the skill to:

   a. Clear the area.

   b. Select an entry altitude that allows the task to be completed no lower than 3,000 feet above ground level (AGL).

   c. Retard the throttle and configure the airplane for landing.

d. Establish a normal glide airspeed and trim the airplane.

e. Advance the throttle to the maximum allowable power as in a go-around.

f. Acknowledge the cues at the first indication of a stall (e.g., aircraft buffet, stall horn, etc.).

g. Recover at the first indication of a stall or after a full stall has occurred, as specified by the evaluator.

h. Adjust trim and return to the desired flight path.

i. Describe and demonstrate conditions that lead to an elevator trim stall for future avoidance.

j. Analyze and correct common errors related to this task.

Note: The applicant and evaluator must brief the recovery prior to stall execution. A realistic scenario includes a simulated short-field approach at altitude trimmed for approach airspeed, low power, and full flaps.

6. What common errors can occur when demonstrating and explaining an elevator trim stall? (FAA-H-8083-3)

a. Failure to adequately clear the area before beginning the maneuver.

b. Failure to present simulated learner instruction that adequately emphasizes the hazards of poor correction for torque and up-elevator trim during go-around and other maneuvers.

c. Not adequately explaining the "what, why, and how" of elevator trim stalls.

d. Failure to establish selected configuration prior to entry.

e. Improper or inadequate demonstration of the recognition of and the recovery from an elevator trim stall.

- Not allowing the pitch attitude to increase above the normal climbing attitude.

- Reducing power during recovery; not maintaining control of aircraft while retrimming and retracting flaps.

H. Secondary Stall Demonstration

1. What is a secondary stall? (FAA-H-8083-3)

This stall is called a secondary stall since it may occur after a recovery from a preceding primary stall. It is caused by attempting to hasten the completion of a stall recovery before the airplane has regained sufficient flying speed.

2. Explain why secondary stalls occur at low altitudes. (FAA-H-8083-3)

If a primary stall should occur at low altitude, the pilot's natural impulse is to bring the nose up as soon as possible and to do so abruptly. This reaction is amplified as proximity to the ground increases. To demonstrate how this occurs at altitude, the pilot makes an abrupt recovery after one stall and exceeds the critical AOA a second time.

3. How should a flight instructor demonstrate a secondary stall? (FAA-H-8083-3)

Secondary stalls can be demonstrated during the recovery phase of any of the basic stalls. The secondary stall can be induced by simply pulling the nose up more rapidly than necessary during the recovery from a full stall.

Note: The flight instructor normally demonstrates this task to learners for the purposes of familiarization and stall/spin awareness. Private and commercial pilot certification does not include this task.

4. Identify the hazards a learner should consider when performing secondary stalls. (FAA-S-ACS-25)

a. Stall recovery procedure.

b. Effect of environmental elements on airplane performance related to cross-controlled stalls (e.g., turbulence, microbursts, and high density altitude).

c. Collision hazards.

d. Aircraft limitations.

e. Distractions, task prioritization, loss of situational awareness, or disorientation.

5. What are the skill standards expected when demonstrating a secondary stall? (FAA-S-ACS-25)

The applicant exhibits the skills to:

a. Clear the area.

b. Select an entry altitude that allows the task to be completed no lower than 3,000 feet above ground level (AGL).

c. Enter a stall in a specified configuration and exceed the critical angle of attack a second time during the recovery.

d. Recover promptly and appropriately after a secondary stall occurs.

e. Describe and demonstrate conditions that lead to a secondary stall for future avoidance.

f. Analyze and correct common errors related to this task.

Note: Secondary stalls include a full stall.

6. What common errors can occur when demonstrating and explaining a secondary stall? (FAA-H-8083-3)

a. Failure to adequately clear the area before beginning the maneuver.

b. Failure to establish selected configuration prior to entry.

c. Improper or inadequate demonstration of the recognition of and recovery from a secondary stall. Not applying sufficient back pressure to induce secondary stall.

d. Failure to present simulated learner instruction that adequately emphasizes the hazards of poor procedure in recovering from a primary stall.

e. Not adequately explaining the "what, why, and how" of secondary stalls.

I. Spin Awareness and Spins

1. Describe a spin. (FAA-H-8083-3)

A spin may be defined as an aggravated stall that results in what is termed "autorotation" wherein the airplane follows a downward corkscrew path. As the airplane rotates around a vertical axis, the rising wing is less stalled than the descending wing, creating a rolling, yawing, and pitching motion. The airplane is basically being forced downward by gravity, rolling, yawing, and pitching in a spiral path. Mishandling of yaw control during a stall increases the likelihood of a spin entry.

2. Why is it important for the flight instructor to demonstrate spins and spin recovery? (FAA-H-8083-3)

Fear of and aversion to spins are deeply rooted in the public's mind, and many pilots have an unconscious aversion to them. If one learns the cause of a spin and the proper techniques to prevent and/or recover from the spin, mental anxiety and many causes of unintentional spins may be removed.

Note: The intentional spinning of an airplane, for which the spin maneuver is not specifically approved, is *not* authorized by the regulations. Refer to the aircraft's FAA-approved POH/AFM.

3. How should spins and spin recovery be demonstrated? (FAA-H-8083-3)

Entry:

a. Establish the appropriate altitude; high enough to complete recovery at or above 4,000 feet AGL.

b. Clear the flight area above and below the airplane for other traffic.

c. Apply carburetor heat and reduce the throttle to idle.

d. Configure the aircraft for a power-off stall (no flaps).

e. As the airplane approaches a stall, smoothly apply full rudder in the direction of the desired spin rotation and continue to apply back elevator to the limit of travel. The ailerons should be neutral.

f. Maintain full rudder deflection and elevator back pressure throughout the spin.

g. Allow the spin to develop (approximately 2 to 3 rotations).

Recovery:

a. Close the throttle (if not already accomplished).

b. Neutralize the ailerons.

c. Apply full opposite rudder against rotation.

d. Apply positive, brisk, and straight forward elevator (forward of neutral).

e. Neutralize the rudder after spin rotation stops.

f. Apply back-elevator pressure to return to level flight and adjust power as appropriate.

4. Identify the hazards that a learner should consider when performing spins and spin recovery procedures. (FAA-S-ACS-25)

a. Factors and situations that could lead to inadvertent spin and loss of control.

b. Range and limitations of stall warning indicators (e.g., aircraft buffet, stall horn, etc.).

c. Spin recovery procedure.

d. Effect of environmental elements on airplane performance related to spins (e.g., turbulence, microbursts, and high density altitude).

e. Collision hazards.

f. Distractions, task prioritization, loss of situational awareness, or disorientation.

5. What are the skill standards expected when demonstrating a spin and spin recovery procedures? (FAA-S-ACS-25)

The applicant demonstrates and simultaneously explains how to:

a. Clear the area.

b. Select an entry altitude that allows the task to be completed no lower than 4,000 feet AGL.

c. Enter and recover from an intentional spin if requested by the evaluator.

d. Analyze and correct common errors related to this task.

6. **What common errors can occur when demonstrating a spin?** (FAA-H-8083-3)

   a. Failure to apply full rudder pressure (to the stops) in the desired spin direction during spin entry.

   b. Failure to apply and maintain full up-elevator pressure during spin entry, resulting in a spiral.

   c. Failure to achieve a fully stalled condition prior to spin entry.

   d. Failure to apply full rudder (to the stops) briskly against the spin during recovery.

   e. Failure to apply sufficient forward elevator during recovery.

   f. Waiting for rotation to stop before applying forward elevator.

   g. Failure to neutralize the rudder after rotation stops, possibly resulting in a secondary spin.

   h. Slow and overly cautious control movements during recovery.

   i. Excessive back-elevator pressure after rotation stops, possibly resulting in secondary stall.

   j. Insufficient back-elevator pressure during recovery, resulting in excessive airspeed.

Basic Instrument
Maneuvers

10

A. Straight-and-Level Flight

1. Briefly explain the performance of straight-and-level flight by reference to instruments. (FAA-H-8083-15)

Straight-and-level flight by reference to instruments under simulated instrument conditions involves using the basic flight instruments to maintain a constant heading and altitude. This is accomplished by:

a. Establishing a definite altitude.

b. Establishing a definite heading.

c. Establishing a cruise power setting and airspeed.

d. Trimming aircraft for "hands off" flight.

e. Maintaining level flight by positioning the miniature aircraft in relation to the horizon bar on the attitude indicator. Cross-check with the altimeter and vertical speed indicator.

f. Maintaining straight flight by occasionally referencing the directional gyro for any indication of heading change. Cross-check with the attitude indicator and turn coordinator.

g. Cross-checking the instruments, interpreting what they are telling you, and controlling the aircraft.

2. Explain the value of learning basic maneuvers under simulated instrument conditions. (FAA-H-8083-3)

Developing the ability to maneuver an airplane for limited periods of time solely by reference to instruments and to follow radar instructions from ATC may become invaluable to a pilot when outside visual references are lost due to unexpected adverse weather. It must be emphasized to students that this training does *not* prepare them for unrestricted operations in instrument weather conditions.

3. Explain the two basic methods used for learning attitude instrument flying. (FAA-H-8083-15)

The two methods are the *control and performance method* and the *primary and supporting method*. Both methods utilize the same instruments and responses for attitude control. They differ in their reliance on the attitude indicator and interpretation of other instruments.

4. When using the primary and supporting method of attitude instrument flying, how does the pilot determine which flight instrument is primary for a specific basic instrument maneuver? (FAA-H-8083-15)

The primary instrument will be the one that depicts the most accurate indication for the aspect of the aircraft attitude being controlled. This is usually the instrument that should be held at a constant indication. For example, when the pilot is maintaining a constant altitude, the primary instrument for pitch is the altimeter.

5. Identify the hazards that a learner should consider when practicing straight-and-level flight by reference to instruments. (FAA-S-ACS-25)

   a. Instrument flying hazards, including failure to maintain visual flight rules (VFR), spatial disorientation, loss of control, fatigue, stress, and emergency off-airport landings.

   b. When to seek assistance or declare an emergency in a deteriorating situation.

   c. Collision hazards.

   d. Distractions, task prioritization, loss of situational awareness, or disorientation.

   e. Fixation and omission.

   f. Instrument interpretation.

   g. Control application solely by reference to instruments.

   h. Trimming the aircraft.

6. What are the skill standards expected when demonstrating straight-and-level flight by reference to instruments? (FAA-S-ACS-25)

The applicant demonstrates and simultaneously explains how to:

   a. Maintain straight-and-level flight using proper instrument cross-check and interpretation and coordinated control application.

   b. Maintain altitude ±100 feet, heading ±10°, and airspeed ±10 knots.

   c. Analyze and correct common errors related to this task.

7. **What common errors can occur when a learner is performing straight-and-level flight by reference to instruments?** (FAA-H-8083-15)

   a. Fixation, omission, and emphasis errors during instrument cross-check.

   b. Improper instrument interpretation.

   c. Improper control applications.

   d. Failure to establish proper pitch, bank, or power adjustments during altitude, heading, or airspeed corrections.

   e. Faulty trim technique.

B. Constant Airspeed Climbs

1. **Explain the procedure for performing a straight, constant airspeed climb.** (FAA-H-8083-15)

   A straight, constant airspeed climb involves a climb in which a constant heading is maintained at a predetermined airspeed. To accomplish this, the learner should:

   a. Raise the miniature aircraft to the approximate nose-high indication appropriate to the predetermined climb speed.

   b. Apply light back elevator pressure to initiate and maintain the climb attitude. The pressures will vary as the airplane decelerates.

   c. Power may be advanced to the climb power setting simultaneously with the pitch change or after the pitch change is established and the airspeed approaches climb speed.

   d. Once the airplane stabilizes at a constant airspeed and attitude, the airspeed indicator is the primary instrument for pitch and the heading indicator is primary for bank.

2. **Explain the procedure for leveling off at an assigned altitude after a constant airspeed climb.** (FAA-H-8083-15)

   To level off from a climb, and maintain an altitude, it is necessary to start the level off before reaching the desired altitude. The amount of lead varies with rate of climb and pilot technique. An effective practice is to lead the altitude by 10 percent of the vertical speed shown (e.g., 500 fpm/50-foot lead; 1,000 fpm/100-foot lead).

3. **What instruments are considered primary for pitch and bank in a constant airspeed climb?** (FAA-H-8083-15)

   Once the airplane stabilizes at a constant airspeed and attitude, the ASI is primary for pitch and the heading indicator remains primary for bank.

4. **Identify the hazards that a learner should consider when performing constant airspeed climbs by reference to instruments.** (FAA-S-ACS-25)

   a. Instrument flying hazards, including failure to maintain visual flight rules (VFR), spatial disorientation, loss of control, fatigue, stress, and emergency off-airport landings.

   b. When to seek assistance or declare an emergency in a deteriorating situation.

   c. Collision hazards.

   d. Distractions, task prioritization, loss of situational awareness, or disorientation.

   e. Fixation and omission.

   f. Instrument interpretation.

   g. Control application solely by reference to instruments.

   h. Trimming the aircraft.

5. **What are the expected skill standards when performing constant airspeed climbs by reference to instruments?** (FAA-S-ACS-25)

   The applicant demonstrates and simultaneously explains how to:

   a. Transition to the climb pitch attitude and power setting on an assigned heading using proper instrument cross-check and interpretation and coordinated flight control application.

   b. Climb at a constant airspeed to specific altitudes in straight flight and turns.

   c. Level off at the assigned altitude and maintain altitude ±100 feet, heading ±10°, and airspeed ±10 knots.

   d. Analyze and correct common errors related to this task.

6. **What common errors can occur when a learner is performing a constant airspeed climb by reference to instruments?** (FAA-H-8083-15)

   a. Fixation, omission, and emphasis errors during instrument cross-check.

   b. Improper instrument interpretation.

   c. Improper control applications.

   d. Failure to establish proper pitch, bank, or power adjustments during heading and airspeed corrections.

   e. Improper entry or level-off technique.

   f. Faulty trim technique.

C. Constant Airspeed Descents

1. **Explain the procedure for performing a constant airspeed descent by reference to instruments.** (FAA-H-8083-15)

   A straight, constant airspeed descent involves a descent in which a constant heading is maintained at a predetermined airspeed. To accomplish this, the learner should:

   a. Reduce power to a predetermined value.

   b. Maintain back pressure until the airspeed slows to the desired descent airspeed.

   c. Lower the miniature aircraft on the attitude indicator to the approximate nose-low indication appropriate to the predetermined airspeed/rate of descent.

   d. Once the airplane stabilizes at a constant airspeed/rate of descent and attitude, retrim the aircraft.

   e. Control airspeed with pitch and rate of descent with power.

2. **During a constant airspeed descent, does power or aircraft pitch control airspeed?** (FAA-H-8083-15)

   During a constant airspeed descent, any deviation from the desired airspeed calls for a pitch adjustment.

3. **Assuming a 500 fpm rate of descent, what is the procedure for leveling off from a descent at a speed higher than the descent speed?** (FAA-H-8083-15)

Lead the altitude by 100–150 feet for a level off at an airspeed higher than the descent speed. At the lead point, add power to the appropriate level flight cruise setting.

4. **Identify the hazards that a learner should consider when performing a constant airspeed descent by reference to instruments.** (FAA-S-ACS-25)

    a. Instrument flying hazards, including failure to maintain visual flight rules (VFR), spatial disorientation, loss of control, fatigue, stress, and emergency off-airport landings.

    b. When to seek assistance or declare an emergency in a deteriorating situation.

    c. Collision hazards.

    d. Distractions, task prioritization, loss of situational awareness, or disorientation.

    e. Fixation and omission.

    f. Instrument interpretation.

    g. Control application solely by reference to instruments.

    h. Trimming the aircraft.

5. **What are the skill standards expected when demonstrating a constant airspeed descent by reference to instruments?** (FAA-S-ACS-25)

The applicant demonstrates and simultaneously explains how to:

    a. Transition to the descent pitch attitude and power setting on an assigned heading using proper instrument cross-check and interpretation, and coordinated flight control application.

    b. Descend at a constant airspeed to specific altitudes in straight flight and turns.

    c. Level off at the assigned altitude and maintain altitude ±100 feet, heading ±10°, and airspeed ±10 knots.

    d. Analyze and correct common errors related to this task.

6. **What common errors can occur when a learner is performing a constant airspeed descent by reference to instruments?** (FAA-H-8083-15)

   a. Fixation, omission, and emphasis errors during instrument cross-check.

   b. Improper instrument interpretation.

   c. Improper control applications.

   d. Failure to establish proper pitch, bank, or power adjustments during heading and airspeed corrections.

   e. Improper entry or level-off technique.

   f. Faulty trim technique.

D. Turns to Headings

1. **What is the procedure for performing turns to headings by reference to instruments only?** (FAA-H-8083-15)

   Performing turns to headings solely by reference to instruments involves changing or returning the aircraft heading to a desired heading. The process is as follows:

   a. Apply coordinated aileron and rudder pressure in the desired direction of turn.

   b. On the roll-in, use the attitude indicator to establish the approximate angle of bank, then check the turn coordinator for a standard rate turn indication.

   c. During the roll-in, check the altimeter, vertical speed indicator, and attitude indicator for pitch adjustments necessary as the vertical lift component decreases with an increase in bank.

   d. When rolling out, apply coordinated aileron and rudder pressures opposite the direction of turn.

   e. Lead the rollout by approximately 1/2 bank angle prior to the desired heading.

   f. Anticipate a possible gain in altitude on rollout and adjust pitch attitude as appropriate.

2. What are the two fundamental flight skills that must be learned during attitude instrument training? (FAA-H-8083-15)

Instrument cross-check and instrument interpretation.

3. Explain the term *instrument cross-check*. (FAA-H-8083-15)

Instrument cross-checking (also called *scanning* or *instrument coverage*) is the continuous and logical observation of instruments for attitude and performance information. In attitude instrument flying, the pilot maintains an attitude by reference to instruments, producing the desired result in performance. Observing and interpreting two or more instruments to determine attitude and performance of an aircraft is called cross-checking.

4. Identify the hazards that a learner should consider when performing turns to headings by reference to instruments. (FAA-S-ACS-25)

a. Instrument flying hazards, including failure to maintain visual flight rules (VFR), spatial disorientation, loss of control, fatigue, stress, and emergency off-airport landings.

b. When to seek assistance or declare an emergency in a deteriorating situation.

c. Collision hazards.

d. Distractions, task prioritization, loss of situational awareness, or disorientation.

e. Fixation and omission.

f. Instrument interpretation.

g. Control application solely by reference to instruments.

h. Trimming the aircraft.

5. **What are the skill standards expected when demonstrating turns to headings by reference to instruments?** (FAA-S-ACS-25)

The applicant demonstrates and simultaneously explains how to:

a. Perform turns to headings, maintain altitude ±100 feet, maintain a standard rate turn, roll out on the assigned heading ±10°, and maintain airspeed ±10 knots.

b. Analyze and correct common errors related to this task.

6. **What common errors can occur when a learner is performing turns to headings by reference to instruments?** (FAA-H-8083-15)

a. Fixation, omission, and emphasis errors during instrument cross-check.

b. Improper instrument interpretation.

c. Improper control applications.

d. Failure to establish proper pitch, bank, and power adjustments during altitude, bank, and airspeed corrections.

e. Improper entry or rollout procedure.

f. Faulty trim procedure.

E. Recovery from Unusual Flight Attitudes

1. **What is meant by the term *unusual flight attitudes*?** (FAA-H-8083-15)

When outside visual references are inadequate or lost, the VFR pilot is apt to unintentionally let the airplane enter a critical attitude (sometimes called an *unusual attitude*). In general, this involves an excessively nose-high attitude in which the airplane may be approaching a stall, or an extremely steep bank that may result in a steep downward spiral.

2. **Discuss the importance of instrument training for recovery from an unusual attitude.** (FAA-H-8083-3)

Since unusual attitudes are not intentional, they are often unexpected, and the reaction of an inexperienced or inadequately trained pilot is usually instinctive rather than intelligent and deliberate. However, with practice, the techniques for rapid and safe recovery from these critical attitudes can be learned.

3. Explain procedures used for recovery from unusual flight attitudes by reference to instruments.
(FAA-H-8083-3)

Nose-high decreasing airspeed:

a. Indicated by:
   - Decreasing airspeed on airspeed indicator.
   - Increasing altitude on altimeter and positive rate on vertical speed indicator.
   - Bank on attitude indicator, heading indicator, and turn coordinator.

b. Recover by:
   - Reducing pitch attitude.
   - Simultaneously increasing power.
   - Leveling the wings as necessary.

Nose-low increasing airspeed:

a. Indicated by:
   - Increasing airspeed on airspeed indicator.
   - Decreasing altitude on altimeter and negative rate on vertical speed indicator.
   - Bank on attitude indicator, heading indicator, and turn coordinator.

b. Recover by:
   - Reducing power.
   - Leveling the wings.
   - Raising the nose gradually.

Note: The attitude indicator is normally the most useful instrument in determining the aircraft's attitude. However, extreme unusual attitudes may cause the gyros in the attitude indicator and heading indicator to tumble. In this situation the pitch attitude may be determined through combined use of the information provided by the airspeed indicator, altimeter, and vertical speed indicator. The turn coordinator may be used as the primary instrument in detecting bank angle.

4. **Identify the hazards that a learner should consider when performing recovery from unusual attitudes.** (FAA-S-ACS-25)

   a. Situations that could lead to loss of control in-flight (LOC-I) or unusual attitudes in flight (e.g., stress, task saturation, inadequate instrument scan distractions, and spatial disorientation).

   b. Assessment of the unusual attitude.

   c. Control input errors, inducing undesired aircraft attitudes.

   d. Collision hazards.

   e. Distractions, task prioritization, loss of situational awareness, or disorientation.

   f. Interpreting flight instruments.

   g. Control application solely by reference to instruments.

   h. Operating envelope considerations.

5. **What are the skill standards expected when demonstrating recovery from unusual attitudes?** (FAA-S-ACS-25)

   The applicant demonstrates and simultaneously explains how to:

   a. Use proper instrument cross-check and interpretation to identify an unusual attitude (including both nose-high and nose-low) in flight, and apply the appropriate flight control, power input, and aircraft configuration in the correct sequence, to return to a stabilized level flight attitude.

   b. Use single-pilot resource management (SRM) or crew resource management (CRM), as appropriate.

   c. Analyze and correct common errors related to this task.

6. What common errors can occur when a learner is performing recoveries from unusual attitudes? (FAA-H-8083-3)

a. Failure to recognize an unusual flight attitude.

- Not interpreting the information provided correctly.
- Not sure of which instruments provide pitch, bank, and power information.

b. Consequences of attempting to recover from an unusual flight attitude by feel rather than by instrument indications; not trusting instrument indications can lead to rapid altitude loss as a result of inadvertent steep spirals or power-on/power-off stalls.

c. Inappropriate control applications during recovery:

- Not following the correct sequence of actions in recovery.
- In descents: increasing back pressure before leveling the wings, not reducing power in descent; overcompensating on recovery by increasing pitch attitude past that for level flight.
- In climbs: not lowering the nose fast enough; lowering the nose too far; not adding power.

d. Failure to recognize, from instrument indications, when the airplane is passing through a level flight attitude:

- Not cross-checking instruments.
- Not using the attitude indicator and/or airspeed indicator/ altimeter to determine level flight.

Emergency
Operations

11

A. Emergency Descent

1. Describe an emergency descent procedure.
(FAA-H-8083-3)

An emergency descent is a maneuver for descending as rapidly as possible to a lower altitude or to the ground for an emergency landing. The need for this maneuver may result from an uncontrollable fire, a sudden loss of cabin pressurization, or any other situation demanding an immediate and rapid descent.

2. What is the objective when performing an emergency descent procedure? (FAA-H-8083-3)

The objective of this maneuver is to descend the airplane as soon and as rapidly as possible within the structural limitations of the airplane.

3. Describe the procedure for conducting an emergency descent. (FAA-H-8083-3)

a. Simulated emergency descents should be made in a turn to check for other air traffic below and to look around for a possible emergency landing area.

b. A radio call announcing descent intentions may be appropriate to alert other aircraft in the area.

c. When initiating the descent, establish a bank of approximately 30 to 45° to maintain positive load factors (G forces) on the airplane.

d. Except when prohibited by the manufacturer, reduce the power to idle, and place the propeller control (if equipped) in the low pitch (high RPM) position. This will allow the propeller to act as an aerodynamic brake to help prevent an excessive airspeed buildup during the descent.

e. Extend the landing gear and flaps as recommended by the manufacturer. This will provide maximum drag so that the descent can be made as rapidly as possible, without excessive airspeed.

f. Do not allow the airplane's airspeed to pass the never-exceed speed (V_{NE}), the maximum landing gear extended speed (V_{LE}), or the maximum flap extended speed (V_{FE}), as applicable. The descent should be made at the maximum allowable airspeed consistent with the procedure used.

g. Initiate the recovery from an emergency descent at a high-enough altitude to ensure a safe recovery back to level flight or a precautionary landing.

Note: Emergency descent training should be performed as recommended by the manufacturer, including the configuration and airspeeds.

4. What factors should be taken into consideration when selecting the appropriate airspeed for an emergency descent? (FAA-H-8083-3)

In the case of an engine fire, a high-airspeed descent should be established to extinguish the fire. However, weakening of the airplane structure is a major concern and descent at a lower airspeed would place less stress on the airplane. If the descent is conducted in turbulent conditions, the pilot must also comply with the design maneuvering speed (V_A) limitations. This will provide increased drag and therefore loss of altitude as quickly as possible.

5. Identify the hazards that a learner should consider when performing an emergency descent. (FAA-S-ACS-25)

a. Altitude, wind, terrain, obstructions, gliding distance, and available landing distance considerations.

b. Collision hazards.

c. Configuring the airplane.

d. Distractions, task prioritization, loss of situational awareness, or disorientation.

6. What are the skill standards expected when demonstrating an emergency descent procedure? (FAA-S-ACS-25)

The applicant demonstrates and simultaneously explains how to:

a. Clear the area.

b. Establish and maintain the appropriate airspeed and configuration appropriate to the scenario specified by the evaluator and as covered in the POH/AFM for the emergency descent.

c. Maintain orientation, divide attention appropriately, and plan and execute a smooth recovery.

    d. Use bank angle between 30° and 45° to maintain positive load factors during the descent.

    e. Maintain appropriate airspeed +0/−10 knots, and level off at a specified altitude ±100 feet.

    f. Complete the appropriate checklist(s).

    g. Analyze and correct common errors related to this task.

7. What common errors can occur when a learner is conducting a practice emergency descent procedure? (FAA-H-8083-3)

    a. Failure to identify the reason for executing an emergency descent.

    b. Delaying the decision to execute the emergency descent procedure (seconds matter).

    c. Failure to reduce power to idle (can't get down as quickly).

    d. Failure to move propeller control (if equipped) to high RPM (increases drag).

    e. Improper use of emergency checklist to verify procedures for initiating the emergency descent.

    f. Improper use of clearing procedures before initiating and during the emergency descent.

    g. Improper procedures for recovering from an emergency descent.

B. Emergency Approach and Landing

1. What are the different types of emergency approach and landing procedures? (FAA-H-8083-3)

    a. *Forced landing*—an immediate landing, on or off an airport, necessitated by the inability to continue further flight.

    b. *Precautionary landing*—a premeditated landing, on or off an airport, when further flight is possible but inadvisable.

    c. *Ditching*—a forced or precautionary landing on water.

2. What is the objective of teaching simulated emergency approach and landing procedures to a learner? (FAA-H-8083-3)

The objective is to instill in the pilot the knowledge that almost any terrain can be considered suitable for a survivable crash landing if the pilot knows how to use the airplane structure for self-protection and the protection of passengers.

3. Explain the procedures for performing a simulated emergency approach and landing. (POH/AFM)

a. Reduce power to idle

b. Establish pitch for best glide airspeed.

c. Begin a scan for an appropriate field for landing. Fly towards it.

d. Complete the "Engine Failure During Flight" checklist.

e. Set your transponder to "7700" (simulated).

f. Transmit a "mayday" message on either the frequency in use or 121.5 (simulated).

g. Begin to spiral down over the approach end of the selected landing site.

h. Arrive at downwind key position, at pattern altitude for selected landing area.

i. From the key point on, the approach is a normal power-off 180° accuracy approach.

j. On final, complete the forced landing checklist.

Note: During all simulated emergency landings, keep the engine warm and cleared. During a simulated emergency landing, either the instructor or the pilot should have complete control of the throttle. There must be no doubt as to who has control, since many near accidents have occurred from such misunderstandings.

4. **Identify the hazards that a learner should consider when performing an emergency approach and landing procedure.** (FAA-S-ACS-25)

   a. Altitude, wind, terrain, obstructions, gliding distance, and available landing distance considerations.

   b. Following or changing the planned flight path to the selected landing area.

   c. Collision hazards.

   d. Configuring the airplane.

   e. Low-altitude maneuvering, including stall, spin, or controlled flight into terrain (CFIT).

   f. Distractions, task prioritization, loss of situational awareness, or disorientation.

5. **What are the skill standards expected when demonstrating emergency descent and landing procedures?** (FAA-S-ACS-25)

   The applicant demonstrates and simultaneously explains how to:

   a. Establish and maintain the recommended best glide airspeed, ±10 knots.

   b. Configure the airplane in accordance with the pilot's operating handbook (POH)/airplane flight manual (AFM) and existing conditions.

   c. Select a suitable landing area considering altitude, wind, terrain, obstructions, and available glide distance.

   d. Plan and follow a flight path to the selected landing area considering altitude, wind, terrain, and obstructions.

   e. Prepare for landing as specified by the evaluator.

   f. Complete the appropriate checklist(s).

   g. Analyze and correct common errors related to this task

   Note: Execution of this task must allow for a safe landing in the event of an actual engine failure.

6. **What common errors can occur when a learner is practicing simulated emergency approach and landing procedures?** (FAA-H-8083-3)

   a. Improper airspeed control.

   b. Poor judgment in the selection of an emergency landing area.

   c. Failure to estimate the approximate wind speed and direction.

   d. Failure to fly the most suitable pattern for the existing situation.

   e. Failure to accomplish the emergency checklist.

   f. Undershooting or overshooting the selected emergency landing area.

C. Systems and Equipment Malfunctions

1. **What is the objective of teaching simulated system and equipment malfunctions?** (FAA-H-8083-3)

   The objective is to develop the learner's ability to detect, analyze, and apply the appropriate procedure for a given system or equipment malfunction. The key to successful management of an emergency situation (or preventing a progression into a true emergency) is a thorough familiarity with, and adherence to, the procedures developed by the airplane manufacturer and contained in the FAA-approved AFM or POH.

2. **What are several psychological factors that may interfere with a pilot's ability to act promptly and properly when faced with an emergency?** (FAA-H-8083-3)

   a. Reluctance to accept the emergency situation.

   b. Undue concern about getting hurt.

   c. Desire to save the airplane.

3. **Describe common system and equipment malfunctions that you will teach your learners to detect and respond to with the appropriate procedures.** (FAA-S-ACS-25)

   a. Causes of partial or complete engine power loss.

   b. Electrical system malfunction.

   c. Vacuum/pressure and associated flight instrument malfunctions.

   d. Pitot-static system malfunction.

(continued)

e. Electronic flight deck display malfunction.

f. Landing gear or flap malfunction.

g. Inoperative trim.

h. Causes and remedies for smoke or fire on board the aircraft.

i. Malfunctions of other systems specific to the aircraft (e.g., supplemental oxygen, deicing).

j. Inadvertent door or window opening.

4. Describe several commonly experienced in-flight abnormal engine instrument indications you will teach your learners to detect and respond to with the appropriate procedures. (FAA-H-8083-3)

a. Loss of RPM during cruise flight (non-altitude engine).

b. Loss of manifold pressure during cruise flight.

c. Gain of manifold pressure during cruise flight.

d. High oil temperature.

e. Low oil temperature.

f. High oil pressure.

g. Low oil pressure.

h. Fluctuating oil pressure.

i. High cylinder head temperature.

j. Low cylinder head temperature.

k. Ammeter indicating discharge.

l. Load meter indicating zero.

m. Surging RPM and overspeeding.

n. Loss of airspeed in cruise flight with manifold pressure and RPM constant.

o. Rough-running engine.

p. Loss of fuel pressure.

Exam Tip: A thorough review of your aircraft's AFM/POH is vital to you demonstrating instructional knowledge in this task. Specifically, your knowledge of everything in Section 3: Emergency Procedures and Section 7: Description and Operation of the Airplane and Its Systems and your ability to teach that knowledge will be evaluated.

5. **Explain why specific system and equipment malfunctions training is needed to operate aircraft with electronic flight instrumentation systems (EFIS).** (FAA-H-8083-3)

   a. The failure indications of EFIS may be entirely different from conventional instruments, making recognition of system malfunction much more difficult for the pilot.

   b. Lack of system standardization compounds the problem, making equipment-specific information and knowledge an important asset when analyzing electronic display malfunctions.

   c. The inability to simulate certain failure modes during training and evaluation could make the pilot less prepared for an actual emergency.

6. **Identify the hazards that a learner should consider when simulating system and equipment malfunctions.** (FAA-S-ACS-25)

   a. Startle response.

   b. Checklist usage for a system or equipment malfunction.

   c. Distractions, task prioritization, loss of situational awareness, or disorientation.

   d. Undesired aircraft state.

7. **What are the skill standards expected when simulating system and equipment malfunctions?** (FAA-S-ACS-25)

   The applicant demonstrates and simultaneously explains how to:

   a. Determine appropriate action for simulated emergencies specified by the evaluator, from at least three of the elements or sub-elements listed in ACS AOA XII, Task C, K1 through K5.

   b. Complete the appropriate checklist(s).

   c. Analyze and correct common errors related to this task.

8. **Describe the common errors that can occur to learners when responding to simulated system and equipment malfunctions.** (FAA-H-8083-3)

   a. Failure to recognize/detect the system or equipment malfunction.

   b. Inadequate knowledge of aircraft systems and equipment.

   c. Failure to accomplish the appropriate checklist or procedure.

D. Emergency Equipment and Survival Gear

1. **What is the objective of teaching a learner about emergency equipment and survival gear?** (FAA-H-8083-3)

   The objective is to educate the learner on the equipment and gear appropriate for operation in various climates, over various types of terrain, and over water as well as provide knowledge on the purpose, method of operation or use, servicing, and storage of appropriate equipment.

2. **What additional equipment is required if an aircraft is operated for hire over water and beyond power-off gliding distance from shore?** (14 CFR 91.205)

   If an aircraft is operated for hire over water and beyond power-off gliding distance from shore, approved flotation gear readily available to each occupant and at least one pyrotechnic signaling device are required.

3. **Explain how various materials on board an aircraft can be used to aid in survival.** (CAMI OK-06-033)

   a. The compass will keep you going in one direction.

   b. Gasoline will help make a fire.

   c. Oil can be used for smoke signals.

   d. Seat upholstery may be used to wrap around feet or hands.

   e. Wiring may be used for tie strings.

   f. The battery may be used to ignite fuel.

4. Identify several hazards that a learner should consider on the use of emergency equipment and survival gear. (FAA-S-ACS-25)

a. Survival gear (water, clothing, shelter) for 48 to 72 hours.

b. Use of a ballistic parachute system.

c. Use of an emergency auto-land system, if installed.

5. What are the skill standards expected when instructing about the use of emergency equipment and survival gear? (FAA-S-ACS-25)

The applicant demonstrates and simultaneously explains how to:

a. Identify appropriate equipment and personal gear.

b. Brief passengers on proper use of onboard emergency equipment and survival gear.

c. Simulate ballistic parachute deployment procedures, if equipped.

d. Analyze and correct common errors related to this task.

Note: For airplanes that include a ballistic parachute, applicants must follow the manufacturer's procedures for arming and disarming the system before and after flight. Testing of an applicant's knowledge regarding how and when to use the system and how to manage associated risks may include simulation and briefing of procedures but not actual deployment of the system.

6. What common errors are associated with the emergency equipment and survival gear task?

The learner fails to exhibit knowledge of:

a. When it would be prudent to carry emergency and survival equipment.

b. What type of emergency and survival equipment is appropriate for different climates and terrain.

c. The purpose, method of operation or use, servicing, and storage of appropriate equipment.

Postflight Procedures

A. After Landing, Parking, and Securing

1. After landing, when is it considered safe to begin performing the after-landing checklist items? (FAA-H-8083-3)

The after-landing checks should be performed only after the airplane is brought to a complete stop beyond the runway holding position markings. There have many cases of a pilot mistakenly grasping the wrong handle and retracting the landing gear instead of the flaps due to improper division of attention while the airplane was moving.

2. After landing at an airport with an operating control tower, when is an airplane considered clear of the runway? (AIM 4-3-20)

A pilot or controller may consider an aircraft that is exiting or crossing a runway to be clear of the runway when all parts of the aircraft are beyond the runway edge and there are no restrictions to its continued movement beyond the runway holding position markings.

3. While taxiing to parking, what are several examples of collision avoidance procedures a pilot might employ to mitigate risk and avoid an accident? (FAA-H-8083-3)

a. Be familiar with the parking, ramp, and taxi environment. Have an airport diagram, if available, out and in view at all times.

b. The pilot's eyes should be looking outside the airplane, scanning from side to side while looking both near and far to assess routing and potential conflicts.

c. Be vigilant of the entire area around the airplane to ensure that the airplane clears all obstructions. If there is any doubt about a safe clearance from an object, the pilot should stop the airplane and check the clearance.

d. A safe taxiing speed should be maintained. The speed should be slow enough so when the throttle is closed, the airplane can be stopped promptly.

e. When yellow taxiway centerline stripes are present, the pilot should visually place the centerline stripe so it is under the center of the airplane fuselage.

4. **When approaching the ramp for parking and maneuvering with power into or near the parking spot, what precautions should be taken?** (FAA-H-8083-3)

   Maneuver the airplane so that the tail is not pointed at an open hangar door, toward a parked automobile, or toward a group of bystanders in the area. Blowing dirt, small rocks, and debris is not only discourteous and thoughtless but could result in personal injury and serious damage to the property of others.

5. **On an unfamiliar ramp, why would a pilot want to inspect their tie-down spot prior to parking and shutdown?**

   Foreign object debris (FOD) and other unknown objects can be a significant hazard that could cause damage to the aircraft and subject other aircraft and/or people nearby to the flying FOD.

6. **After parking and shutdown, what are several considerations a pilot should have when securing the aircraft?** (FAA-H-8083-3)

   a. Unless parking in a designated, supervised area, the pilot should select a location and heading that will prevent the propeller or jet blast of another aircraft from striking the aircraft broadside.

   b. Consider the existing (or forecast) wind when parking the airplane. Whenever possible, the aircraft should be parked headed into the existing wind.

   c. Consider allowing the airplane to roll straight ahead enough to straighten the nose wheel or tail wheel.

   d. Consider whether the tie-down method actually secures the aircraft. Check rope, chain, and hook integrity.

   e. If using ropes as tie-downs, consider whether the knot used will be effective.

7. **After the aircraft is safely hangered or tied down, what other actions can a pilot take to further enhance safety and security of the airplane?** (FAA-H-8083-3)

   Flight controls should be secured and any security locks in place. Also consider utilizing pitot tube covers, cowling inlet covers, rudder gust locks, window sunscreens, and propeller security locks to enhance safety.

8. **Describe inspections and procedures a pilot should perform when conducting a post-flight inspection of an aircraft.** (FAA-H-8083-3)

A pilot should always use the recommended procedures in the airplane's POH/AFM. A post-flight inspection is similar to a preflight inspection and should include the following:

a. Inspect near and around the cowling for signs of oil or fuel streaks and around the oil breather for excessive oil discharge.

b. Inspect under wings and other fuel tank locations for fuel stains.

c. Inspect landing gear and tires for damage and the brakes for any leaking hydraulic fluid.

d. Inspect cowling inlets for obstructions.

e. Check oil levels and bring quantities to POH/AFM levels.

f. Add fuel based on the immediate use of the airplane.

g. If the airplane is going to be inactive, it is a good operating practice to fill the fuel tanks to prevent water condensation from forming inside the tank.

9. **If a possible mechanical problem is detected during a post-flight inspection, what procedure should be followed?** (FAA-H-8083-3)

Document the problem and notify maintenance personnel. A maintenance problem that is detected during a post-flight inspection and appropriately documented will allow maintenance personnel more time to make appropriate repairs and prepare the aircraft for subsequent flights. If the airplane is a rental or belongs to a flying club or flight school, there is usually a "squawk" sheet or book for the airplane where the pilot can document the discrepancy.

10. When boarding or deplaning passengers, what is the safest, most effective procedure to follow to reduce the possibility of an accident? (FAA-H-8083-3)

The engine of a fixed-wing aircraft or of a helicopter should always be shut down prior to boarding or deplaning passengers. The pilot can be most effective in ensuring that his or her passengers arrive and depart the vicinity of the airplane safely by stopping the engine completely at the time of loading and unloading, or in instances when the engine must be running, by providing a definite means of keeping them clear of the propeller if it is left in motion.

Scenario-Based Training

Training

13

by Arlynn McMahon

Introduction

Pilot examiners are encouraged by the FAA to develop scenarios as part of the "Plan of Action" used during the practical tests they conduct. The evaluator is not required to follow the consecutive order of tasks as they appear in the Airman Certification Standards (ACS) or Practical Test Standards (PTS). Therefore, questions in this chapter are presented as they might appear in an actual oral exam, rather than in the order given in the ACS/PTS. However, these questions alone do not make a complete oral exam. Usually, the examiner will first ask a scenario-based question, and then building from your response, construct additional questions as he or she goes in order to further probe into your knowledge of a ACS/PTS task.

Scenario-based questions are intentionally open ended. Don't get frustrated. They are designed to allow you to go freely in any direction you feel is pertinent. You should formulate an answer that displays the **practical application of your instructional knowledge**.

The examiner doesn't expect a textbook answer to a scenario-based question. He or she wants to feel that you have seriously considered *how* you will do the job of an instructor. **Your answer should include specific examples of things that you plan to do with or for your learners**. When you are asked, "How will you..." the examiner means *you*—specifically how are *you* going to do it—whatever "it" is. Feel free to tell a personal flying story if it will illustrate an example.

Scenario-based questions don't have one universal correct answer. Your correct answer will depend on the specifics of the scenario and the aircraft used for the practical exam. For that reason, the question-and-answer material in this chapter provides suggestions for what your answers could include.

Instructors are expected to draw, list, and diagram for learners— so you should have a pencil and scratch paper to use in answering questions, just as you would when instructing. Answers to scenario questions can be lengthy, and paper will also help you to organize your thoughts before answering.

The examiner will test your instructional knowledge by asking you to demonstrate *how* you will respond to a specific scenario and *why* it's important But even if you aren't specifically asked, you should freely include the *how* and *why* in your answers. Many flight instructor candidates are well equipped with the answers for *what* to do but are sorely lacking in describing *how* to do it. This is the *Practical Test*. To perform your best, you must show the **practical application of *what* to do, *when* to do it, *how* to do it, and *why* do it**.

Show, through your answers, that you are professional, thoughtful, careful, diligent, and work-ready. By all means, include elements that you feel make good instructors and pilots, rather than ones who just meet minimum standards. Demonstrate that you care about your learners and that you intend to graduate them as responsible aviation-citizens.

Scenario-Based Questions

1. **Use V_X to give me an example of how your learner could demonstrate each level of learning.**

   When my learner can state the correct definition of V_X, he is at the Rote level of learning. When he can explain when to use V_X, then he is at Understanding. When he can perform a V_X climb and hold a constant V_X speed in the plane, he is at Application. A few days later, after practicing a simulated engine failure, if he pulls up into the V_X climb on the go-around to gain altitude to clear trees ahead, he's demonstrated Correlation by showing he's able to apply the skill in a way other than how he originally learned it.

2. **This is the fifth time you've reviewed steep turns with your learner, Katy, but she still doesn't "get it." Her steep turns are getting worse rather than improving. What will you do?**

   Katy may be in a learning plateau and would benefit from a break from practicing steep turns. I'll move her to another place in the syllabus and work on something else—maybe ground reference maneuvers. This will help her relax, start to have fun again, and get back in the groove. I'll bring her back to steep turns at a later point after she has regained her confidence.

3. **Your learner has rushed from work to the airport and received a speeding ticket along the way. He also says that he *must* finish today's lesson on time, as his wife is mad at him for not getting the yard mowed yesterday. How will you conduct his lesson?**

This learner is not ready to learn because he has too much on his mind. I could cancel the lesson, but he might not want to cancel after all of his effort to get to the airport. I would reduce the flight lesson to include less content (make it a review lesson) or use it as a teaching opportunity for a ground lesson in risk management and the "I'M SAFE" checklist.

4. **Considering Maslow's hierarchy of needs, how will you meet the needs of your learner?**

I will meet my learner's physiological needs by giving her a tour of the facility, showing her the restrooms, kitchen area, and water fountain. I'll meet her need for security and safety by teaching her to perform a thorough preflight inspection with a review of the maintenance discrepancy system for fixing items. I'll meet her need for belonging by introducing her to others around the airport and encouraging her to attend the next WINGS seminar. I'll meet her need for self-esteem by praising her in public and correcting her in private, and by posting her solo photo on the flight school website. I'll meet her need for self-actualization by continuously raising the bar—providing small challenges that I know she will be successful at.

5. **How will you change your normal instructional style for a learner who consistently exhibits resignation?**

Resignation is a hazardous attitude. If I'm teaching a person with consistent resignation, I will have to give her opportunities to be successful and continuously remind her of her successes. I'll build her confidence by incorporating small challenges that she can conquer, in a wide variety of training situations. She will need a more detailed, all-inclusive checklist. I'll encourage her to create workable tools to help her remain organized in the cockpit. At some point, after I've earned her trust, we'll discuss all of the hazardous attitudes and their antidotes so that she'll develop self-sufficiency and self-confidence.

6. **When it's time to move on to a new job, what will you do as a professional instructor for the learners who are left behind?**

I had several instructors leave in the middle of my training, and this can be tough on learners. What I plan to do is give my learners ample warning so they can mentally prepare for the change. I will then review each learner's logbook and endorsements to make sure that everything is up-to-date and properly completed. I will attempt to locate another instructor to refer my learners to, and with each learner's permission, discuss my training plan for the learner with the new instructor to ensure the learner's seamless transition. I'll also provide learners with my contact information in case of future questions.

7. **During the engine run-up, you notice that one magneto has no apparent drop in RPM. What is the probable cause and what will you do?**

The probable cause is either a failure in the mag switch or a problem with a grounding wire on the magneto. It could indicate that the engine is running on one mag or it could be the inability to turn a mag off. In any case, this is an airworthiness no-go situation. We must return to the flight school, report the discrepancy, and be dispatched a different plane.

8. **How would your learner detect an electrical failure and what actions would you expect him to take?**

Your specific answer will depend on your training aircraft, but it should demonstrate how you expect your learner to detect electrical system failure and the proper responses when on the ground or in the air. For example:

There are several ways my learner might detect an electrical failure in this airplane. He might see the alternator annunciator illuminate or the ammeter discharging. He might notice the low voltage readout on the GPS. Whichever way he detects the problem, I would expect him to verify it with other indications. Then I'd expect him to cycle the master switch off for 2 or 3 seconds and then back on, to reset the over-voltage relay. I'd expect him to determine if that fixed the problem or not. If not, I'd want him to review the POH checklist for other possible actions. If the electrical system has failed:

- on the ground, then I expect him to return to the flight school, record the problem in the discrepancy log, and be dispatched in a different plane for his flight.
- in flight, I'd expect him to turn off all unnecessary electrical items to preserve battery power and land as soon as practical:
  - › If in the traffic pattern/practice area, I want him to land at our home airport and prepare for possible light gun signals from the tower.
  - › If on cross-country, he should land at the next planned destination and call me. He should know not to take off again until he talks to me.

9. A learner provides his own Cessna 152 for private pilot training. As the instructor teaching in this plane, how will you ensure that it is airworthy?

First, I'll verify that the airworthiness certificate and other pertinent papers are in order. I'll check the inspection status of the annual, emergency locator transmitter (ELT), and transponder check. I'll also check the status of any reoccurring ADs and inoperative equipment. Lastly, I'll conduct a thorough preflight to ensure the overall condition of the aircraft is safe for flight.

10. In the event that the learner provides his own training airplane, what are your responsibilities and the responsibilities of the learner pertaining to maintenance?

The learner as the owner/operator is responsible for having the repairs done.

If the learner is not a current, certificated pilot, then as the instructor I am also the pilot-in-command and am responsible for ensuring that repairs are done and properly documented.

As an instructor, I am also responsible for knowing what to look for and helping the learner to learn how to be a responsible aircraft owner.

11. It's 4:30 p.m. on Friday. The maintenance shop is closed for the weekend. Your learner reports the aircraft's cigarette lighter (12V power source) is INOP. What will you do?

My INOP checklist is:

- Is there an approved MEL? On this plane, there is not.
- Is the INOP item on the required VFR day or night equipment list (TOMATOFFLAAMES)? The cigarette lighter is not.
- Is it on the VFR type certificate? It is not.
- Is it on the Kinds of Operations List (usually Chapter 2 in the POH)? The cigarette lighter is not.
- Is there an airworthiness directive requiring the equipment? There is none.
- Can I operate the aircraft safely without it? In my opinion, yes, I can.
- I could remove it or placard it. I will placard it and we will fly, but the INOP equipment must be fixed at least with the next scheduled inspection.

12. What factors will you take into consideration when choosing an area to practice maneuvers?

I'll choose an area away from low clouds; busy airspace and congested areas; and airports, VORs, or other areas where traffic converges. I'll choose an area with good landmarks, ground references, and emergency landing areas. I'll also look for a place not too far from the airport so that the learner doesn't waste time getting to and from the practice area.

13. As the instructor, what specific steps will you take in collision avoidance during training?

I'll make sure to clean the windshield, and I'll recommend that the learner use goggles rather than a big hood. I'll make sure not to get so engrossed inside the cockpit (especially in a technically advanced aircraft) that I forget to look outside. I'll observe the learner's collision avoidance techniques and continually remind the learner to look outside to scan for traffic or other potential collision threats.

14. How could you demonstrate longitudinal stability to a learner while in the air?

I could trim the airplane to straight-and-level flight and remove both hands from the control wheel, and point out how the airplane remains (on average) in the straight-and-level attitude. Then without re-trimming, I would pull the nose up a bit, maybe to a cruise climb attitude, and observe. I'd point out to the learner how the airplane continues to porpoise but that each oscillation gets smaller until the aircraft has returned itself, once again, to straight-and-level flight.

15. How will you explain to your learner the concept of zero fuel weight?

Zero fuel weight is the weight of an aircraft with all of the useful load not including the weight of the fuel on board. It is a payload limitation placed on the aircraft by the manufacturer. The airplane without fuel cannot be loaded to more than its zero fuel weight, or another way to say it is that all weight over the zero fuel weight must be fuel.

16. What syllabus will you use in teaching your learners? Tell me what you like about it.

Describe specific elements of your chosen syllabus and why you think they are important. An example using a fictional "A-B-C syllabus":

I have chosen the A-B-C syllabus. I like it because the lesson plans contain things like risk management, aeronautical decision making, and other items not related specifically to maneuvers that I might otherwise forget. I also like that the syllabus is part of a total kit containing a textbook so the ground portion of training is organized and works hand-in-hand with the flight portion.

17. Your learner, Katy, can't choose between a Sport Pilot and a Recreational Pilot Certificate. What will you tell her?

I'll tell her that she can start training before choosing. Sometimes it's easier to make a decision after training begins. She should ultimately choose after considering which rating will help her achieve her goals. In this case, would she rather be limited to flying only a light-sport airplane or limited to flying within 50 NM from her airport? I'll also explain that she can achieve any rating, and with additional training can have privileges upgraded or limitations removed.

18. Katy returns from the Aviation Medical Examiner (AME) saying that she was found ineligible due to color blindness. The AME suggested she obtain a SODA. What will you do?

I can help Katy by explaining the Statement of Demonstrated Ability (SODA) and the process for getting one, and by making contact with the FSDO. They will conduct an evaluation for the issuance of her SODA, but I would go with her for general support.

19. When flying straight and level, Katy has great trouble holding a heading. What advice will you give her to become more consistent on heading control?

I will suggest that she pick a landmark out ahead, on the horizon, in the direction she wants to fly and then keep the airplane pointed toward that landmark. This will do two things: keep her going straight and keep her head up and looking outside of the cockpit.

20. Katy appears very anxious about stalls and has even cancelled two previously scheduled lessons knowing that stalls were on the agenda. What will you do?

I will confirm her fear and share how I didn't used to like stalls either. I'll build her trust by reaffirming that I would never do anything to scare her. I will make sure my first demonstration in the plane is a very gentle, straight-ahead, power-off stall with a clean break. I'll delay the recovery from the stall to show her that she still has control (the falling leaf maneuver). I'll just take it one step at a time until her anxiety eases.

21. **Upon recovery from a stall, Katy applied full power and the aircraft rolled abruptly to the left. What is the likely reason for this and the corrective action to avoid this in the future?**

Katy probably applied full power before breaking the stall. Her sudden application of full power—torque and P-factor—caused a left-turning tendency. To avoid this in the future, I'll ensure that Katy separates the actions, first lowering the angle of attack to break the stall, and then applying power to minimize altitude loss in the recovery. While the ACS/PTS requires that the learner simultaneously lower the nose and apply power, the learner can't always meet practical test standards in the introductory lesson of the maneuver. I'll take it one step at a time until she gets it.

22. **When evaluating Katy after flight lesson #10, what criteria will you use?**

Without knowing what flight lesson #10 is, I can't be specific, except to say that the after-flight evaluation should be based on the objectives of the lesson. By lesson #10, I would hope that Katy is able to evaluate herself to start with—using a learner-centered grading method.

23. **Have you prepared a pre-solo knowledge exam that you will ask your learners to complete before initial solo?**

Show the examiner your prepared pre-solo knowledge exam. Your response should include an explanation of what sections you included in your exam and why, and what you expect of your learners.

Yes, it's right here. This portion covers questions that I copied from the FAA question database on FARs. These questions are about our airport. See this big blank box? I ask the learner to draw a rough taxi diagram including runway markings. This section reviews information on our training aircraft, but rather than making it multiple choice, I ask them to write their answers in the box. Here is a date and signature line indicating that I graded it and reviewed wrong answers with them. I even put the endorsement here so I can remember what to write in their logbook.

24. Many places in Federal Aviation Regulations require that the instructor determine "that the learner is proficient to operate the aircraft safely." How will you do this?

I can determine that the learner is proficient to operate the aircraft safely when he can consistently perform maneuvers correctly, and when he makes mistakes, he catches and fixes them without my intervention. He is able to prioritize tasks and maintain situational awareness. By this point, the learner should no longer need much help from me.

25. What criteria will you use to determine that Katy is ready for first solo? Be specific.

To determine that Katy is ready for first solo, I will have had at least one lesson where she conducted landings without any help whatsoever from me. I would be completely hands-off and not say a word. I consider this lesson a practice session for her being in the airplane solo. I also want to know that she has good airspeed control and will make a prompt decision to go-around if needed.

26. Regulations say that a soloing learner may not operate in a manner contrary to limitations placed in the logbook by an authorized instructor. What limitations will you put in your learner's logbook?

I'll include limitations based on the ceiling, visibility, and winds. Those limitations might be different for solo flight in the traffic pattern versus practice area or solo cross-countries. I'll also limit the use of distracting electronic devices (audio players, cameras, etc.). And I'll require that the learner and I meet at the airport to formally dispatch each flight so that I can supervise his or her flight preparations.

27. Katy has been studying the Knowledge Exam Guide and asks you for an endorsement to take the FAA Knowledge Exam. What will you do?

My endorsement certifies that I find her prepared to pass the test, so I must first determine that she is ready. I would orally quiz her on several test questions or give her a written exam that I created to establish that she is ready to pass the FAA exam. If she answers at least 80 percent of my questions correctly, then I would consider her ready to pass the FAA's exam and I would provide her with an endorsement.

28. **Daren's original instructor endorsed his initial solo but has since moved out of state. Daren is asking you to renew his solo authorization for an additional 90 days. You've never flown with him. What will you do?**

    I will not give a solo endorsement renewal if I haven't flown with him. We'll have to go fly together so I can evaluate Daren's readiness for solo flight. Besides, it looks like Daren needs a new instructor—maybe he'll hire me!

29. **Tonight is Daren's first dual night flight. What are the key issues that you will teach him?**

    I have a lesson plan specifically for night flight. It breaks down each phase of flight and reviews the differences between day and night flying techniques. It also includes terrain and obstacle awareness, visual illusions, preservation of night vision, airport and aircraft lighting, and FARs pertaining to night flight. We might also cover other topics specific to night flight, but I think those are the key issues.

30. **During Daren's night cross-country, he abruptly pulled the aircraft nose up and rolled to the right. Why did this happen and what is the corrective action to avoid this in the future?**

    Daren probably had spatial disorientation with an optical illusion from the lights on the ground. The way to avoid this in future flights is to emphasize a higher reliance on cross-checking instruments during night flight.

31. **At one point during Daren's dual cross country, you feel that he is lost. What will you do?**

    If I simply inform Daren that he is lost, then I've robbed him of a learning opportunity. Instead, I will use guided discussion in such a way that he can discover for himself that he is lost (he might already know it), and I will hint that now is the time to use his skills to get unlost. I'll ask him to pinpoint his position on the chart and to verify his position with radials or landmarks. I'll give him time to think and to develop a plan and make a decision on how to get back on course. He is an advanced learner; his ADM is part of his training. I want to see his ability to make decisions like this so that I have confidence to send him on solo cross-country.

32. Daren is a large guy. During dual cross-country flights, he found the C-152 too uncomfortable. He is requesting to upgrade to the C-172 for solo cross-country and the remainder of his training. How will you proceed?

Daren will have to earn solo authorization in the C-172. I can help him do this by giving him a pre-solo knowledge exam on the C-172, evaluate him as he performs the required pre-solo maneuvers in the C-172, and when ready, provide an endorsement in his logbook. Then the procedures required before solo cross-country must be completed by Daren in the C-172 (for example, C-172 aircraft performance charts). And, of course, Daren must demonstrate that he is proficient to operate the C-172 safely.

33. You authorized Daren on a solo cross-country this morning. He is now on the phone, saying that he made an unscheduled landing at XYZ airport to go to the restroom and will now be continuing on his flight from there. What will you say?

I'll say, "No. You can't take off. Your cross-country authorization was specific and now you're at a different airport. We have to get you authorized from your present position to the authorized destination." Then, I might be able to work with a local instructor to authorize him, or if there is no CFI at that airport, I could talk with Daren on the phone to review his flight planning and fax a new logbook endorsement.

34. Daren experiences a mechanical failure while on a solo cross-country. A local maintenance technician diagnosed the problem and says the airplane will have to be repaired at another location. What actions are necessary?

A special flight permit must be obtained from the FSDO to fly to the maintenance location. A certificated pilot must fly the aircraft to maintenance, and Daren must be retrieved. One option is for another pilot and me to fly a second airplane to Daren's location, and then the pilot takes the aircraft with the special flight permit to maintenance while Daren and I fly home together in the second airplane. This assumes Daren is not authorized to solo the second plane, or is not mentally "up" to finishing his flight.

35. **John is enrolled at your flight school. You haven't flown with him, but you know who he is and have seen him around over the past few months. His regular instructor is not available today, and John asks you for permission to solo to the practice area for an hour. What will you do?**

I will review his logbook to ensure that it has been endorsed for initial solo and is within 90 days. I will also look at his logbook to find a renewal of the 90-day solo authorization if necessary. This assumes that the flight is not at night or in Class B airspace, etc. Then we'll discuss where he's going, what he will be practicing, and what time he will return. If I will not be around, I'll ask him to call me when he lands so I can supervise his safe return.

If his solo endorsements are not proper or current, then I won't give him permission to solo.

36. **The flight school needs to reposition an aircraft to another airport for routine inspection. You have agreed to reposition the aircraft but are looking for another pilot to fly a second aircraft to return you home. John, a learner pilot with a practical exam scheduled next week, volunteers to fly the second aircraft for extra practice before the checkride. How will you proceed?**

John can't fly the second aircraft because he has not yet passed his Private Pilot checkride. A learner pilot flying a flight school airplane in that way might be considered "in furtherance of business." We will need to make another plan or find another pilot.

37. **Jim has been pursuing flight training at another school but now would like you to finish his training and prepare him for a Private Pilot checkride. What is your plan?**

I would get out the FARs and compare his logbook to the requirements to create a list of outstanding tasks, and do this in front of him so that he understands what I'm doing. I would review the hours and cross-country destinations. By looking at the words that describe what was completed during each lesson, I could compare those words to the requirements for pre-solo maneuvers and solo cross-country requirements. I would double-check the math on the totals column. I'd also examine his ground training in the same way. I would review his endorsements to make sure they are proper and current and look at his Knowledge Exam Report. By now, I would know if he meets the age requirement, if he is a U.S. citizen, and if he has any problem with English.

Once I have a complete picture of what training is still necessary for Jim to meet the requirements, I'd look at the dates of his lessons: How consistent was his training, how old is his training, has he flown recently, etc. This will give me some indication of his proficiency today and how much review time might be needed. Now I can give him my best estimate of the number of hours and the cost for him to complete his training.

Before starting his training, I'll get a copy of his proof of citizenship. Once we begin, I can use the list that I made as a checklist of items to complete for his training.

38. In reviewing Jim's logbook you find flights that were logged as dual but not properly endorsed by an instructor. What will you do?

I will inform Jim that flights that are not properly endorsed will not meet the requirements for required training. If he is still in contact with the instructor that accompanied him on those dual flights, perhaps he can arrange to get the needed endorsements. If he can't obtain the proper endorsements, then the required training must be repeated with me as his instructor so that I can properly endorse it.

39. In preparing Jim for his practical exam, how will you ensure that your copy of the ACS/PTS is still the most current edition?

I would visit faa.gov to cross check my ACS/PTS book with the edition and effective date the FAA lists as the most current.

40. Jack has asked you to instruct him for a complex aircraft endorsement. How will you proceed?

In a complex plane, the biggest concern is teaching the learner to develop safety habits for the retractable gear. I have a copy of the advisory circular that makes recommendations on transitional training. I'll use that recommended training as a basis for making my lesson plan specific to Jack's airplane. I'll also call on another instructor at my airport who is a very experienced instructor, and I'll ask him to mentor me the first time I teach a learner for a complex aircraft endorsement.

41. Jenny has called you because she is in need of a flight review. How will you proceed?

At FAASafety.gov, I printed a booklet titled *Conducting an Effective Flight Review*. I'll use that as a basis for making my plan. My basic approach will be to send Jenny to FAASafety. gov for the free Flight Review Prep Guide Course, then we'll do a flight preparation ground session followed by a short cross-country segment including some maneuvers. The FAA booklet has recommendations for how many hours it may take if she's not current and needs an extended flight review. I'll leave her with my recommendations for a plan of continued improvement.

42. Jenny is scheduled to depart this afternoon on a weekend SCUBA vacation and has just found that she needs a flight review. Her vacation is already paid for and she'll lose her money if she doesn't go. There is no time to complete the flight review before her departure. She is a longtime good friend and a very experienced pilot. She suggests that you record the flight review in her logbook so she can depart, and then complete the review first thing when she returns, only two days from now. How will you proceed?

I can't endorse a flight review without doing it. It's not legal, it's not ethical, and I could lose my certificates. I would convince Jenny to let me do the minimum flight review requirements of one hour on the ground and one hour in the air. That's the minimum I must do to give her the endorsement. Then we'll arrange to meet when she gets back to do anything else that is safety-related and needs to be done.

43. Mike is requesting training in the FAA Pilot Proficiency WINGS program. How will you proceed?

I'll sit with Mike in front of the computer and log on to the WINGS website. Together, we can see what level of WINGS he is looking to achieve and the requirements he has to meet. While there, I'd have him print the lesson plans so I can begin looking at them. Then we'll be ready to make appointments and fly.

44. **Donna wants you to instruct her for a Commercial Pilot Certificate. She does not have an Instrument Rating and she understands the limitations placed upon her. What are your limitations in training her?**

For the issuance of a Commercial Pilot Certificate, she is required to have 10 hours of flight by reference to instruments. Without having an Instrument Rating, it's doubtful that she has that and I can't give it to her. By not having a CFII, my limitation is that I can't do the instrument training for the issuance of a Commercial Pilot Certificate.

45. **Bob asks you to conduct training toward his Airline Transport Pilot Certificate. Can you do that?**

Yes, no, and maybe. Legally, yes, I can do that. The Airline Transport Pilot (ATP) Certificate does not require an endorsement for the checkride and there are no specific training requirements. But it wouldn't be smart for me to conduct his training. I wouldn't be helping Bob because I don't have enough experience to guide him. The best thing I can do for him is to recommend a more experienced instructor. I may also be able to help by familiarizing him with the training plane (I hold a Single Engine Rating; is Bob training for a SEL ATP?) and local area before turning him over to an experienced instructor for more specific training on ATP-related topics.

46. **Will the successful completion of this initial Flight Instructor Practical Exam renew your flight review?**

No. A Flight Instructor Practical Exam is not a pilot practical exam, so it will not apply. However, I'm sure that I worked enough with the instructor who recommended my practical exam to ask him to endorse a flight review. Also, if I let the examiner know in advance that I'd like to have a flight review endorsement, he or she would probably do it (assuming I'm successful in passing the practical exam).

47. When the time comes, which method do you anticipate using to renew your Flight Instructor Certificate?

I prefer to rotate through all of the choices for renewal—they each have a benefit. Attending a flight instructor refresher course (FIRC) will keep me up-to-date with new trends. Passing a renewal checkride and even preparing to pass a checkride will keep my flight proficiency top notch. Renewing through activity means that I'm actively engaged in training and that my learners are passing their checkrides, which is really the true test that I'm an effective instructor.

Applicant's Practical Test Checklist

Appendix 1

407

Applicant's Practical Test Checklist

Appointment with Examiner

Examiner's Name _____

Location _____

Date/Time _____

Acceptable Aircraft

Aircraft Documents
___ Airworthiness certificate
___ Registration certificate
___ Operating limitations

Aircraft Maintenance Records
___ Logbook record of airworthiness inspections and AD compliance
___ Pilot's Operating Handbook, FAA-approved Airplane Flight Manual
___ Current weight and balance data

Personal Equipment
___ View-limiting device
___ Current aeronautical charts (printed or electronic)
___ Computer and plotter
___ Flight plan form and flight logs (printed or electronic)
___ *Chart Supplement U.S.*, airport diagrams, and appropriate publications
___ Current FAR/AIM

Personal Records
___ Identification—photo/signature ID
___ Pilot certificate
___ Current medical certificate
___ Completed FAA Form 8710-1, Airman Certificate and/or Rating Application, with instructor's signature (or IACRA equivalent with applicant's FTN and application ID)
___ Original Knowledge Test Report
___ Pilot logbook with appropriate instructor endorsements

___ FAA Form 8060-5, Notice of Disapproval of Application
   (if applicable)
___ Letter of Discontinuance (if applicable)
___ Approved school graduation certificate (if applicable)
___ Evaluator's fee (if applicable)

Safety of Flight
(from FAA-S-ACS-25)

Appendix 2

Flight Instructor for Airplane Category Airman Certification Standards (FAA-S-ACS-25)
Appendix 2: Safety of Flight

General

Safety of flight must be the prime consideration at all times. The evaluator, applicant, and crew must be continually alert for other traffic. If performing aspects of a given maneuver, such as emergency procedures, would jeopardize safety, the evaluator will ask the applicant to simulate that portion of the maneuver. The evaluator will assess the applicant's use of visual scanning and collision avoidance procedures throughout the entire test.

Stall and Spin Awareness

During flight training and testing, the applicant and the instructor or evaluator must always recognize and avoid operations that could lead to an inadvertent stall or spin and inadvertent loss of control.

Use of Checklists

Throughout the practical test, the applicant is evaluated on the use of an appropriate checklist.

Assessing proper checklist use depends upon the specific Task. In all cases, the evaluator should determine whether the applicant demonstrates CRM, appropriately divides attention and uses proper visual scanning. In some situations, reading the actual checklist may be impractical or unsafe. In such cases, the evaluator should assess the applicant's performance of published or recommended immediate action "memory" items along with his or her review of the appropriate checklist once conditions permit.

In a single-pilot aircraft, the applicant should demonstrate the crew resource management (CRM) principles described as single-pilot resource management (SRM). Proper use depends on the specific Task being evaluated. If the use of the checklist while accomplishing elements of an Objective would be either unsafe or impractical in a single-pilot operation, the applicant should review the checklist after accomplishing the elements.

Positive Exchange of Flight Controls

A clear understanding of who has control of the aircraft must exist. Prior to flight, the pilots involved should conduct a briefing that includes reviewing the procedures for exchanging flight controls.

The FAA recommends a positive three-step process for exchanging flight controls between pilots:

- When one pilot seeks to have the other pilot take control of the aircraft, they will say, "You have the flight controls."
- The second pilot acknowledges immediately by saying, "I have the flight controls."
- The first pilot again says, "You have the flight controls," and visually confirms the exchange.

Pilots should follow this procedure during any exchange of flight controls, including any occurrence during the practical test. The FAA also recommends that both pilots use a visual check to verify that the exchange has occurred. Doubt as to who is flying the aircraft should not occur.

Use of Distractions

Numerous studies indicate that many accidents have occurred when the pilot has been distracted during critical phases of flight. The evaluator should incorporate realistic distractions during the flight portion of the practical test to evaluate the pilot's situational awareness and ability to utilize proper control technique while dividing attention both inside and outside the flight deck.

Aeronautical Decision-Making, Risk Management, Crew Resource Management, and Single-Pilot Resource Management

Throughout the practical test, the evaluator must assess the applicant's ability to use sound aeronautical decision-making procedures in order to identify hazards and mitigate risk. The evaluator must accomplish this requirement by reference to the risk management elements of the given Task(s), and by developing scenarios that incorporate and combine Tasks appropriate to assessing the applicant's risk management in making safe aeronautical decisions. For example, the evaluator may develop a scenario that incorporates weather decisions and performance planning.

In assessing the applicant's performance, the evaluator should take note of the applicant's use of CRM and, if appropriate, SRM. CRM/SRM is the set of competencies that includes situational awareness, communication skills, teamwork, task allocation, and decision-making within a comprehensive framework of standard operating procedures (SOP). SRM specifically refers to the management of all resources onboard the aircraft, as well as outside resources available to the single pilot.

If an applicant fails to use aeronautical decision-making (ADM), including SRM/CRM, as applicable in any Task, the evaluator will note that Task as failed. The evaluator will also include the ADM Skill element from the Flight Deck Management Task on the Notice of Disapproval of Application.

Multiengine Considerations

On multiengine practical tests, where the failure of the most critical engine after liftoff is required, the evaluator must consider local atmospheric conditions, terrain, and type of aircraft used. The evaluator must not simulate failure of an engine until attaining an altitude of at least 400 feet AGL and at least minimum single-engine speed (V_{SSE}), best single-engine angle-of climb speed (V_{XSE}), or best single-engine rate-of-climb (V_{YSE}).

The applicant must supply an airplane that does not prohibit the demonstration of feathering the propeller in flight. However, an applicant holding an unrestricted AMEL rating may take a practical test for the addition of an AMES rating in an AMES without propeller feathering capability. Practical tests conducted in a flight simulation training device (FSTD) can only be accomplished as part of an approved curriculum or training program pursuant to 14 CFR part 61, section 61.64. Any limitations or powerplant failure will be noted in that program.

For safety reasons, when the practical test is conducted in an airplane, the applicant must perform Tasks that require feathering or shutdown only under conditions and at a position and altitude where it is possible to make a safe landing on an established airport if there is difficulty in unfeathering the propeller or restarting the engine. The evaluator must select an entry altitude that will allow the single-engine demonstration Tasks to be completed no lower than 3,000 feet AGL or the manufacturer's recommended altitude (whichever is higher). If it is not possible to unfeather the propeller or restart the engine while airborne, the applicant and the evaluator should treat the situation as an emergency. At altitudes lower than 3,000 feet AGL, engine failure should be simulated by reducing throttle to idle and then establishing zero thrust.

Engine failure (simulated) during takeoff should be accomplished prior to reaching 50 percent of the calculated V_{MC}.

For safety reasons, the evaluator will not request a simulated powerplant failure in a single-engine airplane unless it is possible to safely complete a landing.